Wild West 2.0

Wild West 2.0

How to Protect and Restore
Your Online Reputation on the
Untamed Social Frontier

Michael Fertik and David Thompson

ⵙAMACOM

American Management Association
New York • Atlanta • Brussels • Chicago • Mexico City • San Francisco
Shanghai • Tokyo • Toronto • Washington, D.C.

Bulk discounts available. For details visit: www.amacombooks.org/go/specialsales
Or contact special sales: Phone: 800-250-5308. E-mail: specialsls@amanet.org
View all the AMACOM titles at: www.amacombooks.org

This publication is designed to provide accurate and authoritative information in regard to the subject matter covered. It is sold with the understanding that the publisher is not engaged in rendering legal, accounting, or other professional service. If legal advice or other expert assistance is required, the services of a competent professional person should be sought.

Library of Congress Cataloging-in-Publication Data

Fertik, Michael.
    Wild west 2.0 : how to protect and restore your online reputation on the untamed
social frontier / Michael Fertik and David Thompson.
        p.   cm.
    Includes bibliographical references and index.
    ISBN-13: 978-0-8144-1509-2
    ISBN-10: 0-8144-1509-1
      1. Personal information management.   2. Online identities.   3. Rumor.
4. Internet in publicity.   5. Public relations.   6. Corporate image.   I. Thompson,
David, 1979–   II. Title.
    HD30.2.F495   2010
    659.20285'4678—dc22

                                                                          2009042255

About AMA

American Management Association (www.amanet.org) is a world leader in talent development, advancing the skills of individuals to drive business success. Our mission is to support the goals of individuals and organizations through a complete range of products and services, including classroom and virtual seminars, webcasts, webinars, podcasts, conferences, corporate and government solutions, business books and research. AMA's approach to improving performance combines experiential learning—learning through doing—with opportunities for ongoing professional growth at every step of one's career journey.

Printing number
10   9   8   7   6   5   4   3

Contents

CHAPTER 1:

Welcome to the New Digital Frontier   1

CHAPTER 2:

Your Online Reputation Is Your Reputation   16

CHAPTER 3:

The Internet Is the New Wild West   30

CHAPTER 4:

The Forces Driving Online Reputation   44

CHAPTER 5:

Anonymous Cowards   61

CHAPTER 6:

Google Gone Wild: The Digital Threat to Reputation   82

CHAPTER 7:

Why People Attack Each Other Online   100

CHAPTER 8:

Types of Internet Attacks   123

CHAPTER 9:

How to Measure Damage to Your Internet Reputation   150

CHAPTER 10:

Your Reputation Road Map and Online Reputation Audit   162

CHAPTER 11:

Getting Proactive: The Best Defense Is a Good Offense   188

CHAPTER 12:

Recovering from Online Smears: Restoring Your Reputation
After the Damage Has Been Done   207

CHAPTER 13:

Protect Your Small Business and Your Professional Reputation   234

CHAPTER 14:

Conclusion: Embrace the Internet   249

Glossary   251

Index   255

Wild West

2.0

CHAPTER

Welcome to the New Digital Frontier

Imagine a place where anonymous vandals can spray repugnant graffiti about you or your business without any consequence. They may call you a criminal, accuse your business of fraud, or reveal your most personal secrets. And this graffiti is viewed not only by a handful of passersby—instead, it is spread worldwide and instantly broadcast to anyone who looks for information about you. You can't remove the smear, and copies of it are permanently saved around the world.

Sound frightening? You don't have to imagine this scenario. It happens every day on the Internet. The victims are innocent people—parents, teachers, students, managers, workers, craftsmen, business owners, and more. Real personal reputations are being trashed with just a few mouse clicks, real businesses are losing thousands of customers due to false reports online, and real relationships are being destroyed by anonymous gossip.

1

The Internet has changed the rules for reputation. Once, reputation was hard-earned and carefully guarded. Today, your reputation can be created or destroyed in just a few clicks. And there are plenty of people who seek to destroy your reputation: bullies, people jealous of your success, competitors for jobs or customers (or even loves), and gangs of disaffected teenagers. The Internet gives them the power to permanently scar your reputation. They harness the power of Google™ and the Web to broadcast false and distorted information about you and your business to your closest friends and most distant customers. They can manipulate your photos, steal your secrets, and ruin your credit. If you are prepared, you can defend yourself from these attacks. But if you aren't careful, you can just make matters worse by fanning the flames.

Don't even think of ignoring the Internet's impact on your reputation. The Internet is not some passing fad; it is here to stay. It is the primary source of information about people, products, services, and companies. Even if you don't use the Internet, your boss, your customers, your neighbors, your friends, and your family do. What they find online will shape how they think about you, for better or worse: they could find slanderous allegations or shocking photos posted by a digital Peeping Tom; your business might be the subject of an online boycott or an urban legend about your business might spread through social discussion sites; or your relationships might be poisoned by false gossip. The worst part is that once false information about you is spread online, it can start a self-sustaining cycle that spreads it further and faster than you thought possible.

Luckily, the well prepared can still prosper on this new digital frontier. The Internet is not something to be afraid of; instead, it is a tremendous opportunity to shape the way that people see you or your business. Careful monitoring of your online reputation (or that of your business) combined with delicate intervention can help you make sure that your online image is a true reflection of reality. Often, by acting quickly you can stop online attacks and set the record straight. And careful seeding of positive truthful content will help you improve your social standing, get more clients, or grow your business. Thanks to the Internet, *you* have the chance to take direct control of the way people see you.

This book will teach you what you need to know to prosper in the new Wild West of online reputation. It will explain the rules of the new digital frontier, teach you to measure and analyze your reputation, and then give you the tools you need to defend yourself from online reputation attack. It will also explain special considerations and tactics for small businesses and professionals. In short, not all hope is lost: by learning the tricks of online reputation, you can defend—or even improve—your online image.

The Internet Is a New Digital Frontier

The Internet today resembles the Old West of American history. Like the Old West, the Internet is rich with opportunity and hope, but it is also still a rough-and-tumble place with many hidden dangers. There is a chance for individuals to express themselves or strike it rich, but the unprepared also face immense dangers. And, just like in the Old West, law enforcement is weak, and traditional society has not yet adapted to the strange new technology, social norms, and culture of the Internet. In short, the Internet is a new digital frontier that echoes the Wild West of American history. Call it "Wild West 2.0."

Just like in the original Wild West, countless people have struck it rich on the new digital frontier. From the Google founders—now among the richest people on Earth—to microbloggers who supplement their incomes with a few hundred dollars a month in advertising revenues, the Internet has created a modern gold rush. And the frontier is still open: There is still a chance for ordinary people to change their lives forever with new and creative business ventures.

Thanks to the Internet, there are useful new services like powerful search engines capable of finding any document on the planet (Google), the largest and most comprehensive encyclopedia in the history of mankind (Wikipedia), and countless other sites that provide news, entertainment, and commerce. With just a few clicks it's possible to find out nearly any information, from the chemical formula for caffeine ($C_8H_{10}N_4O_2$) to the name of the Red Sox' third baseman in 1912 (Larry Gardner). Research that would once have required a trip to the local public library can now be conducted online in seconds from anywhere in the world; a student sitting in class in Calcutta can research any topic using the California-based Wikipedia, and a student at home in California can just as easily look up the weather in Calcutta.

The Internet has forever changed politics. Now, it is possible for an anonymous whistleblower to reveal corruption to an audience of millions. Sites that provide outlets for classified documents (such as Wikileaks.org) exist because thousands of people want to reveal the truth about government wrongdoing. Political dissenters in Iran have organized their opposition to their government using e-mail and social sites like Twitter. Closer to home, supporters and opponents of local or national political candidates can anonymously express their deepest and most fervent beliefs. The power to speak anonymously has generated wide-ranging debate on the biggest issues of the day, free from constraints of political correctness and peer pressure.

Even more important, the world has become more closely connected. Electronic mail has replaced postal letters: you can send an e-mail across the globe in seconds for free rather than pay to send a "snailmail" letter that might be delivered days or weeks later. Skype and other Internet telephone services have slashed the cost of long-distance phone calls, allowing far-flung families and lovers to connect for pennies (rather than dollars) per minute. The ability to send videos and photos electronically has allowed closer communication between friends, parents, and others. Thousands of Web-based discussion forums allow far-flung people to discuss the issues most important to them and to find like-minded souls spread around the world.

For all the praise heaped upon the Internet for opening up political and social thought, it might be just as useful for the mundane.

The ability to get answers to basic questions has saved countless college students from pink laundry and burnt macaroni; the ability to get phone numbers of local businesses has saved millions in "411" phone charges; and the ability to plot driving routes electronically has prevented countless drivers from getting lost.

The Dangers of Frontier Life Are Real

But, also as in the old Wild West, the frontier has expanded faster than the law and our culture, which have proven unable to keep up. There is no sheriff in town, and Internet users have been left with rough frontier justice. Innocent reputations can be ruined by anonymous attackers, and the victims are often greeted with blank stares by law enforcement. Disputes are settled at the ends of virtual pitchforks and torches instead of at a negotiation table or in a court of law. People suspected of wrongdoing are run out of town on an electronic rail, often before there is time to figure out whether they are really guilty or innocent. And, all too often, the victims are innocent people, who have done nothing wrong other than venturing online without fully understanding the unique culture of the Internet.

The increase in connectivity that allows instantaneous research and positive connections also brings with it the capability to do immense harm. Popular search engines like Google that allow students to research their homework also allow anybody anywhere in the world to search for your name and find nasty commentary written by a bitter ex-lover. Internet forums that empower positive discussions also allow insular communities to gossip and spread lies about outsiders. The power to instantly transmit data also allows malicious software to spread worldwide instantaneously. The power to speak anonymously about corrupt politicians also allows anonymous attacks on private people who have done no wrong.

The Internet has grown too fast for social norms and common sense to keep up. Special software makes it possible for malevolent users to access the Internet anonymously without leaving any digital fingerprints; society has not yet come to grips with truly anonymous untraceable speech. Social norms have not yet evolved to create a code of conduct for acceptable online behavior—and may never do so. The psychology of the Internet creates a feeling that the targets are somehow distant or unreal and therefore less sympathetic—this problem has been known since the psychologist Stanley Milgram demonstrated the effect of social distance on human behavior, but, has been accentuated and made nearly universally applicable by modern technology.

Law enforcement also lags behind the Internet. In the United States, online law enforcement has generally been focused on major fraud and child pornography. Many victims of "routine" online attacks cannot obtain help from the legal system, either because the attackers have disappeared into the digital night or because local courts and lawyers simply don't know how to deal with complex online attacks that might have come from the far side of the world.

Developments in the law itself have also lagged far behind the evolution of Internet technology. Today, the law of the Internet is controlled by two major federal statutes: the Communications Decency Act (CDA) and the Digital Millennium Copyright Act (DMCA). These laws were enacted in 1996 and 1998, respectively, and they have not been updated, even though the Internet today would be unrecognizable to politicians of 1996. A legal loophole in the Communications Decency Act makes it impossible to force a website to remove anonymous attacks, no matter how false and damaging they may be. The result of the CDA and the DMCA is perverse and bewildering: Viacom can send one letter to YouTube and force it to remove 50,000 videos for copyright violations, but if an anonymous attacker were to upload a lie-filled video about your kid sister to the same site, she would have no power to force the site to take the undoubtedly illegal video down.

As a result, false rumors are spreading with lightning speed. Intimate photographs, videos, and personal details are being leaked worldwide. Gossip and innuendo are replacing honesty and truth. And, thanks to the power of the Internet, attackers and gossipmongers enjoy instant global audiences and powerful anonymity. They work from the shadowy corners of the Web to sabotage reputations, careers, and families. Loopholes in the law protect them from being found or prosecuted.

Of course, anonymous gossip and lies are as old as civilization. But, thanks to the Internet, smears that would once have been limited to a bathroom stall or a hand-passed note can now be seen by employers, friends, families, dates, clients, and anyone else with access to the Web. Before the Internet, a smear campaign based on a personal grudge would last only as long as it took for scrawled notes to find their way to the trash can or as long as it took to paint over graffiti. But today, notes posted on the Web are broadcast to a worldwide audience, preserved into the distant future, and spread to thousands by Google.

For too many people, the Web has become a permanent scarlet letter. Who is going to hire a victim of an online smear when there is a similar candidate up for the job who is not accused, however nonchalantly and anonymously, of being a liar, thief, or cheating husband? Too often, the attack is hard to undo, even if the smears are untrue: how does one rebut an allegation of sexual impropriety? Can one forget the emotional damage caused by being crassly reminded of the loss of a loved one? How is it possible for an everyday person to prove that a photograph is a forgery, let alone inform everyone who has seen it?

The harm caused by electronic attacks extends into the "real" world of flesh-and-blood interactions. Nothing separates the "virtual" and the "real" worlds; an online smear impacts face-to-face interactions just as much as a hushed comment or a passed note. A false claim about your business—accusations of bias or of a lack of patriotism, claims that your product is dangerous, or even claims that employees made offensive comments to customers—can send customers running in droves away from your business and even tie up your phone lines or flood your e-mail with howling protests.

These online attacks are happening more and more frequently. Bullies, jerks, jilted lovers, and sociopaths have realized that they can wreak far more havoc with far less accountability by using the Internet to launch their barbs. The attackers seek explosive revenge for petty differences and jealousies, censorship of their critics through humiliation, destruction of political and business opponents, and sometimes schadenfreude or just nerdy self-celebration from the ability to inflict pain on unsuspecting people hundreds of miles away.

The Machine Is Amoral

The problems caused by the Internet are amplified by its structure. The computers that run the Internet—including the big network switches that control the flow of data and the computers that store the content of websites—do not know or care what information is being transmitted. To a computer, it is all just digital bits. A computer doesn't know if information is true or false, kind or hurtful, public or private. There is no way for a computer to realize that real people are being hurt by a website. A computer is amoral—it just does not have any sense of what is "good" or "bad." (The Internet is not *immoral*—of bad morals—but rather merely *amoral*, meaning that it has no regard for morals either way.) If a computer is programmed to repeat information that it finds, then it will do so no matter whether the information it finds is true ("the moon is made of rock"), false ("the moon is made of cheese"), or completely nonsensical ("the moon cheeses the rock").

The most obvious example is Google's search results. No matter what terms you search for, the results you see will be selected by a computer without human intervention. The details of the algorithm used by Google to rank search results are a closely guarded secret, but the general outlines have been made public. In short, Google's algorithm ranks "popular" sites higher and less "popular" sites lower. The algorithm does not make any judgment about the correctness of a page; it just finds the most popular pages. Google is notorious for refusing to alter the results provided by the algorithm, no matter how compelling the circumstances. Sometimes this policy leads to painful results. For some time, a search for "Jew" on Google returned a hateful anti-Semitic site as the first result, rather than information about the Jewish faith or people. Google apologized and blamed the algorithm's result on the popularity of the hate site, but refused to intervene directly.[1] Just because the hate site was popular, Google's algorithm assumed it must be important. Other results of the algorithm's single-minded focus on popularity are more comical: A search for "miserable failure" used to return a link to the White House, and a search for "French military victories" still returns a link to a page suggesting that the user should have been searching for "French military defeats."

The danger of the automated Web is not limited to search engines: The "social Web" or "Web 2.0" is a group of increasingly interconnected websites that are based around active user participation. This "Web 2.0" model relies on users to create large amounts of content, which is then displayed to other users. The new "Web 2.0" model stands in sharp contrast to the older generation of websites (call it "Web 1.0" or even the "old Web"), which relied on a top-down content model: a paid author would write content and then hope that users would read it. The basic functions of sites like CNN.com or FoxNews.com are classic examples of "Web 1.0" sites: content (like news stories and photographs) is developed by a professional staff, and average users play an entirely passive role when reading the site.

On the other hand, Facebook.com and its adult cousin, LinkedIn.com, are paradigmatic examples of "Web 2.0" websites in that they are both sites where most of the content comes from active user interactions: the sites both allow people to connect online with friends and co-workers in order to share photos and life updates. There is very little content that is created by employees of Facebook or LinkedIn; instead, the sites simply create an open space where users can determine for themselves how to interact. Discussion sites like Slashdot, Digg, and Reddit are also classic examples of "Web 2.0" sites. These sites allow users to submit news stories for others to view and discuss; there is no editor who picks news stories or puts an official spin on the news—instead, it is up to users to submit news and commentary for other users to view. Hundreds of thousands of people visit

these sites to get an eclectic view of current events and to discuss the social issues of the day, and most of the value comes from other users.

These Web 2.0 sites allow (and encourage) positive user interaction. But they also create grave risks to personal reputation. Back
in the days of Web 1.0, the reputation of most private individuals
was pretty safe: most highly visible content was created by professional journalists (or at least by serious amateur ones), and a big
news website like CNN.com had no reason to spread rumors about
individual people (the big sites had other news topics to cover) and
a big financial reason not to smear individuals (the threat of a libel
lawsuit). But, in the days of Web 2.0, everyone is a publisher, and
everyone can distribute content. Your enemies have been armed with
new weapons: blogs, easy "WYSIWYG" website editing ("What
You See Is What You Get" editors that allow everyday people to create fancy-looking sites), extensive discussion forums, and a massive
social echo chamber to repeat it all. And, most important, all of these
enemies have been armed with the power of Google to index everything they say. Disgruntled customers no longer have to rely on professional journalists to carefully research their claims against your
company; now, customers can directly blog about their experience or
write negative reviews on consumer sites—and then these sites will
appear in a Google search for the name of your business. Bitter ex-
lovers or rejected suitors can create online attacks that have the same
impact as buying a massive billboard above a freeway, but at a frac-
tion of the price—and with the possibility of doing it anonymously.
Kids who would once end their mischief with prank phone calls can
now leave a permanent scarlet letter on your reputation by publiciz-
ing a rumor or lie just for kicks and giggles. The power of Web 2.0 to
create positive connections among its users also creates the danger of
misuse to attack and smear reputations.

The open nature of Web 2.0 sites can also create a system of interconnected websites, algorithms, and search systems that no one
person or company is responsible for. Call it a "machine" of sorts,
with parts spread around the world. Often the system works for

good: information is found, packaged, and presented to users. But, the system can also spin out of control when users feed it false information. With one bad input, the connections between the sites can cause the entire system to amplify and echo false information. The amplification starts when one user copies bad information to a "Web 2.0" site, that website automatically spreads it to others, and then another user repeats the process—the cycle repeats uncontrollably until the false information has been distributed far beyond where it should be. For example, a false story posted on the social news site Digg might be shared by users of the social networking site Facebook, which might be "tweeted" by users of the short-form messaging site Twitter.com, where other users will post it to the news site Reddit, where an automated software "robot" will display it on other popular websites without any human intervention, and so on. The sites start to resemble a game of "telephone"—one person posts a story, which gets transformed a little bit as it is relayed to another site, then a little more, then a little more, until complete fiction has been accepted as reality. Often, the story moves so far away from its original source that readers have no way to find out if it is false or incomplete.

The out-of-control Internet "machine" has caused millions of dollars in real-world losses. One day, a "citizen journalist" participating in CNN's "iReport" experiment posted a prank article claiming that Apple CEO Steve Jobs had been rushed to the hospital after suffering a heart attack. The news automatically spread from CNN's site to others and was quickly visible on hundreds of websites that provide stock news and trading information. Apple stock dropped $10 (nearly 10 percent) on the news, and millions of dollars of value was destroyed. Apple was later able to correct the rumors, but the stock still ended the day lower.[2]

Or take the example of the website Spock.com, which was purchased in 2009 by the public records and background-check company Intelius. Spock.com attempts to aggregate information about everyday people. If you were to search Spock.com for the authors of this book, you would likely find a little profile about each of us. Much of the content on Spock.com is based on a robot's automated exploration of a variety of directories. The site then uses other software to cross-reference the results that the robot finds in order to compile an automated dossier on as many people as it can identify. There is generally no human intervention and no way for the robot to verify whether any content it finds is true. In one infamous incident, the robot mistook John Aravosis (a prominent blogger) for a pedophile, because of the robot's inability to tell whether Aravosis was *writing about* a pedophile or whether he was one himself. (For the record, John Aravosis is not a pedophile.) Nonetheless, the site tagged his profile as "pedophile," and his name appeared whenever somebody searched for "pedophile" on the site. The problem was instantly compounded when news reporters mentioned the robot's error. The robot, lacking any irony detector whatsoever, interpreted news stories about the error—many of which contained the words "John Aravosis" and "pedophile"—as confirmation that it got it right the first time around. The link was reinforced, and Aravosis was reduced to pleading with Spock.com's customer service team to get his name cleared. In that case, Spock.com was willing to override the robot's actions, probably because Aravosis is a powerful blogger and could create massive bad publicity for the company. Future victims might not be as lucky.

Another example of false amplification occurred when Google News—an automatic newsbot that searches the Internet to find the important news of the day without any human intervention—got out of control. The results that the newsbot calculates to be the most important (usually the most popular stories that appear in the most news sources) are displayed on the Google News homepage. One morning in late 2008, a software glitch occurred, and an outdated article about United Airlines' 2002 bankruptcy filing suddenly appeared in the Google News system as if it were new. The sudden appearance of a new-seeming article led a writer at the "Income Securities Advisor" newsletter to mention the possibility of a bankruptcy in his own article. That article was then automatically distributed by the Bloomberg wire to hundreds of websites. Once a (false) story about the new United bankruptcy rumor appeared on hundreds of sites, the Google newsbot mistook the story's popularity as confirmation of its importance and made the story even more prominent on the Google News site. The cycle continued. Stock traders immediately reacted, sending UAL stock into a tailspin that ended with a 76 percent drop in the company's value before trading was automatically halted. By afternoon, United was able to deny the rumor, but UAL stock still closed down 10 percent on the day. Of course, all parties involved claim that somebody else was responsible for the error.[3]

These stories are vivid, but they are neither unique nor rare. Similar events happen all the time to everyday people who have done nothing wrong and done nothing to attract attention to themselves. Sometimes these events go without publicity because they are less egregious, but just as often extreme errors go unnoticed by the media because they happen to everyday people and small businesses, rather than to big companies or powerful bloggers. Unfortunately, the effect of one of these incidents on a private individual or small business can be even larger than on a big company or famous person: most everyday people don't have millions of dollars to spend on PR or their own blog through which to correct the record.

The machine can cause great harm even when it is working as designed. A number of well-known companies are in the business of aggregating and selling enormous amounts of personal information: social security numbers, phone numbers, current and old addresses, spousal information, information about children, medical histories and insurance claims, income data, and other revealing details. They often gather this information from widely dispersed sources, ranging from phonebooks to innocent-seeming consumer surveys to state governments. This information is often used for good purposes, such as rooting out credit card fraud and providing background checks for teachers and medical professionals. But some data brokers also sell their lists to less scrupulous companies, like telemarketers and small-time scammers. Their data has been used by identity thieves and stalkers to help find details about victims. And, because these database companies possess such rich stores of data, they become targets of opportunity for fraudsters and computer hackers.

There Is Hope

Thank goodness, there is hope for the average Internet user. Despite all the threats and changes, millions of people have positive online images and live in peace with their Internet neighbors. Through a few simple steps, everyday people like you can still guard your reputation on the digital frontier and even improve your online image in order to increase your success in dating, socializing, getting a job, or getting more clients. By understanding how the Internet is different from other communications media, you will begin to understand the rules of reputation online and the online reputation dangers faced by individuals and small businesses. Then, by learning specific tactics to measure and analyze your own online reputation, you will be able to assess your online reputation priorities—and the gaps that need to be filled to meet those priorities. Next, by learning the techniques used by professionals to repair and improve online reputations, you will learn the active steps you can take to improve your reputation today—and why you should act *before* you have suffered a reputation attack at all (especially if you hope to get more customers, meet new people, or just generally present a positive appearance to the world). Finally, by discovering steps to take in case of an online reputation attack, you will learn how to protect yourself in a worst-case attack and how to start down the road to reputation recovery.

Hold tight; traversing the new digital frontier can still be a rough ride, but the rewards are powerful.

A Note About Notes

For your convenience, the authors have provided many links to additional information or to the full text of sources. In order to save space and avoid the need for you to retype some dreadfully long URLs, all links to additional information are provided through the official website of the book: WildWest2.com. Links of this kind appear in the format "**Go:** http://wildwest2.com/go/101." When you come across one of these links, it is a signal that there is more information available online. Simply type the URL in your web browser and you will be automatically forwarded to the original source of additional information. The authors might not agree with anything (or everything) that a source says, but the links are provided so that you can gather information for yourself. Of course, the authors do not control any linked websites, which may have different privacy policies—please browse cautiously.

Notes

1. Google, Inc., "An Explanation of Our Search Results." **Go:** http://wildwest2.com/go/101.

2. Eric Schonfeld, "Citizen 'Journalist' Hits Apple Stock with False (Steve Jobs) Heart Attack Rumor," *TechCruch*, October 3, 2008. **Go:** http://wildwest2.com/go/102.

3. Jackson West, "Google News Glitch Helps Cause United Stock Selloff," *ValleyWag*, September 8, 2008. **Go:** http://wildwest2.com/go/103.

CHAPTER 2.0

Your Online Reputation
Is Your Reputation

Your online reputation is your reputation. Period.

Your online reputation determines how people look at you. Your online reputation determines who is willing to hire you, buy from you, or sell to you. Your online reputation determines if you will get a second date, or even a first. Your online reputation can be the source of gossip and rumors that can spin a whirlwind around your personal life. And you probably know less about your online reputation than you should.

Your Reputation Shapes Your
Real-World Interactions

Reputation is reality.

—UPDATING A CLASSIC QUOTE

It does not matter whether your reputation is accurate or not; people are going to judge you by it and make their decisions on it. It is an unfortunate fact that the world is too crowded and hectic for most people to stop and take the time to make a careful judgment about you or your business after collecting and weighing all of the evidence available. Instead, people are far more likely to rush to a snap judgment based on the first information they see—and then use that judgment to decide whether they will date, befriend, do business with, hire, or trust you.

Your reputation is the sum total of how you are seen by the public. It is all of the facts and judgments that people make about you. It can be based on news, gossip, rumors, public records, photos, personal experience, and anything else people use to form their opinions.

Reputation is more than just "good" or "bad," although both are part of reputation. Reputation is all of the judgments people make about you: Are you considered an innovator or a leader? Do people think of you as trustworthy and loyal? Do you have a reputation for being good with details or a master of the big picture? Are you seen as stoic or emotional? The list of all the parts of your reputation could stretch many pages.

If you are a small business owner, the same concerns apply. Is your company compared to a Ford Pinto or to a Mercedes Benz? Is it seen as down-market like Wal-Mart or cheap-chic like Target? Positive like Johnson & Johnson or negative like Enron? Growing like Google or shrinking like Alcoa? A leader in customer satisfaction like Southwest Airlines or a laggard like United? The reputation of a business drives sales and growth; customers are unlikely to buy from a business with a tarnished reputation, especially if there are other alternatives available. Some investors even think that almost two-thirds of a company's value is driven by its reputation.[1] This figure has been confirmed on Wall Street; in many corporate buyouts, billions of dollars are attributed to "goodwill"—Wall Street jargon for having a good reputation that encourages consumers to buy whatever the company is selling.

Sometimes, reputation is earned through a combination of many observations over time. Your reputation among your close friends is likely formed this way; they have seen you through thick and thin, and they know your true character. But, other times, a reputation can be made or lost on one event: Captain "Sully" Sullenberger, pilot of the U.S. Airways jet that landed safely in the Hudson River in early 2009, has a reputation as a skilled airman solely because of that one incident.[2] On the other side of the ledger, the supermarket chain Food Lion suffered from a bad reputation for years after one report that the company was selling expired meat. Many athletes have made their reputations on the basis of just one failure success or failure in the clutch: the name Bill Buckner reminds all too many fans of a crucial error in the 1986 World Series, rather than his consistent play across his twenty-year, 1,000-RBI career, and the 1980 U.S. Olympic hockey team is remembered for its "Miracle on Ice" win over the Soviet Union in the medal round instead of its uninspired play in international exhibition matches.

Reputation Matters Because People Take Shortcuts

Every day, thousands of judgments are made on the basis of reputation: Is this person trustworthy? Does this company make reliable products? Will this politician be honest in office? Will this adviser manage my money responsibly? Those judgments lead to countless real-life decisions with serious consequences: whom to hire, what products to buy, how to vote, whom to befriend or date.

This heavy reliance on reputation is probably inevitable. Reputation gives us a fast way to make decisions. We all interact with so many people and companies on a daily basis that it would be impossible to thoroughly investigate each interaction from scratch. And, many times, there is no way to take a person, product, or business partner for a "test drive" to experience them firsthand; you can't safely test the food from a restaurant known for food poisoning, and you certainly would not test entrusting your children to a school bus driver known for alcoholism. Instead, we rely on the collected wisdom of others. This distilled wisdom is known as reputation and makes it possible to make fast decisions.

In more scientific terminology, people rely on so-called heuristics. A *heuristic* is nothing more than a rule of thumb used to make a decision in the face of uncertainty. Some heuristics are easy to spot: when all else is equal, most people assume that expensive products are of higher quality than cheaper products, even to the point of telling their doctors that a $2.50 sugar pill was more effective than an identical $0.10 sugar pill.[3] Obviously, the heuristic is wrong when applied to the sugar pill, but it is understandable how it came about: our life experience tells us that expensive products are usually of higher quality than cheap products.

Sometimes, real-world use of heuristics can be manipulated to comical result. The "social proof" heuristic—a rule of thumb suggesting that there is often wisdom in crowds—has been heavily used by "candid camera" TV shows. The formula is simple: place the unsuspecting target (the "mark") in an unfamiliar environment, surround the mark with actors who behave strangely, and then watch as the mark conforms his own behavior to whatever odd manner the actors are adopting. The mark might face the wrong way in an elevator because everyone else is also facing the wrong way,[4] or walk right past a world-famous artist playing a $2.3 million violin in a subway because everyone else is treating the violinist as a common busker.[5] The application to reputation is straightforward: Most people will follow the crowd when deciding whom to trust, whom to befriend, and whom to do business with. If you ever need proof that this works in practice, then look at the way that many nightclubs artificially create a line outside their front door in order to appear more popular and exclusive; many people subconsciously assume that the club must be better simply because so many people are willing to wait in line to go inside.

Another common heuristic related to reputation is the so-called halo effect. It was first studied by the psychologist Edward Thorndike in the U.S. Army in 1920.[6] He discovered that once a military officer formed a positive impression of a soldier, the officer was likely to give that soldier good scores in all evaluation categories, even if an objective observer would have scored the soldier lower in some categories. And once the officer formed a negative impression of a soldier, the officer was likely to give that soldier a negative evaluation across all evaluation categories, even if the solider deserved high marks in some categories. The explanation was simple: the officer dealt with hundreds of soldiers, so he formed a mental image of each soldier as either a "good" or "bad" soldier and viewed all of the soldier's actions in that light.

Combining social proof with the halo effect creates a powerful basis for social reputation. It is a common rule of thumb to trust people with a good reputation in the community and to distrust people with a bad reputation in the community. This heuristic makes sense: It is efficient to learn from the experiences that other people have had. If a poker player had a reputation for cheating, only a fool would sit down and play a high-stakes game with him. If a company had a reputation for selling unsafe products, it would be foolish to trust its product without inspecting it first. The halo effect makes this form of social reputation even more powerful: Just like most people would not play poker against a gambler with a reputation as a cheater, most people also would not trust him to watch their children.

Unfortunately, this use of reputation as a heuristic is not always accurate. Many reputations are undeserved, especially in the age of digital media and Web 2.0 socialization. There are people and companies that have been unfairly smeared and that do not deserve their negative reputations. And there are people and companies that have positive reputations beyond what they have earned. But the inaccuracy of many reputations does not stop people from using reputation to judge each other. Instead, let this serve as a reminder of why you must carefully guard your reputation if you hope to succeed at any pursuit in life.

Online Content Can Make or Break Your Reputation

The Internet is the instant universal research source.

If nobody relied on the Internet, online smears and attacks would not matter. To paraphrase a Zen master, "if a vandal scrawled insults on a bathroom wall and there was nobody there to read it, would it really be graffiti?" Anonymous lies and smears would go unnoticed, inaccurate information would not be repeated, and reputations would be earned the old-fashioned way.

But, unfortunately, the Internet is *the* source of every kind of information imaginable. It is hard to overestimate the impact of the Internet. Millions upon millions of people use the Internet to learn about the people they meet and the businesses they interact with. The Internet is the primary source of news, research, entertainment, and information for innumerable people. Almost everyone in the developed world relies either directly or indirectly on the Internet for research into *something*. The difference between the pre-Internet era and today is the difference between graffiti in a bar bathroom and graffiti on a billboard overlooking Highway 101 in downtown Los Angeles. It is the difference between a classroom note and a full-page advertisement in *USA Today*. It is the difference between lies that would have once faded into obscurity and a permanent scarlet letter (see Figure 2-1).

The Internet Is Given Too Much Trust

The Internet has the power to shape reputation only because many Internet users trust it. This trust is often misplaced. Anyone can create Internet content, often anonymously (as is described in Chapters 4 and 5). There is no person or computer that verifies that Internet content is complete, balanced, or even vaguely truthful.

Figure 2-1. "Who Might Be Searching for You?

If you are a ...

Parent	Salesperson	Student	Boss	Anybody
↓	↓	↓	↓	↓
Teachers	Your boss	Teachers	Your boss	Friends
PTA board members	Co-workers	Classmates	Co-workers	Nosy neighbors
Other parents	Potential customers	College admissions offices	Subordinates	Acquaintances
Your child's peers	Past customers	Your parents	Recruiters	Identity thieves
Private school admissions offices	Competing companies	Other parents	Competitors	Disaffected strangers
Guidance counselors	Competing salespeople	Summer jobs	Disaffected customers	
			Political protestors	

... these people might be searching for information about you online! What will they find?

Nonetheless, vast swaths of Internet content are accorded at least some degree of trust, which is far more than a lot of Internet content probably deserves.

The fact that most Internet content is in print (rather than spoken) and the way that it is presented (through a computer, rather than scrawled on a bathroom wall) encourage blind faith in online content, even though much online content is given about as much thought when posting as a bathroom artist gives when scrawling a drunken graffito. Even if readers take online content with a grain of salt, they still often give too much credit to a false or malicious story; it is a false compromise to assume that the truth must be somewhere between two (or more) anonymous stories, when everything online might be entirely groundless.[7]

At the same time that users are giving too much trust to content found on the Internet, they are also giving too much meaning to its absence. Today, a "Google trail"—a long history of information that can be found about you or your business through Google—is necessary for you to be seen as legitimate. A company with no Google trail is viewed as possibly fraudulent; people wonder why there is no recorded mention of the company.[8] Similarly, an individual who claims to be a leader in her field is viewed with skepticism if there are no trade journal publications about her, blog posts or Twitter "tweets" from conferences, or other relevant online content. It doesn't matter how many people know about you offline or how many local newspapers wrote about you in the pre-Internet era: if it doesn't show up in Google, then it doesn't count. Many people think that if something doesn't exist in Google, then it probably doesn't exist at all.

The Internet also provides such an easy way to perform research that it has replaced many more traditional sources. Before the Internet, researching a company or product often involved a trip to the local public library to dig up old newspapers on microfilm, check the volumes of the *Encyclopedia Britannica*, or at least dig through dusty issues of *Consumer Reports* magazine. These sources were never completely accurate, but at least they were written and edited by professionals, subject to corrections, vetted by librarians, and published by companies concerned with their own reputations for accuracy and completeness. But, today, it is possible to perform nearly any kind of research online, from the comfort of one's home, at any hour of the day. You can wake up early to perform research or stay up late. Frankly, you don't even need to wear clothes to perform research online. It is so easy to perform research online that few people bother to check offline sources anymore. But many Internet users still have not learned how to apportion trust to online sources that might not be trustworthy, complete, or accurate. Of course, there are plenty of websites that present reliable information written and edited by dedicated amateurs, but there are also websites stocked with half-truth, bias, slander, and outright lies—and few ways to tell the difference between the good and the bad.

Today, even professional journalists have been caught cribbing their stories entirely from the Internet. The prestigious *The Times*

(London), founded in 1785, was caught red-handed relying exclusively on Internet research when it published a list of the "Top 50 Rising Stars" in European soccer. The paper listed a Moldavian player named Masal Bugduv as the thirtieth hottest soccer star. It turns out that there is no "Masal Bugduv" anywhere in the world; he was nothing more than an elaborate Internet hoax. But, because the author relied exclusively on online research, he was easily fooled by a series of fake news releases. Had the newspaper performed even a tiny amount of offline research—perhaps by making a phone call to "Bugduv's" alleged coach—it could have avoided major embarrassment.[9] Fortunately for fans, local coaches took the time to perform their own research before signing "Bugduv" to a contract.

Of course, if an anonymous hoaxster can fool the *Times* into reporting on a fictional soccer star, other tricks can fool millions of others. And many tricks are not nearly as innocent as pulling a newspaper's leg. False reports started online can destroy real-life reputations, break up families, and shorten careers. And, as the "Masal Bugduv" story shows, false information online can quickly be echoed in print publications. The print publication then supports the false online information, leading to a cycle of self-reinforcing false information. This is the so-called Wikipedia echo effect, based on the tendency of lazy journalists to collect their "facts" from the online encyclopedia Wikipedia and then the tendency of Wikipedia to cite those same journalists as proof of the (possibly false) facts.

A Bad First Impression Might Be Your Only Impression

First impressions matter. The first thing somebody knows about you gives context to all subsequent interactions. If you make a positive first impression, that positive impression will provide a positive background for all future interactions—remember the power of the "halo effect" to reinforce a positive image. But a negative first impression will sabotage your future interactions and leave you playing at a disadvantage.

There is extensive experimental evidence supporting the common wisdom that first impressions create a powerful impact. In job interviews, it is possible for an observer to correctly predict which candidates will get the job by looking at only the first thirty seconds of a thirty-minute interview.[10] In just thirty seconds, enough social cues are exchanged that a powerful first impression is formed. First impressions are just as important in social life: college freshmen could tell within the first three minutes of interaction whether a classmate would become a friend or stay an acquaintance.[11]

There is even more evidence that people make very quick decisions online. One study showed that consumers could decide within 0.05 seconds—not much longer than it takes to blink—whether they were interested in reading a web page or if they wanted to leave for another site.[12]

In other words, many people do not take the time to slowly and deliberately research all possible information before making their decisions about whom to trust, especially online. Instead, in less than three minutes (and sometimes in just the time that it takes to blink), people come to snap decisions about whom to hire, fire, befriend, or ignore. It is crucial to make that first impression count if you hope to achieve success.

Your Online Résumé Is Your Online First Impression

Your online résumé is the first blast of content that people find when they look for information about you. If your reputation is a book, your online résumé is its cover; it is what too many people will use to judge you at a glance. It is the most prominent information about you, and it shapes your personal brand.

Your online résumé is the information that can be quickly found and skimmed through a quick search using a general search engine like Google, a social site like Facebook, a photo-specific site like Flickr, a professional site like LinkedIn, or a people-specific engine like Pipl.com. In short, it is the first blast of content that a curious Internet user could find when looking for you or your business.

Within your online résumé, some content is more important than the rest. Content that is more prominent online makes up a larger part of your online résumé. For example, content found at the very top of a search engine search for your name will make up an important part of your online résumé. Content that is less prominent is a smaller part of your online résumé. Content that cannot be found by an average user in five minutes or less is not part of your online résumé at all; for example, information about you that can be found only through a detailed query in a very specific government database might make up some part of your online reputation, but it is not part of your online résumé.

The metaphor behind the term "online résumé" is simple: in a job search, your professional résumé provides a summary of your qualifications. Hiring managers quickly flip through résumés and weed out résumés with obvious flaws; someone with a bad résumé is unlikely to get an interview or a job. Similarly, your online résumé provides what appears to be a summary of who you are, and it is used to quickly make a judgment about you and your character. Web searchers quickly flip through your online résumé, looking at the first few items that come up. They may investigate some items further, or they may simply make their final judgment about you on the basis of the limited information available at first glance.

Unfortunately, you don't have the same control over your online résumé that you have over your professional résumé. It is easy enough to update your professional résumé: just fire up a copy of Microsoft® Word™ (or any other word processing software) and add or delete whatever information suits you. But control over your online résumé is much more difficult; it is not entirely up to you what appears in a

Google search for your name. You can exert some control over your online résumé, as will be described in Chapters 10–13, but it takes careful planning and detailed execution.

If all online résumés were always accurate, then it would be easy to have a positive online résumé: just live a good life, achieve great things, be kind to others, and clean up after your own messes.[13] But, unfortunately, your online reputation often does not reflect the complete truth about you. It might be incomplete. It might reflect inaccurate statements or distortions. It might be obsolete or outdated. It might focus on only one event, rather than on the entirety of your life and career. Or it might contain outright lies and nasty attacks. These distortions might be accidental—the result of a similarity in name or a computer error—or might be caused by malicious users with their own agendas.

In short, your online reputation does not necessarily reflect the truth. Instead, it reflects the "*Google Truth.*" The Google Truth looks like the authoritative truth, but it is often incomplete, inaccurate, or just plain wrong. It is what happens when computers try to guess who you are and what you do. But computers cannot always tell what is really you and what is truly important. And if there is inaccurate information about you online, all too often the Google Truth will reflect it. There is an old adage about computer algorithms, and it applies fully to the output of search engines like Google: "garbage in, garbage out."

Chapter 9 covers, in great detail, the way to measure and analyze your online résumé. It gives you step-by-step instructions how to understand your online résumé by carefully analyzing who is looking for information about you or your business, where they are likely to search, and what they are likely to find.

Your Total Online Profile Is Everything About You Online

In contrast to your online résumé, your total online profile is the sum of what people can learn about you or your business through detailed online research. It includes everything in your online résumé, plus everything that would take a more substantial search to find, including information that can be found only indirectly or only through proprietary data services.

Your total online profile can be vast. It can include everything from news articles to blog posts about you, to photos of you, to information in phone-number and address databases, to criminal records, to land deed records, and much more.

In many ways, your total online profile is like a painting. Much like a painting, it is a stylized interpretation of reality—you hope more like a Renoir and less like a Picasso. Because not everything you have ever done is online, it does not include everything that is part of your life; instead, it represents only one angle or perspective on you. And, also like a painting, it is composed of hundreds of tiny details that add up to a larger image. Just as paintings have small brush strokes that add up to a scene, your total online profile is the sum of many small bits of content that add up to a snapshot of your life. The content that is most readily available to someone searching your name makes up a big part of your total online profile, whereas content that is hard to find is a small part. Someone just glancing at your online profile will see only the big picture and will not see most of the small details, but a dedicated searcher can find and examine each individual brush stroke.

Chapter 9 explains how to take inventory of your total online profile, and Chapters 10 through 13 help you improve your total online profile by painting over the worst content and drawing attention to the best content.

Notes

1. Weber Shandwick, "Safeguarding Reputation," at 2. **Go:** http://wildwest2.com/go/201.

2. For example, his "fan page" on Facebook. **Go:** http://wildwest2.com/go/202.

3. Justin Wolfers, "More Expense = Less Pain," Freakonomics (blog), in *New York Times*, March 6, 2008, via nytimes.com. **Go**: http://wildwest2.com/go/203.

4. Dan Lockton, "London Design Festival: Greengaged," Design with Intent (blog), September 18, 2008, via danlockton.co.uk. **Go**: http://wildwest2 .com/go/204.

5. Gene Weingarten, "Pearls Before Breakfast," *Washington Post*, April 8, 2007, via washingtonpost.com. **Go**: http://wildwest2.com/go/205.

6. E. L. Thorndike, "A Constant Error in Psychological Rating," *Journal of Applied Psychology* 4 (1920): 25–29.

7. Perhaps a grain of salt is outdated. Internet users should be issued burlap sacks of salt.

8. Chadwick Matlin, "The Way We Beg," The Big Money (blog), February 5, 2008, via thebigmoney.com. **Go**: http://wildwest2.com/go/207.

9. Brian Phillips, "Fictional Moldavian Soccer Player Tells All," *Slate*, January 23, 2008, via slate.com. **Go**: http://wildwest2.com/go/208.

10. Martha Brockenbrough, "First Impressions: How Much Do They Really Matter?" *Encarta*, via Encarta.com. **Go**: http://wildwest2.com/go/209.

11. Ibid.

12. Martha Brockenbrough, "First Impressions Count for Web," BBC News (online), January 16, 2006, via news.bbc.co.uk. **Go**: http://wildwest2.com/go/210.

13. If it really were that easy, the authors would simply direct readers to a popular self-help book, such as *The Purpose Driven Life*, by Rick Warren (Grand Rapids, Mich.: Zondervan, 2002), **Go**: http://wildwest2.com/go/211; or *Living a Life That Matters*, by Harold Kushner (New York: Knopf, 2001). **Go**: http://wildwest2.com/go/212.

CHAPTER

The Internet Is the
New Wild West

The Internet is a new frontier. In many ways, the experience of the Internet today echoes the experience of the American Old West. To understand why the Internet is the way it is today, one must understand how it got its start and how it has changed over time.

In a frontier environment like the early Internet, the only certain thing is that everything is subject to change. Frontiers often start with rapid expansion. In American history, expansion started with the early "Wild West" days, when land was cheap, there was always something new over the horizon, and settlement moved rapidly westward. There were no established interests that had an incentive to preserve the status quo. And, like all frontiers, the West had little government regulation—which also meant little formal law enforcement and a strong need for self-defense (which often became rough vigilante justice). Innovation and experimentation thrived in the Old West; frontiers are always known for spurring entrepreneurs to create new and useful products and services. And the West was a place where new forms of social expression were accepted.

But the story of the American West did not end with rapid growth. Frontiers don't stay wild forever; eventually, the frontier either becomes civilized or fades away. Later phases of frontier development in the West created tensions between new and old, between "civilized" and "wild," and between early pioneers and late arrivers. Towns that were once on the margins of the frontier quickly found themselves becoming interior cities. Sturdy buildings replaced canvas tents. Law and order began to replace frontier violence as the growth of wealth and stability prompted residents to replace vigilante committees with formal law enforcement. And other changes were forced by late arrivers who were not accustomed to the frontier way of doing things.

The recent history of the Internet closely echoes this stylized history of the American West, simply substituting an electronic frontier for a physical one.

The Internet Is a New Frontier: Call It Wild West 2.0

Those who cannot remember the past are condemned to repeat it.

—George Santayana[1]

The similarity between the original Wild West and the Internet of today is striking. Both started as outposts at the edges of civilization that were known for their lawlessness: gambling, prostitution, and petty scams dominated both the American West and the early Internet. Both were known for having wide-open societies that tolerated behavior previously condemned by "civilized" society. Both enabled the creation (and loss) of spectacular fortunes, and both prompted the development of many wondrous new technologies.

But, as more people migrated to the American West and more people started to connect to the Internet, law enforcement started to catch up to the outlaws. Entrenched interests began to slow the growth of new industries. It became harder to strike it rich overnight. And a flood of late arrivers from the "old world" brought morals and social norms that clashed with the frontier's wild ways.

The Internet has captured the global imagination, just like the original Wild West. Many people see the Internet as more than just a technological innovation; instead, many people view it as a revolutionary frontier experience. Proposals to change the Internet are met with emotional protests that defend the current state of the Internet as if it were an idealized representation of freedom, just as many residents of the Wild West protested vigorously against changes to the frontier culture of the early wild days. Many people project their dreams and aspirations of freedom onto the Internet, even if many expressions of that "freedom" are harmful or prevent other people from making full use of the Internet.

Even the technical history of the Internet mimics that of the Old West frontier.[2] Very few people even knew about the Internet in its early days, and even fewer were able to access it. In the 1970s and 1980s, dedicated lines and expensive computer terminals were required to connect to the fledgling network. But, by the early 1990s it was possible to use a home computer and a dial-up line to access the Internet through a new class of Internet Service Providers (ISPs). These early connections were slow and primitive, and early users had to be very tech-savvy in order to configure their home computers to work with the network. The World Wide Web did not exist yet, so most of the social value of the early Internet came through a free-ranging discussion system known as Usenet and through a few file-transfer systems sites that shared simple programs or games through a text interface.

But, just like the Old West, the Internet had its own gold rush that opened the frontier to all. In the early 1990s, the World Wide Web was invented, allowing users to navigate the Internet visually instead of by typing arcane commands into a text interface. Entrepreneurs recognized an opportunity and started to find ways to profit from the accelerating growth of the Internet. On August 9, 1995, Netscape was the first Internet company to go public.[3] Its initial public offering (IPO) marked the official start of the Internet gold rush. At its IPO, Netscape's most visible founder, Marc Andreessen, was only twenty-four years old. The company had never reported a profit, and its main product (the now-forgotten Mosaic Internet browser) was given away free. But antiquated concerns like "profit" and "revenue" could not stop the speculators; there were more than 100 million requests for the 5 million shares that Netscape was willing to sell.[4] Its stock opened trading at $26 dollars per share, already double the price that bankers thought it was worth. At one point during the first day of trading, Netscape shares were selling for more than $75, which meant that Netscape—a company that recorded less than $25 million in total revenue before going public—had a market value of more than $2 billion, large enough to put it in league with then-Fortune 500™ companies like the New York Times Company (NYSE: NYT).[5] The IPO made multimillionaires out of kids who were barely out of college and who would normally have been working at entry-level jobs in faceless corporations—as Malcolm Gladwell explains in *Outliers*, the Internet gold rush was one of the rare moments in history when ordinary people could strike it extraordinarily rich.[6]

The media frenzy rivaled that of the original Wild West promoter Samuel Brannan: MSNBC tried to get a live feed of the NASDAQ trading floor, Netscape founder Marc Andreessen was on the cover of *Time* magazine, and new magazines sprung up to cover the rapidly growing Internet IPO market. Netscape was to the dot.com boom what Sutter's Mill was to the 1848 gold rush. And, in a peculiarly close echo of the first gold rush, thousands of migrants again moved west to join the early Internet pioneers in California. But this wave of Internet entrepreneurs bypassed San Francisco (the heart of the old gold rush) and instead settled just thirty miles south in Silicon Valley and San Jose (see Figure 3-1).

Figure 3-1. Sand Hill Road in Silicon Valley, the heart of the 1990s technology bubble. Credit: Mark Coggins (via Flickr).

Just as in the original Wild West, a boom followed the first discovery of (electronic) gold. In 1999, there were more than 300 technology IPOs, creating instant paper millionaires out of thousands of entrepreneurs. And, just like in the old West, the overheated market collapsed within a few years; the only difference is that Netscape founder Marc Andreessen took home at least $500 million, while Old West gold rush originator James Marshall went broke and eventually relied on the state for assistance.[7]

The Internet Developed a Frontier Culture

As a result of its cultural isolation, the young Internet developed its own manners, rules, and conduct apart from the culture of the "off-line" society. The most obvious signal that things were different online was the unique vocabulary of the Internet; most users quickly began to use and understand emoticons like ":)" and ":("and new acronyms like "LOL" (which morphed from "lots of love" in handwritten letters to "laugh out loud" online) and "ROFL" ("rolling on the floor laughing"). More advanced users developed a specialized vocabulary, extending all the way to "leetspeak," a complex language that substitutes symbols for letters in words (the word "leetspeak" itself might be written as "l33tsp33k").[8]

But the cultural differences of the Internet extend far beyond linguistics. For example, the early Internet's heavy reliance on self-policing created a culture of governmental noninterference that continues to this day. In the very early days, only academic researchers had access to the Internet. They had little need for oversight because they were all bound by their academic interests and personal connections. These first pioneers were amazed by the potential of the network and thought that any restrictions on the network would hinder its growth; their views echoed those of the cattlemen of the Old West who thought that absolute freedom to move their cattle would lead to riches for all. Disputes on the early Internet were resolved by massive "town hall" discussions and direct democracy, another hallmark of frontier societies.

This frontier culture of self-policing and self-reliance matured somewhat over time. Early online disputes were settled under a code of behavior that bore only a loose resemblance to offline law or offline behavioral norms. A unique rough-and-tumble character emerged: Users would take great pride in gently competing to undermine each other's security. Actual malicious use was rare, but pranks were common; one well-known prank was to chide a user who left his account insecure by accessing the victim's computer and broadcasting a standard message under the negligent user's name: "I have very baggy pants."[9] The victim of the prank was embarrassed by the message, but there was no permanent harm done.

The Internet soon grew into a larger community than could support gentle "baggy pants" trickery. The network spread outside the personal networks that initially restrained behavior. The first obvious bumps occurred in 1978, when the first "spam," or unsolicited commercial e-mail, was sent to 393 early e-mail users. The message advertised a demonstration of new computing hardware by Digital Equipment Corporation.[10] The response, however, was a typical frontier response: Instead of imposing technical or legal limits, the community encouraged restraint and social enforcement of vague norms. Law enforcement was frowned upon: "Any censorship can only lead to worse things later on," said one debate participant.[11]

The Internet also quickly took on many other qualities of the lawless Old West frontier. Just as in the first Wild West, prostitution and gambling were rampant online by the late 1990s. Of course, any transaction for prostitution still had to be consummated offline, but online advertising of services offered was plentiful; even the mainstream classified site Craigslist had an "erotic services" section. For years, law enforcement turned a blind eye: There were simply other priorities that it considered more important than obscure electronic advertisements for prostitution.[12] Similarly, online gambling blossomed, with online casinos raking in tens of millions of dollars from players worldwide. The game of Texas Hold 'Em poker experienced a renaissance in the early twenty-first century largely because of the sudden availability of online poker. And, again, the law looked the other way.

And, just like the Old West, the digital Wild West had its share of petty con men, starting with the infamous "419" advance-fee scammers who promised a share of a (nonexistent) fortune if only the victim would pay a small tax or transfer fee required to release (non-existent) lottery winnings or the (nonexistent) estate of a deceased businessman. As early as 1997, the U.S. government confirmed that individuals had lost almost $100 million to this scam, and actual losses were probably much higher. And, just as in the original Old West, there were accusations of rigged card games—one charlatan was confirmed to have stolen roughly between $400,000 and $700,000 after just forty days of "work" rigging an online poker website.[13]

In another echo of the Old West, there were substantially more men than women on the early digital frontier. While there are few statistics about the very early days of the Internet, as late as 1996 there was a roughly seven-to-three ratio of men to women online, meaning that there were more than twice as many men as women online.[14]

The result was an online culture that was vastly different from the offline culture: Gambling was effectively legal, prostitution was openly advertised, countless con men and scam artists worked the virtual streets, and the law turned a blind eye to it all. For these early pioneers, the only form of defense was self-defense; the law was simply unable (or unwilling) to track down scammers and spammers working in far-off countries or to crack down on the proliferation of online vice.

The Culture of the Internet is in Conflict with Offline Culture

The Internet boom also put a limit on the Internet's cultural isolation. This too is an echo of the original gold rush, which created the infrastructure that allowed late-arrivers to flock to mining boomtowns like San Francisco and Denver. Online, the digital " '49-ers" of the dot.com era cleared a path that made it easier for everyday citizens to access the Internet today. To take one example, the Mosaic Internet browser itself has been long forgotten, but it introduced a world of visual browsing that has become the foundation for the Web and for modern programs like Internet Explorer, Mozilla Firefox, and Google Chrome. In fact, the Firefox browser is a direct descendant of Netscape's Mosaic browser thanks to Netscape's decision to release the source code for Mosaic. Similarly, the founders of Google made a massive fortune, but their efforts also made it possible for everyday users to find nearly anything online through a simple search interface. Early users who played obscure online games through dial-up modems spurred the technology now used by senior citizens to play online hearts and bridge. The demand for high-speed connections to view "adult" videos sparked the creation of high-bandwidth connections that allow services like Netflix to stream mainstream movies directly to the home. And countless other technologies have been adapted for mainstream use thanks to the contributions of the Internet pioneers.

But, the expansion of the frontier has not always been peaceful. The explosive growth of the Internet through the 2000s has created a massive clash between the new and old cultures of the Internet. Hundreds of thousands of new users have flooded the Internet, unaware of the unique history of the network or the culture that had developed online. Many of these new users did not grow up with the Internet. They never internalized the unique language of the Internet and never worked within its strange social norms. When these new users connected, they expected an environment like the offline world—secure, safe, and governed by the same offline manners and standards of behavior. They were shocked to find an Internet filled with scams and con artists, unsecure websites, devious pranksters, and plentiful hoaxsters. And these users were even more shocked to find out that law enforcement was doing virtually nothing to reduce the dangers online (especially the petty scams and viruses that make up "online street crime"). The results were painful for many new users: loss of money to scammers, embarrassment at being pranked, time spent fixing identity theft, and so forth. Even physical harm is possible when online cultures collide. To take an extreme (but entirely true) example, a group of pranksters decided to attack a website used by people with photosensitive epilepsy. The motive appears to have been nothing more than a cruel desire to get laughs at the expense of a less technologically savvy group. The method? The pranksters filled the website with flashing images intended to trigger epileptic migraines—or even epileptic seizures—in anybody who viewed them.[15] The resulting outrage among "offline" society was entirely predictable, as was the backlash among Internet natives who thought that it was nothing more than a prank that revealed the need for users (the victims) to invest more energy in self-defense and computer security.

To new users of the Internet, who were accustomed to a relatively safe and familiar offline world, the need to take active technological steps to avoid harm came as a shock. The online world was simply different in a dangerous way. Some new users took their lumps and stuck around long enough to learn how to practice online self-defense, but other users—especially from an older generation—were frightened by what they saw and fled, losing the benefits of the Internet in the process.

Of course, experienced users have been frustrated by the naiveté of the newcomers (sometimes called "newbies" or just "noobs"), just as the newcomers have been frightened of the Internet natives. As early as 1993, long-time users of the Usenet discussion system began to complain about the "Eternal September." The term arose when America Online connected its network to the Usenet system and allowed tens of thousands of new users to flood the existing discussion, disrupting what had been a relatively stable discussion system. The "September" of "Eternal September" was a reference to the annual flood of inappropriate messages and silly questions caused by the wave of new Internet users every September when college freshmen got their first Internet access through their school. The fear underlying the term "Eternal September" was that the sudden flood of AOL users would permanently destabilize the discussion system. The old-timers complained that the new users lacked etiquette ("netiquette"), used the system inappropriately, and did not understand how the system worked. The new users, of course, thought the old users rude, unwelcoming, and unrealistic to think that their idiosyncratic culture would last forever. Of course, the influx of new AOL users in 1993 was a mere trickle compared to what came later, but it represented the first major clash to result from a large group of the general public crashing what had been a private Internet party.

The influx of new users into the formerly insolated Internet culture has re-created many of the same tensions that plagued interactions on the Old West frontier between newcomers and old-timers. The changes created by the Internet culture clash have been obvious in some ways. There has been a massive crackdown on gambling and prostitution online, just as there was at the close of the frontier in the Old West. In 2006, the FBI arrested the owner of a major online gambling site.[16] Digital natives lamented the move as the beginning of the end of the wild Internet. Later that year, Congress passed and the President signed a bill outlawing all monetary transactions with online casinos, effectively making it impossible for U.S. residents to get money into or out of an online casino.[17] Similarly, the online classified site Craigslist removed many of its prostitution advertisements after being investigated by forty state attorneys general,[18] and law enforcement officers started to create fake online prostitution ads as part of a sting operation against johns.[19] Extensive investigations took some malicious websites offline, including the complete shutdown of one server farm that was a haven for spammers and criminals.[20]

But law enforcement online has not yet caught up with offline enforcement, and it may never. Thousands of spammers and malicious websites are still online. International scammers and fraudsters still work with impunity. Vigilante justice remains the only form of justice against many fraudsters; for example, an extensive community of Internet users has sprung up with the goal of playing tricks on "419" fraudsters, often by encouraging the fraudster to take embarrassing photos of himself or by convincing the fraudster to go on a long trip to collect (nonexistent) wire transfer payments from the would-be victim.[21] One can argue until blue in the face about whether this digital vigilantism ("digilantism," if you will) is good or bad, but there's no doubt that it happens frequently.

Long-time Internet users continue to preach self-reliance and technical measures to make the Internet more useable. To take just one example, the well-known Internet developer Paul Graham (responsible for many of the online shopping cart innovations that have become standard practice online) thinks that pure technology is better than law at stopping unsolicited commercial e-mail ("spam"). He elaborated on this theme in his classic book *Hackers and Painters*.[22] To him, it is only natural that the solution for an online problem is a technological solution designed to detect key phrases that appear in spam messages and to delete the offending messages. In contrast, many people more familiar with offline legal systems suggest imposing new laws and controls on the Internet. One leading example is technology lawyer David Baumer, who believes that legal solutions based on the federal CAN-SPAM law and similar state laws that give private citizens an incentive to sue spammers are "within sight."[23] To him, it is only natural that the solution for an online problem is a legal regime. Somewhere in between, leading Internet scholar Jonathan Zittrain suggests that the answer to problems like spam might be a mix of technological and social solutions, such as cooperation between Internet Service Providers and users to identify and block websites that send spam.[24]

The result is a continuing conflict between self-defense and law enforcement, between open and closed borders, and between order and chaos. It is the same debate that raged in the Old West. And it is not clear that either side is entirely "right" or "better." There are fundamental technological limitations in the Internet that mean that it may never be as safe and secure as the offline world, or at least not in the same ways. But there is no reason for it to be a complete free range for fraud, scams, attacks, smears, impersonation, and libel. Too many people are using the Internet these days to continue a world of vigilante justice and aggressive self-defense. But much of the growth of the Internet was spurred by its wide-open nature, free from government interference or rules of any sort. It is inevitable that some balance will be struck between these positions, but it is not yet certain what balance that will be. And, as Internet scholar Lawrence Lessig wisely points out, the final balance might depend a lot on whether the old policy of Internet self-governance is able to avert a massive catastrophe or whether serious government regulation of the Internet starts from the perspective of recovering from a digital terrorist attack.

The Internet is still fundamentally a frontier environment. But it is not the frontier of the early pioneers anymore. Just as the end of the gold rush was not the end of the story for the Old West, the end of the first stage of the Internet's development is not the end of its story. Those who understand the battle over the future of the Internet will be well positioned to preserve their own reputation along the way.

Notes

1. From George Santayana, *Reason in Common Sense*, the first volume of *The Life of Reason*. **Go**: http://wildwest2.com/go/301.

2. For a more detailed history of the Internet, check out the free online bonus chapter detailing the history of the Internet, exclusively available at http://www.WildWest2.com/bonus/history/.

3. "Remembering Netscape: The Birth of The Web," *Fortune*, July 25, 2005. **Go**: http://wildwest2.com/go/302.

4. "Further Fallout from Last Week's Nutty Netscape IPO," *Fortune*, September 4, 1995. **Go**: http://wildwest2.com/go/303.

5. "It's the IPO, Stupid," *Vanity Fair*, January 2000. **Go**: http://wildwest2.com/go/314.

6. **Go**: http://wildwest2.com/go/304.

7. Gary Rivlin, "If You Can Make It in Silicon Valley, You Can Make It . . . in Silicon Valley Again," *New York Times* (magazine), June 5, 2005. **Go**: http://wildwest2.com/go/316.

8. **Go**: http://wildwest2.com/go/305.

9. **Go**: http://wildwest2.com/go/306.

10. Brad Templeton, "Reactions to the DEC Spam of 1978." **Go**: http:// wildwest2.com/go/307.

11. Mark Crispin, in Brad Templeton, "Reactions to the DEC Spam of 1978." **Go**: http://wildwest2.com/go/308.

12. Bruce Lambert, "As Prostitutes Turn to Craigslist, Law Takes Notice," *New York Times*, September 5, 2007. **Go**: http://wildwest2.com/go/309.

13. Mike Brunker, "Online poker cheating blamed on employee," MSNBC.com, October 19, 2007. **Go**: http://wildwest2.com/go/310. Also visit a site dedicated to recounting the scam. **Go**: http://wildwest2.com/go/311.

14. The Internet Encyclopedia, Hossein Bidgoli (ed.), 2004, at 14.

15. WARNING: The following link contains samples of the images used in the attack and may trigger a response in readers with photo-sensitive epilepsy: **Go**: http://wildwest2.com/go/312. Also see a news report at **Go**: http://wildwest2.com/go/313.

16. Simon Bowers, "Online Betting Boss Faces Conspiracy Charges in U.S.," *The Guardian* (UK), July 18, 2006. **Go**: http://wildwest2.com/go/314.

17. Associated Press, "Bush Signs Port-Security, Internet Gambling Bill," *USA Today*, October 13, 2006. **Go**: http://wildwest2.com/go/315.

18. Associated Press, "Craigslist to Crack Down on Prostitution Ads," KDKA.com, November 6, 2008. **Go**: http://wildwest2.com/go/316. Also see Craigslist's response, at **Go**: http://wildwest2.com/go/317.

19. Hector Castro, "Ad on Craigslist Really a Sex Sting," *Seattle Post-Intelligencer*, November 16, 2008. **Go**: http://wildwest2/com/go/318.

20. Jeremy Kirk, "After McColo Takedown, Spam Surges Again," *Network World*, January 26, 2009. **Go**: http://wildwest2.com/go/319.

21. The website is at 419eater.com.

22. Paul Graham, *Hackers and Painters* (Santa Rosa, Calif.: O'Reilly Media, 2004). **Go**: http://wildwest2.com/go/320.

23. David Baumer, "SPAM: Are Legal Solutions Within Sight?" Working paper (2006). **Go**: http://wildwest2.com/go/321.

24. Jonathan Zittrain, *The Future of the Internet and How to Stop It* (New Haven, Conn.: Yale University Press, 2008). **Go**: http://wildwest2.com/go/322.

CHAPTER 4.0

The Forces Driving
Online Reputation

The Internet has turned reputation on its head. What was once private is now public. What was once local is now global. What was once fleeting is now permanent. And what was once trustworthy is now unreliable. These changes are explained by the way that the technology of the Internet has shaped the people's interaction with it. Understanding the unique relationship between technology and culture online is key to understanding how to manage your reputation online. Failure is certain for users who apply offline techniques to their Internet reputation or who use offline assumptions when dealing with online problems. Instead, savvy users must understand the technical and cultural differences between the Internet and the offline world in order to effectively preserve and improve their reputations online.

A Brave New World for Reputation

The Internet is not like other forms of communication. The Internet is not a phone, a radio, a TV, a newspaper, a magazine, a billboard, or a bathroom wall. It is entirely unique: it is simultaneously the largest soapbox in the history of soapbox speeches, the largest library of human knowledge ever created, the biggest party line chat in the history of conversation, and much more. Unlike any medium that has come before it, it offers powerful, global, instant, interactive communication equally to everyone, no matter how young or old, no matter where in the world they are located, and no matter what they have to say. Everyone can broadcast, and everyone can listen.

Thanks to the Internet, we now have more power over one another's reputations than at any point in history. Average everyday citizens have the power to create or destroy almost anybody's good name. But, fortunately, the Internet has also given people the power to monitor, manage, and improve their own reputation, in a way never before seen. Understanding the technical nature of the Internet is the first step toward monitoring and managing your online reputation. The technology of the Internet is dramatically different from the offline world: it allows anyone to publish anything instantly and globally, it is easily searched, search engines don't know or care if something is true so long as it is popular, nearly everything online is permanent, and disparate audiences are thrown together in a way that doesn't often happen in the real world.

Leading scholar Daniel Solove's groundbreaking book *The Future of Reputation: Gossip, Rumor, and Privacy on the Internet* goes into great depth explaining the massive impact of this digital revolution on personal reputation. He examines both the digital causes, many of which are discussed in this chapter, and legal and social factors that can help mitigate the destructive impact of these changes.

Everyone Can Create, and
Everyone Is (Almost) Equal

Everywhere you look on the Internet, you can find content written by other everyday people like yourself. The industry calls this "user-created content," and it appears to be the future of the Internet. In the early days, much Internet content was written by professional journalists and large corporations. This "top-down" model of publishing featured a few trusted content creators who spread their message to many readers.

Today, user-created content is king. Profit-oriented websites like Facebook and Reddit have discovered that it is cheaper to let users create their own content than it is to pay writers and editors to write and edit it. As a result, countless "Web 2.0" sites rely on users to create the content that other users will view. These sites range from blogging sites like LiveJournal and Blogger, to online encyclopedias like Wikipedia, to news aggregation sites like Digg, to short-message sites like Twitter (used for content as banal as "I'm eating a cheeseburger" and as meaningful as political commentary in 140 characters or less).

Everyone Can Create

The result of the Web 2.0 revolution is that everyday people now can create online content that can be viewed by millions of people. It is possible for anyone to set up a free online journal or blog with just a few clicks. An online journal can hold any kind of information, ranging from family photos to political thoughts to gossip and scandal. It is entirely up to the creator to decide what to write on the blank slate he or she is given. This immense power is given to anyone, and it is up to the user to decide whether to use this newfound power for good or for evil.

Similarly, there are hundreds (if not thousands) of sites that focus on discussion and chat. These "forums" and "bulletin boards" usually allow users to read messages left by others and to post their own thoughts in response. Often, discussion sites are organized around a larger theme (like a particular sports team), and allow users to create smaller discussions ("threads") about a particular topic (such as the role of steroids in sports). Any user can post any message, subject only to the whim of the website owner. The result is massively multidirectional conversations about every topic under the sun. To just paraphrase one short list of topics, it is possible to find discussions about parenting, painting, the playoffs, the Partridge Family, Picasso, Proctor and Gamble, Portland (Oregon), Portland (Maine), and myriad other niches. There is probably a discussion group for any identifiable interest. And, even if there isn't, many forums have "off-topic" sections where anything else can be discussed.

The owners of Web 2.0 or discussion websites may choose to moderate discussions by deleting offensive content, or they may simply choose to let users set their own standards. Moderation is time-consuming for site owners; everyone has a different idea of what it means for something to be offensive (consider, for example, the controversy about depictions of the religious figure Mohammed in a series of editorial cartoons), and moderation decisions frequently lead to more bickering and debate among users. As a result of the difficulty of moderation and the natural tendency of humans toward scandal, some user-created content has a tendency to devolve toward the lowest common denominator. Gossip and scandal attracts attention, online and off, and there is a strong temptation for site owners to allow (or even encourage) users to discuss scandalous topics in order to attract more traffic, which usually leads to more ad revenue.

Unfortunately, some users take this freedom and use it to spread gossip, to attack other people out of jealousy or spite, and to repeat misinformation. And, unlike the tabloids of yore, website users often don't limit themselves to discussing celebrities and public figures. The open publishing model of Web 2.0 is the first ingredient of the sometimes dangerous online mix.

Everyone Is (Almost) Equal

To the extent that everyone can create content, everyone is equal. For just a few dollars, anyone can purchase her own ".com" domain name and create a website with almost any conceivable content. Such a site would be visible to users around the world, just the same as sites made by major corporations. There is absolutely no filter on what people can create: someone could make a website claiming that the moon is made of green cheese, and someone else could create a website claiming that there is no such thing as 3-D space.[1]

Unlike most print media, any website can be viewed millions of times by millions of different people. Print distribution is extremely limited; each person who takes a copy of a print message effectively destroys one; to reach an audience of millions would cost hundreds of thousands of dollars in printing costs alone (not to mention the lead time required to coordinate such an effort, the shipping costs such an effort would incur, the staffing that it would take to handle a million pieces of paper, and more). Simple websites that don't include video or extensive graphics almost never exceed the limit of their Web hosting contract, allowing any website to become popular overnight and to reach a massive audience, perhaps even before the site owner realizes it.

Of course, just as in *Animal Farm*, some online publishers are more equal than others. Most major corporations have websites that look substantially better than many personal blogs because major companies can afford professional designers and artists. And most Web users have learned to associate professional design with professional content; a site that features tacky design and rudimentary navigation will often be considered amateurish or untrustworthy. But even that advantage of major sites is limited. It is possible for a skilled designer to mimic the elements of a well-designed site or for a less-skilled designer to outright copy the design of a different site. The ease of copying substantially cuts the design advantage held by major corporations and organizations.

There is no inherent bias within Google (or within most search engines) in favor of large corporate sites or sites that favor the old media establishment. The Google algorithm doesn't appear to have any opinion about the difference between the *New York Times* and the *Onion*, a satirical newspaper; both websites are measured by the same criteria, with no favoritism toward one or the other. Nor does the Google algorithm know the difference between some individual's website and the *Washington Post*; to the algorithm, they're both just websites to be measured along the same scale, even if that means the *Post* will usually win.

Internet scholar Andrew Keen thinks this new egalitarianism will trash our culture, to the point of mindless Youtube clips replacing meaningful movies and plays. In his book, *The Cult of the Amateur*, he predicts that the noise created by amateurish user-created content will drown out the contributions that can be made by skilled and talented experts: He compares the music created by a trained symphony to an average Youtube clip of kids rocking out.[2] Google, of course, is part of the problem because it makes no distinctions between quality and garbage; if you search Google for music, it will bring up the most popular web page rather than the best music. Even if you don't agree with Keen's doom-and-gloom prophecies, it is undeniable that the ever-increasing visibility of user-created content has changed the way we look at each other, and the way that our reputations are shaped.

Everything Is Online Somewhere

Not only is information unfiltered, but there is a vast amount of it online. The combination of individual contributions, corporate media, and government records means that there is more data about private individuals available online than through any other medium in history.

The Internet is without limit. Much like the universe, it is constantly expanding. There is effectively no maximum size to the Internet; new websites can be created, new blogs started, new information added, and new photos uploaded without ever having to remove anything. A prominent politician once verbally stumbled by comparing the Internet to a dump truck and a series of tubes.[3] At the risk of repeating the error, the Internet is more like a black hole than a closet: you can stuff an endless amount of material online without ever having to take anything out.

The infinite capacity of the Internet means that it is possible for an endless amount of information to be provided about even the most obscure topics and for this information to be archived permanently.

Almost everything can be found online somewhere. If it happened in the past ten years, it might be online. If it happened in the past five years, it's probably online. And if it happened in the past two years, it's almost certainly online. Not all of it can be easily found (at least not yet), but it's there—hidden in government databases, corporate databases, blog posts, Facebook updates, Twitter "tweets," MySpace pictures, and all the hundreds of other ways that content is shared online. The data varies from the mundane (the members of local soccer teams) to the dangerous (property records that give stalkers the info they need to find their victims) to the damaging (uncorrected arrest records of people later proved innocent). Even vast amounts of political information is online: All financial contributions to political candidates in the United States made since 2000 are online now, copied across several sites, and readily found by Google; it's easy to find out if your neighbors gave to Democrats, Republicans, Greens, Independents, or even the Marijuana Party.[4]

The depth of information online is also staggering. Want to know who played third base for the Red Sox in 1912? A simple search reveals that Larry Gardner was covering the "hot corner" at Fenway Park's first opening day.[5] Want to know anyone's current address and previous residences? Just search a "whitepages" site online, or at most pay a few dollars to a background-check company for the data. Want to know how much your neighbors paid for their home? Check Zillow.com, which lists past sales and current estimates on millions of homes. Want to know what a particular beachfront home in California looks like? There is a website showing helicopter photos of every beachfront lot along the coast, along with comparison photos dating back to 1979.[6]

The government has been just as aggressive about putting data online; one can easily find Ellis Island immigration records,[7] sex offender registrations,[8] the names of current prison inmates,[9] and even complete land historic ownership and appraisal records for every plot of land in some counties.[10] There are even lots of things online that probably were not meant to be placed online. There have been news stories about curious Web visitors finding lists of passwords,[11] credit card numbers, private phone meetings, and even access codes for buildings.[12]

Archives of old data are also being uploaded. The *New York Times* has digitized its complete archives from 1851 through 1922; any story from that period is available online and visible to anyone who searches using Google. The original contemporary coverage of President Abraham Lincoln's 1860 election can be found through a simple Google search.[13] And, predictably enough, the election coverage shows how the long life of online data can harm reputations; for example, the *Times* article detailing the 1860 election results includes an allegation that a Census Bureau clerk by the name of Goldsborough was plotting to disrupt the counting of the ballots.[14] The clerk is long dead, but the unsubstantiated allegation about his character lingers 150 years later. Even much smaller newspapers, including college newspapers, are placing their archives online. The *Yale Daily News*, the oldest college daily newspaper, has placed online its entire archive back to the first issue in 1878.[15]

Of course, there has been a backlash against the permanent memory of the Internet. A recent book by scholar Viktor Mayer-Schonberger, *Delete: The Virtue of Forgetting in the Digital Age*, proposes that all website data should automatically be deleted unless there is a compelling reason to keep it. He proposes that programmers set up websites so that "old news" is eventually hidden from Google's memory, especially when it does not concern matters of great public importance (e.g., national politics, scientific advancements). While compelling, his ideas are unlikely to be implemented soon, which leaves everyday users the task of trying to control what information about them will be permanently archived.

Everything Is Instant

The Internet creates instant universality. The very moment that something is created online, it is available to be viewed by anyone, anywhere. A newly written blog post can be transmitted around the world, copied digitally to tens or hundreds of websites, and permanently archived—all faster than you can blink. A newly posted photo can be copied, analyzed, and redistributed in the time it takes to sneeze. And a newly penned comment in a forum or blog can become irretrievably permanent in the time it takes for the mouse button to rebound after clicking on "submit." Everything is instantly universal.

Technologies like "Really Simple Syndication" (RSS) make sure that new content automatically gets distributed as fast as computers can process data. Using RSS, it is possible for a blogger to automatically notify other news outlets and news aggregation sites that there is new content available. Those aggregators often immediately scan any new content provided, process it, and display it to their users (like at NewsVine) or pass it on to yet another step (like at Yahoo! Pipes). The next step can display, pass along, or do both. In seconds, a new piece of content can circle the globe and appear on tens or hundreds of sites.

This culture of speed is a sharp break from the old "news cycle." In fact, the concept of a "news cycle" at all is a remnant of the pre-Internet era of news publication. Before the Internet, for a news story to reach a mass audience it had to be published in a morning newspaper or appear on an evening news program. As a result, editors had time to stop, think a story over, and then decide whether to publish it. There was time to gather additional facts, do further research, and perhaps debunk false stories before they were published. Of course, false stories and errors got through, but at least there was time to try to limit their numbers.

Today, the Internet news cycle is constant: at any hour of the day or night, anyone can publish news, which is immediately viewable by millions of readers. There is a never-ending race among news outlets to be first to break a story. All the major news sites update their content 60/24/7/365. Breaking news is posted within minutes. The time to investigate a major scandal is measured in hours rather than days. And big news organizations are not merely competing against each other; they're also competing against thousands of blogs and other small outlets. The legacy news organizations are left to play catch-up; they must investigate and publish every story in the shortest amount of time possible if they hope to compete online, while desperately trying to preserve the journalistic standards of a more leisurely era. One or the other has to give.

This culture of rushing to be first has extended beyond just writing the news. It has also extended to sharing and discussing it. On news discussion sites, like Digg, Slashdot, and Reddit, many users compete to be the first to post a link to a news article or discussion topic; on some sites, users are even awarded "karma" points for being the first to submit a breaking news story. The online culture of speed has even extended so far that, on many blogs, readers race to be the first person to comment on a new post, if only to shout "FIRST" in all-capital letters. (This practice gets old just as fast as you think it would, namely the "FIRST" time you see it.)

In the end, there is little time to consider whether publishing a news article, blog post, or comment is a good idea. The result is that ill-considered and poorly researched content all too often is unleashed after an impulsive mouse click. The race to be first has overcome the quaint desire to be right and appropriate.

Everything Is Permanent

Anything that is said online may be available forever, no matter how hard anyone tries to delete it. Conversations among friends were once conducted in private; they left no permanent trace once the last echo faded, and they could spread only at the speed of interpersonal communication. Classroom notes were passed and trashed or at worst intercepted by a teacher and read aloud before being recycled.

But many of those same conversations are now conducted online in a blog or chat room, in full view of the world, automatically indexed by Google, and broadcast to an audience of millions. Indelicate comments are archived for posterity and presented by Google as if they were as important as newspapers or government reports.

The permanence of the Internet has hit students and jobseekers particularly hard. Those classroom notes have become MySpace posts that are permanently archived in computers around the globe and that are effectively impossible to delete. Pranks and insults that might seem funny to teenagers become visible years later to employers through a simple Google search. Digital photos of the indiscretions of youth are copied around the world and live on long after the acts themselves have faded from memory.

The permanence of the Internet is often caused by the fact that digital data can be copied perfectly and nearly instantaneously. An embarrassing photograph might start on one site, but viewers may copy it to tens or hundreds of other sites within hours or days. Even if the original is removed, the copies will live on. The same is true of any information: the text of a news article or government report can be copied and pasted from place to place just as easily. The act of copying one piece of content (an image, a news story, whatever) across many sites is so common that there is even slang for it: "copypasta."

Even in the absence of user intervention, many sites on the Internet automatically archive vast amounts of content. One not-for-profit project, the Internet Archive, has been creating a permanent historical record of the entire Internet since 1996.[16] The project created a computer program, a "crawler," that wanders from link to link across the Internet and saves everything that it sees. So far, it has saved more than 86 billion web pages. Even when an original web page is deleted, the copy in the Internet Archive will live on forever. A smear today can be found tomorrow in the Internet Archive, images and all. Even the federal government, through the Library of

Congress, is getting into archiving Web content. The Library is working with the Archive to preserve special collections of Internet content that the government finds interesting; right now, the government project is limited to a collection of websites as they stood on September 11, 2001, but other government archives may come in the future.[17]

There are also automatic systems designed to create short-term archives of Internet content. When Google's Web spider reviews a page in order to update its index, it also automatically saves a copy of the page. This cached copy can be viewed by clicking the "cached" button that appears under a Google search result. The Google cache copy is accessible for days (or even weeks) after the original website has been removed or taken offline, regardless of whether the original content was false, defamatory, hurtful, or otherwise wrong—and often the Google cache will stay online even if the original author wants to remove it.

And there are even shorter-term automatic means of copying Internet content. Many Web browsers allow users to utilize caching technology that automatically saves a copy of every web page viewed. For example, there is an "extension" (a helper program) for the Firefox browser that automatically saves a copy of every page a user of the program views; even if the original page is pulled offline, that user will be able to view, share, and duplicate his copy of the web page. Similar technology has even been made social. For example, the Coral Content Distribution Network (better known as "Coral cache") allows users to view the Web through hundreds of distributed caches (storage systems) around the world. If any user has viewed a page through the Coral network, then it continues to be available through the Coral network for some time, even if the original website is taken offline (intentionally or accidentally).

Even in the absence of fancy technology, many things on the Internet end up becoming permanent through sheer inertia. Storage is so cheap these days that it is often easier to simply buy a larger hard drive than to decide whether old data should be kept or deleted. This leads to countless "zombie sites" that are no longer being maintained but that still have content. Often, they are blogs, journals, or other personal sites; they become zombies when the owner loses interest in the site but never bothers to delete it. Or the user may have lost the password, passed away, lost access to the Internet, or forgotten about the site's existence entirely. The site lives on, and the Web host has no incentive to go through the expensive and time-consuming process of sorting out active and inactive sites when it costs only pennies to keep the old sites around. All too often, these zombie sites contain vastly outdated information, and there is often no way to contact the owner—even if an e-mail address is listed on the site, it is probably no longer in service. There are vast ghost towns of inactive sites like these, but Google often has no way to know which sites are frozen in time and which sites are still actively maintained.

Of course, not *absolutely* everything ends up being permanent. Plenty of things drift away into effective obscurity or complete destruction, particularly if they are interesting only to a very small group of people. But anything that piques the interest of a larger community can almost never be destroyed. At best, it will fade in prominence over time, but it will rarely be completely eradicated. In fact, many naive attempts to get rid of content just make matters worse. The "Streisand Effect" describes what happens when an attempt to get rid of content causes it to become even more permanent. The facts are simple: Barbra Streisand was unhappy that a high-resolution photograph of her beachfront home was online, in part because it showed access points that could be used by intruders or burglars.[18] However, her attempts to use heavy-handed legal compulsion to remove the photo from the Internet actually made the problem worse; the photo was copied to hundreds of sites out of spite, and now her name is permanently associated with the photo. Similarly, the Motion Picture Association of America caused more trouble for itself when it used similar tactics to try to eliminate an isolated reference to an encryption key that could be used to copy high-definition DVDs. The Internet backlash against the MPAA's heavy-handed tactics was fierce: the code was copied to more than 200,000 websites and will never be removed from the Internet.[19]

Everything Is Powerful

The power of modern computer technology has been a mixed blessing for reputation. Thanks to vast databases of digital data, fast networks, and powerful computers, it is possible for computers to connect once-separate facts in ways that can be liberating or damaging.

To take one example, millions of people carry cell phones capable of taking photos and uploading them to the Internet. Users often upload their photos to the Internet without identifying the people in the photos in order to preserve some measure of privacy. But, advancements in digital technology mean that facial recognition is now good enough that computers can reliably identify individuals in photos after being "trained" on only a handful of known samples. The result is a world where countless people—friends and strangers—upload photos to photo-sharing sites with the best of intentions, but where the anonymous people in these photos can be quickly identified by computers. The training system for a facial recognition system already exists thanks to photo "tagging" features of sites like Facebook, Flickr, and Picasa. Facebook in particular has a massive set of photo tags—millions of users have each been tagged hundreds of times each.[20] If the security of Facebook is ever broken, it will be possible to identify millions of people in previously anonymous photos spread across the Internet.

There are literally hundreds of millions of photos on the Internet that can become fodder for facial recognition. There are millions of photos of streets, offices, bars, parties, and other events that include images of people. When combined with facial recognition and the power of Google to find obscure information, the possibility of damage to reputation is obvious. Anyone photographed (accidentally or intentionally) near an adult bookstore could be identified by name and made subject to ridicule by his peers. Anyone photographed entering a family planning clinic could be located and subjected to pillory by anti-abortion activists. Anyone photographed near a gay bar is at risk of being named and having his sexual orientation falsely reported or accurately revealed to his employer and peers, especially in less-tolerant areas of the country. Any attempt to explain away any of the photos—"I was going to the business next door" or "it isn't me"—is likely to be lost in the clutter.

Other Internet applications endanger reputations by aggregating a vast amount of data that was once scattered across the Internet. These applications are often "neat" or interesting but create real risks to reputation. To take just one example, there is a website that attempts to find random personal photos scattered across the Internet.[21] The photos found by the site are often very personal, and many appear to have never been meant for a public audience. The application can find such photos because it searches for the default filenames used by digital cameras and is thus able to find photos uploaded to all kinds of personal sites that were never meant to be revealed to the browsing public as a whole. This site could have already found photos that you, a friend, a relative, or even an acquaintance uploaded—and it could be broadcasting these private photos to the Internet as a whole right now.

Notes

1. View one such website at TimeCube.com.

2. Andrew Keen, *The Cult of the Amateur: How Today's Internet Is Killing Our Culture* (New York: Doubleday, 2007).

3. Noam Cohen, "Cyber Ignorance Not Bliss for Public Servants," *New York Times*, June 5, 2007. **Go**: http://wildwest2.com/go/401

4. Center for Responsive Politics, "Money in Politics," via.opensecrets.org. *Go*: http://wildwest2.com/go/402.

5. Unnamed Wikipedia contributors, "1912 Boston Red Sox season," via Wikipedia.com. *Go*: http://wildwest2.com/go/403.

6. The California Coastal Records Project. *Go*: http://wildwest2.com/go/404.

7. National Archives, "Immigration Records (Ship Passenger Arrival Records and Land Border Entries)," via archives.gov. *Go*: http://wildwest2.com/go/405.

8. Family Watchdog, "National Sex Offender Registry," via familywatchdog.us. *Go*: http://wildwest2.com/go/406.

9. Federal Bureau of Prisons, "BOP: Inmate Locator Page." *Go*: http://wildwest2.com/go/407.

10. For example, Jefferson County Clerk's Office, "Online Land Records." *Go*: http://wildwest2.com/go/408.

11. CyberInsecure Blog, "5534 Stolen Ebay Logins and Passwords Accidentally Found Online by Security Firm." *Go*: http://wildwest2.com/go/409.

12. Brian Krebs, "A Word of Caution about Google Calendar," *SecurityFix* (blog). *Go*: http://wildwest2.com/go/410.

13. *New York Times*, "Affairs of the Nation; Highly Important News from Washington. The Electoral Vote Counted," p. 1. *Go*: http://wildwest2.com/go/411.

14. Ibid.

15. *Yale Daily News*, "Yale Daily News Historical Archive," via library.yale.edu. *Go*: http://wildwest2.com/go/412.

16. Internet Archive Foundation, "Internet Archive." *Go*: http://wildwest2.com/go/413.

17. Library of Congress, "Library of Congress, Internet Archive, webarchivist.org and the Pew Internet & American Life Project Announce Sept. 11 Web Archive." *Go*: http://wildwest2.com/go/414.

18. Unnamed Wikipedia contributors, "Streisand Effect," Wikipedia.com. *Go*: http://wildwest2.com/go/415.

19. Brad Stone, "In Web Uproar, Antipiracy Code Spreads Wildly," *New York Times*, May 3, 2007. *Go*: http://wildwest2.com/go/416. Website count estimated via Google search for the text of the code (verified February 1, 2009).

20. Erick Scholfeld, "Who Has the Most Photos of Them All?" *TechCrunch*, April 7, 2009. **Go**: http://wildwest2.com/go/417.

21. One such site is called the "Random Personal Picture Finder." WARNING: the site often shows images that are controversial or R-rated. **Go**: http://wildwest2.com/go/418.

CHAPTER

5.0

Anonymous Cowards

The power of online anonymity has turned reputation and privacy on their heads. Before the Internet, everyday conversations were held face-to-face. Natural social cues guided conversation, reducing the risk of misunderstanding and limiting hostility. Gossipers and attackers could be identified and ostracized if they went too far. Social norms deterred people from prying too deep into each others' affairs. People who spread wrong information could be located and corrected. And the threat of libel lawsuits deterred the mass media from spreading outrageous lies to large audiences.

But, online, anonymity rules. Thanks to the technology of the Internet, most people don a veil of anonymity when they go online. People post, read, share, talk, link, and sometimes even buy and sell anonymously. Online, it is often impossible to know if the person you're chatting with is half a block or half a world away. The owner of a website might be your neighbor, or it might be someone in Azerbaijan. The person spreading company secrets through a blog could be the mailroom clerk, the CEO's child, or even the CEO herself—and, lest you think it unlikely for a CEO to be posting anonymously, the CEO of a major supermarket chain was recently caught writing anonymous comments online in an attempt to lower the stock price of a rival.[1]

Anonymity Is Limited in the Physical World

The ability to interact anonymously online is a sharp break from the "offline," face-to-face world. Most people walk around with their faces uncovered. They drive in cars with visible license plate numbers and pay with credit cards embossed with their names. They go to school, show up to work, and attend church alongside other people who know their real names.

In social settings, the vast majority of people identify themselves truthfully by giving their real names—the use of pseudonyms is rare enough as to seem absurd in all but the most privacy-sensitive settings, such as in therapy or support groups for stigmatizing conditions.

Even if some of everyday life seems anonymous, it is anonymous only as long as it is inconsequential. Many everyday interactions have an illusion of anonymity, especially in urban areas: a cash purchase from a retail shop does not leave a paper trail, and the participants are unlikely to know each others' names. But the transaction is anonymous only because it is routine. If the transaction were to ever become important (for example, if the buyer passed counterfeit currency or tried to rob the store), the illusion of anonymity would quickly disappear. The police could quickly use fingerprints, DNA, and security camera footage to try to track down the individual responsible. Even a simple "WANTED" poster with a sketch of the perpetrator might be enough to lead to an arrest. And there is always the chance that a friend or neighbor might see any transaction, instantly destroying the illusion of anonymity—for example, the risk that the title character in

Ferris Bueller's Day Off was going to get caught at a Cubs baseball game when he had claimed to be at home sick.

Conscious attempts to remain anonymous during face-to-face interactions are frowned upon and often ineffective. Some protestors attempt to remain anonymous, but they are able to do so only as long as they don't break the law in front of the police. For example, members of the Ku Klux Klan are infamous for wearing face-covering hoods while marching, but they can still be de-hooded by police if they commit any crimes. And, of course, counterdemonstrators can follow them to see if they ever remove their hoods in view of the public. A recent wave of protestors against the Church of Scientology made a statement by wearing masks resembling the British conspirator Guy Fawkes, but these mask-wearing protestors were often discounted by passersby because of their unusual form of protest. And, of course, anyone bold enough to wear a ski mask into a bank would quickly discover the limit on tolerance for anonymity in the real world.

Online Anonymity Blows Away Social Norms

Online anonymity also empowers lonely, troubled, and spiteful attackers to say things they would never say in person. It allows attackers to smear a victim (or even impersonate the victim) and then to retreat into the shadows without any accountability for their actions. And, because these anonymous and untraceable attackers can reach a massive audience once reserved for the "professional" media, the threat of libel lawsuits no longer deters outrageous lies. Even simple misunderstandings are harder to clear up in an age of anonymity: how do you track down the source of even an innocent mistake if it is being spread anonymously?

The same powerful anonymity also allows everyday people to pry far deeper into the lives of acquaintances, friends, and strangers than they ever would offline. From the comfort of home, it is easy to search Google for a friend's name, check their Facebook and MySpace profiles, follow leads from LinkedIn, cruise popular sites for embarrassing pictures of them, and generally play amateur private detective in a way that would be called "prying" if it were to happen offline. One website even brags that it provides a way to anonymously "uncover personal photos, videos, and secrets . . . GUARANTEED!"[2]

Put aside what you've heard about Google, DoubleClick, and other advertisers tracking you online. It is true that they can collect bits and pieces of information about you as you visit sites with advertisements. And there are some frightening consequences of their data collection policies. But they still don't know the vast majority of what people do online, and they don't share that information with friends, relatives, co-workers, or other people who make judgments about you. In the end, you are anonymous to most of the world, and most of the world is anonymous to you.

This anonymity can be liberating at times. Many online communities have sprung up where people can discuss very personal and private issues—such as living with HIV/AIDS—under the protection of anonymity or a pseudonym (a made-up name, like "SuperBlogGirl" or "VegasGuy1965"). Other online communities have allowed anonymous dissenters to share their concerns about oppressive governments without fear of retribution. And yet other communities, such as "PostSecret," operate as virtual confessionals, allowing users to anonymously share secrets ranging from extramarital affairs to suicidal desires to problems with drugs. These communities are liberating for their participants, and they could not flourish without the anonymity provided by the Internet.

But the anonymity of the Internet can also lead to profoundly negative results. The worst of human behavior is revealed when nobody is watching. Many people allow their worst side to come out when there is no social pressure to behave ethically. Without social checks, anonymity can quickly lead individuals and groups away from their humanity and into depravity. And there is often no way to resolve disputes or disagreements when the other party to the disagreement cannot be found.

Worse, powerful anonymity combined with outdated laws has allowed a complete lack of accountability for online content. Websites knowingly leave false and libelous information online, claiming that they are not responsible for what users write. But when the original author cannot be found, the website's refusal to act leaves the victim without any remedy: the false content stays online, forever staining the victim's reputation.

Anonymity Is the Default Rule

The Internet is fundamentally an anonymous network. There is no standard for user identification built into the Internet or the World Wide Web. Many of the decisions that foster anonymity can be traced back to the very early days of the network. Back then, it was thought that the Internet would be used exclusively by people in small research laboratories associated with major universities. The designers assumed that user identification would be performed by the individual laboratories connected to the network and that accountability would be enforced by the personal connections among users. (For more information about the way the history of the Internet shaped the Internet today, see the online bonus chapter of *Wild West 2.0*, exclusively available at http://www.WildWest2.com/bonus/history/.)

Individual websites have the option of trying to identify users, but there are few effective ways to do so, and most sites do not even bother to make an attempt unless they are selling something. As a result, you generally browse anonymously, talk anonymously, and interact anonymously until you choose to reveal your own identity. And you don't have any way to know whom you are interacting with until they reveal their identity—but even then you may not be able to verify that they are who they say they are.

A mercifully short explanation of the technology underlying the Internet will help you to understand why there is so much anonymity online. Unlike the phone system, the Internet allows "organic" growth: Anybody in the world can connect to the Internet so long as they can find one other person willing to let them connect.

There is no central authority that monitors or controls connections; as a matter of technology, connecting to the Internet is entirely a private affair. A few governments—in places like China and North Korea—have attempted to outlaw or monitor private connections, with rather limited success. The practical result is that home users can simply call up a local Internet Service Provider ("ISP")—often their cable TV provider or a phone company—and connect to the Internet. Nobody other than the ISP will know the identity of the new subscriber. The government won't know the identity of any users unless it invokes its law enforcement power to subpoena the ISP; websites won't know unless the subscriber reveals her own identity; and other users won't know unless they can convince the user to reveal herself or hire lawyers and obtain a civil subpoena.

Once connected, the new user can communicate with any of the millions of computers on the Internet. This is possible because of a communication system known as "IP," or "Internet Protocol." All data that are transferred over the Internet use Internet Protocol, and it is "Internet Protocol" that gave the Internet its name.

A very short explanation of IP will show why Internet anonymity is so powerful. Internet Protocol is nothing more than a communications language shared among all computers connected to the Internet (see Figure 5-1). Data of any kind (e-mails, pictures, songs, web pages, or videos) can be sent over the Internet by breaking it into small "packets." These packets contain the data that are to be sent, as well as some addressing information known as the "header." Once sent, a packet is automatically forwarded from one computer to another until it reaches its destination. There is no predictable route that any particular packet will follow; the Internet is intentionally designed so that packets are automatically passed toward their destination along whatever route seems fastest at the time. For example, one packet sent from a home user in New York to a website in San Francisco might be passed along a chain of computers from New York to Chicago to San Francisco. The next packet between the same

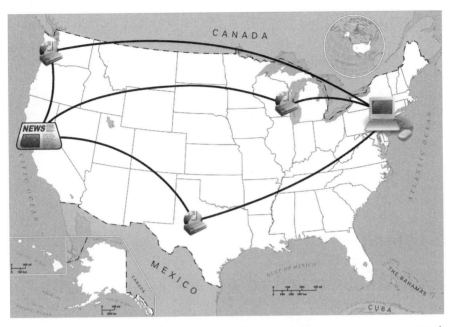

Figure 5-1. Internet Routing. Several possible paths that a computer in New York might use to communicate with a website in San Francisco. In the process of viewing a single Web page, one or all of these paths might be used. Illustration: David Thompson.

computers might pass through Seattle or Houston instead if the Chicago route is too crowded or slow.

Communication across a network of this size is possible because packets are routed on the basis of the "IP address" of the sender and recipient (see Figure 5-2). Each computer or group of computers (such as at an office or university) is associated with an IP address. An IP address is nothing more than a series of numbers—for example, 64.233.169.147—that uniquely identifies one particular computer or group of computers. The IP address of the sender and the recipient are contained in the packet's "header" section, and computers that receive the packet automatically pass it toward the IP address of its destination.

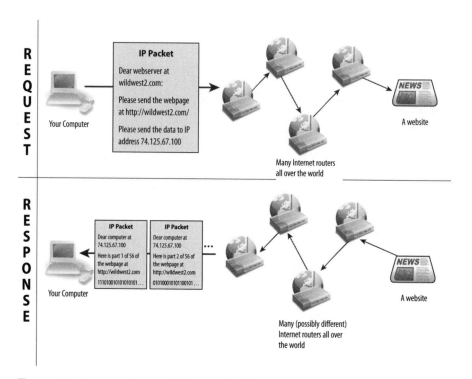

Figure 5-2. Internet Protocol Illustrated. When you want to view a website, your computer sends a short message to the website over the Internet. The message contains very little information: usually just some information about the web page you would like to view, some technical routing information, and your IP address. You are identified only by IP address unless you have disclosed information about yourself. The website then sends the digital files that make up the website back to you, using your IP address to route the information back to you. Your computer assembles these files to display a graphical website. Illustration: David Thompson.

Other than the IP address of sender and recipient, there is no user identification built into IP. Each data packet travelling across the Internet is identified only by the IP address of the sender and the recipient. But these are just numbers; nothing in IP discloses a user's name, location, e-mail address, physical address, or any other identifying information. The IP system is designed only to move data packets from point to point on the Internet and does not even consider user authentication.

When you view a web page, your computer sends a request for that web page to the webserver that "hosts" the website you are viewing. A webserver or webhost is just a computer that responds to requests for website files. A popular website like Google.com may use thousands of webservers, while a smaller site like WildWest2.com is likely to share a webserver with other websites. After getting your request, the webserver returns the files that make up the website or sends back an error message if the page cannot be found.

When your computer sends such a request for a web page, it uses Internet Protocol to transmit the message across the Internet.[3] The packet contains only minimal information—no more than the web page you are requesting, the IP address where your computer can be reached, and some technical routing information. This is true even if you are uploading a file, making a forum post, or using a Web-based e-mail service like Gmail; unless you have disclosed some identifying information (or your computer has been configured or hacked to do so automatically), you are effectively anonymous online.

Internet Protocol Allows and Encourages Anonymity

Often, the only fingerprint Web users leave behind is their IP address. But an IP address does not necessarily correspond to a particular human user. The IP address does not contain any information about the individual user or computer that sent a message; it is, as we noted, just a number. There are Web-based databases that allow an IP address to be linked to a particular ISP (so that you can tell whether your attacker gets his Internet service from Verizon or Comcast), but no publicly accessible database connects individual users to individual IP addresses.

Even if it were possible to know that a particular person was using a particular IP address one day, that does not mean that the same person was using that address some other day. Dial-up Internet connections often assign a different IP address to a user each time the person connects. Cable modem and DSL operators often periodically reassign IP addresses for the security of their users, so one user's IP address today may be another's tomorrow. One IP address may not even uniquely identify one computer: Many corporate LANs have only one externally visible IP address and use "Network Address Translation" ("NAT") technology to mediate requests between many internal computers and the outside Internet. Any user in such a corporate system will appear to have the same address as any other user. Many home cable modem routers do the same; if there are multiple computers inside a house (or apartment, or college dorm room), they may appear to share one IP address. The same goes again for coffee shops and other open wireless connections; all of the users at the shop might share one IP address for most purposes.

Only an ISP will be able to even try to determine who was using an IP address at a given time. Most reputable ISPs keep logs for a period of time (often ninety days to one year) that correlate IP address assignments with real subscriber data. But, most major ISPs will not give out subscriber information without legal process. And understandably so: ISPs don't want to risk a lawsuit for violating the privacy expectations of their subscribers.

If these problems trying to identify users based on IP address weren't enough, many users take steps to intentionally break the link between their identity and their IP address. There are some legitimate reasons to increase anonymity: an activist's fear of an oppressive government or a whistleblower's fear of corporate retaliation. But these same methods are also abused by malicious attackers, hackers, child pornographers, and gossipers.

Some forms of anonymity are simple. Using a neighbor's unsecured wireless network is often sufficient to hide one's identity. Of course, that method requires a neighbor with an unsecured wireless network within range. The effectiveness of that method is also limited: The source of a message can still be located to within the short range of a WiFi connection, and other hints (such as the type of computer being used or the Internet browser software version) may be sufficient to identify an attacker when combined with a rough physical location. Similarly, logging on at a public library may be sufficient if the library doesn't reliably check ID (some do, some don't), or one can use any other insecure connection like that at a coffee shop.

Other technological means also exist to break the connection between Internet-visible IP address and identity when using one's own Internet connection. These methods are generally regarded as legal under current U.S. law. This, too, has a root in the history of the Internet: basic "anonymous remailers" date back to the early days of online discussions. Such remailers allowed users to send messages to the primitive "Usenet" discussion system, without their names, e-mail addresses, or IP addresses being revealed. These were used when discussing controversial or illegal content but were limited in that they worked only for Usenet.

Today, an Internet user can utilize a "proxy server" to hide her identity. There are both free and paid proxy servers that allow users to perform many Internet tasks—including Web browsing—without revealing their real IP address to the destination website.[4] Instead of sending a message directly to the website they wish to view, users send a message to a proxy server. The proxy server then passes the message along but substitutes the proxy server's IP address as the "source." The website then sends the requested material back to the proxy server, which relays it (without the webserver's knowledge) to the original requester.

Newer proxy systems, such as "TOR,"[5] take the concept of anonymous proxy servers even further. "TOR" stands for "The Onion Router," and it is a free software package that was developed in large part by the Electronic Frontier Foundation for the purpose of providing a robustly anonymous system to political activists protesting against oppressive regimes. But nothing about the system limits its use to political activists; it is equally available to hackers, child pornographers, paranoids, and others. Once installed, the program encrypts a user's Internet traffic and forwards it along a chain of several proxy servers. The data are wrapped in layers of encryption; as the data hop from one proxy server to another, each proxy server has only the decryption key required to remove one layer of encryption from the packet. The last proxy server removes the last layer of encryption and sends the packet to its destination. (Hence the "onion" name: the packet of data is wrapped in layers of encryption like the layers of an onion.) Responses are handled in the reverse order; each proxy server adds a layer of encryption as the packet is passed back toward the user. Each link can decrypt no more than is required in order to find the next link in the chain. No single person or computer knows both the sender and the destination because each link can "see" only the link immediately preceding and following it. The first link knows the sender, and the last link knows the destination, but these links are separate computers on opposite sides of the world that are unaware of each other's existence. Intermediate proxy servers cannot access the underlying message and have no clue as to the identity of the sender or recipient. Only the last proxy server has access to the message contents, but it does not know the source of the message or have any way to find out. This complex system reduces the risk that one proxy server could be wiretapped; even if one proxy server were compromised, it would not have enough information to connect a user to a message. The TOR system also prevents an ISP from being able to effectively monitor or track what activities a user is conducting online. In effect, TOR creates a system of technological anonymity that cannot be broken, even by law enforcement.

The Legal System Supports Anonymity

The current legal system supports anonymity online. At least in the United States, there is no requirement that websites, webhosts, ISPs, or anybody else collect or store any information that could be used to connect online activity to a real human being, whether directly (such as storing a name) or indirectly (such as storing an IP address).[6]

Some sites do keep logs of the IP addresses of visitors; by default, several popular webserver software packages create basic IP address logs. After proper legal process, it is sometimes possible to use these logs to determine who uploaded illegal content: One subpoena is issued to the website to find the IP address of the miscreant, and a second subpoena is issued to an ISP to identify a real user based on that IP address. But IP logs are often deleted automatically after a few weeks, and many websites turn off logging entirely. Most ISPs almost never keep track of what sites are visited by their users, let alone what actions their users have taken on those sites; they would have to store large (but not impossible) amounts of data, and ISPs may be hesitant to even appear as if they are monitoring the activities of their users, no matter what technical and legal restrictions they put on use of the data they collect.

What is truly odd about current law is that there is no duty on websites or ISPs to deal with harmful anonymous content. If a website does not keep IP address logs (or any other form of logs), then it has no way to know who uploaded or created harmful content. But, even if a website has kept no information about the user who created offensive content, it will often refuse to remove it if asked by the victim and presented with irrefutable evidence that the content is wrong. The website will often point to Section 230 of the Communications Decency Act of 1996 (CDA), which provides immunity for user-created content, no matter how false or offensive. Even if given absolute proof that the content is libelous, false, or otherwise inaccurate, many websites will still continue to claim to have no duty to remove or alter it.

What's even stranger is that harmful attacks on individuals are treated worse by the law than the copyrights owned by major corporations. A different law, the Digital Millennium Copyright Act of 1996 (DMCA), creates a "notice-and-takedown" system for alleged copyright violations. If a user has uploaded a copyrighted film, song, or photograph, then the copyright owner (usually a movie studio or record label) can force the website to remove the copyrighted material by just sending a letter. The website must remove the allegedly copyrighted material immediately or become subject to claims for money damages for copyright infringement.

The DMCA has been used to remove vast swaths of content. Viacom (the owner of MTV, VH1, and Comedy Central) once sent a letter to the video-sharing website YouTube identifying more than 100,000 instances of alleged copyright infringement.[7] When there was not a satisfactory response, Viacom sued YouTube's parent company, Google, seeking billions of dollars in damages.[8] The lawsuit alleges that YouTube is responsible for the copyright infringements of its users because YouTube encouraged and promoted copyright infringement. There is no allegation that YouTube itself uploaded or edited videos that violated Viacom's copyrights; the only allegation is that YouTube failed to adequately police the actions of its users.

But nobody has been successful in claiming that a website is responsible for the libel or personal attacks of its users because it promoted or encouraged libel or other forms of personal attack. Even the foulest dens of inequity have—thus far—been able to escape liability by simply pointing to Section 230 of the Communications Decency Act.

The Result: A Culture of Anonymity

Because of the technical limitations of IP and the lack of a legal requirement to verify identity or remove harmful anonymous content, there is no custom of online disclosure of real identities. Most websites that allow user-created content either don't ask for a real name at any point in the "signup" process or do absolutely no verification of the name submitted by a user ("John Doe" usually is accepted without question).

The result is that it is possible for users to surf the Web, search for information, e-mail each other, post comments, upload photos, blog, and create websites—all while staying completely anonymous.

The only trace left behind by most users is an IP address, but even that footprint can be removed by use of proxy servers. This anonymity can be liberating if it is used for good—to explore new ideas or identities. But it can also be evil: It is possible for anonymous attackers to slander the good name of innocent victims without fear of being traced, for credit card scammers to peddle their wares online without fear of prosecution, for child pornographers to trade smut in anonymous back alleys of the Internet. And everyone is at risk from anonymous hackers.

This culture of anonymity has even reached pop culture—as the saying goes, "On the Internet, nobody knows you're a dog."[9] Or, as one Wikipedia editor expounded to ironic excess, "cyberspace will be liberatory because gender, race, age, looks, or even 'dogness' are potentially absent or alternatively fabricated or exaggerated with unchecked creative license for a multitude of purposes both legal and illegal."[10]

Internet Anonymity Destroys Accountability

As a result of online anonymity, often nobody claims responsibility for malicious or damaging Internet content. Websites and blogs can be started anonymously and often leave no way to track down the creator. Google claims that it is not responsible for the results produced by its search engine. ISPs claim they are not responsible for the sites created or viewed by their customers. Video- and photo-sharing sites may respond to requests to remove content because of copyright violations but often refuse to do so in response to claims of privacy violations or libel. Even reputable blogs run by major publishers often claim that they are not responsible for content submitted by other users and refuse to remove harmful comments. Some site owners even encourage misuse—owners know that they can profit by creating virtual tabloid newspapers where users compete to sling the most scandalous rumors with no holds barred.

The direct impact of anonymity on many Internet users is obvious. Freed from the social constraints of direct accountability for their actions, users feel free to attack other users at will. In a world with no consequences, many users think there is little reason to avoid profane or malicious behavior. A hypothetical Web user contemplating a malicious attack knows that he is unlikely to be found by the victim, so he does not fear the risk of a lawsuit for defamation (or even more rough forms of justice). And he is also anonymous to his real-world friends and colleagues who would otherwise apply social pressure to prevent socially unacceptable behaviors like malicious attacks and mean-spirited gossip. The stereotype of the Internet user working alone in his parents' basement is probably outdated, but it remains true that most Internet users surf alone and therefore lack many of the social pressures that limit offline behavior.

There are also other, less direct impacts of anonymity. Anonymity creates a form of social isolation from the victim that allows many otherwise normal people to engage in behavior that would seem cruel if performed face-to-face. Because the victim cannot be seen or heard, a form of social distance is created between attacker and victim that empowers behavior that would not otherwise be possible.

There is a long history of study of anonymity and social distance. Starting in 1961, the psychologist Stanley Milgram conducted a famous series of experiments. Participants were told that they were administering a test to a volunteer test-taker. Each participant was shown a large machine and instructed to use the machine to administer electrical shocks to the test-taker after every wrong answer. Unknown to the participants, the test-taker was actually an actor, and the machine did not deliver any shocks; instead, the machine just made a buzzing noise and the actor pretended to receive an increasingly painful shock each time the participant pressed the "electric shock" button. Famously, Milgram found that only gentle coaxing was required to get many participants to administer shocks that were labeled as "450 volts" and described as potentially deadly, even while the actor was howling in apparent pain.

Among his more detailed findings, Milgram found that increasing the social distance between the participant and the (actor) test-taker increased the likelihood that the participant would be willing to administer large and painful electric shocks. In the initial experiment, the actor was hidden behind a wall so that the participant could hear the actor's screams but not see his face. Around two-thirds of participants were willing to administer the maximum shock three times. But, when the participant had to actually hold the actor's arm against the supposed "shock" machine, fewer than half as many participants were willing to apply a shock they believed could be deadly. By this rough measure, the physical presence of the victim cut in half the number of people willing to inflict torture.

Social distance has also been shown to increase the ability of soldiers to kill opposing soldiers, even in the heat of combat. It is well known in the military that even well-trained soldiers resist killing individual enemy combatants, some even going so far as to intentionally or subconsciously fire above the heads of the enemy despite being expert marksmen. Soldiers report the most psychological difficulty in hand-to-hand combat, where both fighters can see each other fully and one must directly perform the physical act of killing. Similarly, snipers—who can see the faces of their targets through high-power magnification—also have to force themselves to kill, even though they possess the tools and training required to do so. In contrast, bomber crews—who see only abstract "targets" on the ground—experience the least resistance. One military scholar cites this psychological aversion to harming another human as the reason why blindfolds are provided at firing-squad executions: it is for the comfort of the shooters, not the victim. "Not having to look at the face of the victim provides a form of psychological distance that enables the execution party and assists in their subsequent denial and the rationalization and acceptance of having killed a fellow human being. The eyes are the window of the soul, and if one does not have to look into the eyes when killing, it is much easier to deny the humanity of the victim."[11] A Vietnam War veteran agreed that emotional distance increased the ability of

soldiers to kill. To him, "'[e]motional distance' includes perceived social, cultural and moral distinctions between the soldier and the enemy, as well as mechanical interfaces . . . which impose some form of
mechanical barrier between the soldier and his victim."[12]

The same inhibitions that keep us from hurting others physically
also apply to nonphysical attacks that cause emotional or psychological pain in the victim. The Internet shares the features found by
the military scholars to increase the willingness of soldiers to harm
others. An online attacker can't see his victim's eyes; instead, all he
sees is (at most) a cartoonish avatar representing his victim. An online attacker is separated by a mechanical interface; he's just typing
into a machine instead of directly saying insults to someone's face.
And the fragmented nature of online discussion groups allows online
attackers to very easily find cultural distinctions that make the victim
part of some "other" group; members of many online communities
strongly self-identify as members of a cultural group of which outsiders are not members.

The combination of direct failures of accountability—such as
the lack of social or legal pressure to conform—and the distancing
effect of the Internet creates a perfect storm of inhumanity. As one
cartoonist put it, "normal person + anonymity + audience = total
f@$%-wad."[13]

Even worse, the anonymity provided by the Internet allows attackers to easily impersonate others. On many sites, the lack of verifiable identity allows malicious (or mischievous) users to enter
somebody else's name as their own. In one political example,
pranksters commented on a blog article under false names in order to
create the appearance of a running dialogue between presidential
candidate John McCain and his running mate, Sarah Palin.[14] The
prank was political theater, and the authors were heavy-handed
enough that few viewers were misled. But there are countless other
instances where a private individual has been more subtly impersonated, often to grave effect. Attacks by impersonation can be par-

ticularly harmful: How do you prove that you didn't really make an offensive comment that appears to be posted under your name? How do you show that it wasn't really you who engaged in a juvenile spat online? In many cases, this kind of impersonation is illegal, but it is often impossible to find the original culprit.

Internet Anonymity Empowers "Google Voyeurism"

Anonymity works on the other end of the equation, as well. Just as anonymity allows users to post content they would never share face-to-face, it also empowers a unique form of online prying: "Google voyeurism." In most social circles, there is a social prohibition against inquiring too far into personal issues and concerns. It is considered impolite to eavesdrop, and the socially accepted response to accidentally walking into a private conversation is to simply walk away.

But online, the anonymity provided by the Internet empowers digital voyeurism. Sitting alone at home, it is very easy to ask Google whether a neighbor named "Joe Smith" has a history of trouble: a user can simply type into a Google search box the words "Joe Smith arrest," "Joe Smith divorce," and "Joe Smith drugs." If those searches come up empty, the user can try searching for Joe's pages on Facebook, My-Space, and other social networking sites. Because web searches do not leave any visible evidence that they ever happened, the searches go unnoticed by their target. Without social pressure to limit intrusion, stories abound of Facebook stalking and other forms of digital eavesdropping.

Luckily for our online reputations, digital anonymity is not complete. In the worst cases of online attack, the attacker inevitably leaves some digital fingerprint or clue behind that allows him or her to be identified. And, if not, it is often easier to dismiss or hide anonymous content: Internet users are learning to recognize that anonymous content is sometimes less trustworthy than identified content. Even if you are attacked by an anonymous coward, you should not despair, because you can still recover your online reputation and get back to your regular life.

Notes

1. Allen Rappeport, "Did Whole Foods CEO Blog Illegally?" *CFO.com*, July 17, 2007. **Go:** http://wildwest2.com/go/501.

2. Spokeo, at http://www.spokeo.com/, website content as of September 2009.

3. It also uses an alphabet soup of other protocols to send the request (ranging from TCP to HTTP), but only IP is relevant to this level of anonymity.

4. For example, Proxify.com.

5. The program is officially known as "Tor" (lowercase) but the usage of "TOR" (uppercase) is more common. Electronic Frontier Foundation, "Tor: Overview." **Go:** http://wildwest2.com/go/502.

6. There is a very limited U.S. requirement that websites that collect personal information attempt to verify that their users are over the age of thirteen, but this is often in the form of a simple checkbox that says "I am over 13" and nothing more.

7. Seth Sutel, "Viacom Sues YouTube for $1 Bllion," *Pittsburgh Post-Gazette*, March 14, 2007. **Go:** http://wildwest2.com/go/503.

8. Anne Broache and Greg Sandoval, "Viacom Sues Google over YouTube Clips," *CNet News*, March 13, 2007. **Go:** http://wildwest2.com/go/504.

9. Peter Steiner, Cartoon: "On the Internet, nobody knows you're a dog," *The New Yorker*, July 5, 1993, via CartoonBank.com. **Go:** http://wildwest2.com/go/505.

10. Unnamed Wikipedia contributors, "On the Internet, Nobody Knows You're a Dog," *Wikipedia*, version of December 6, 2008. **Go:** http://wildwest2.com/go/506.

11. Dave Grossman, *On Killing: The Psychological Cost of Learning to Kill in War and Society* (Boston: Little, Brown, 1995), 128. **Go:** http://wildwest2.com/go/507.

12. Robert A. Hall, *Combat Battalion: The 8th Battalion in Vietnam* (St. Leonards, NSW, Australia: Allen & Unwin, 2000), 138. **Go**: http://wildwest2.com/go/508.

13. Mike Krahulik and Jerry Holkins, "Green Blackboards (and Other Anomalies)," *Penny Arcade*, March 19, 2004. **Go**: http://wildwest2.com/go/509.

14. Unknown comment authors in June Kronholz, "Steelers or Redskins? Obama or McCain?" *Washington Wire* (blog), September 23, 2008. **Go**: http://wildwest2.com/go/510.

Google Gone Wild: The Digital Threat to Reputation

In an ideal world, anyone searching for information about you would find a fair description of who you are and what you do, without too much about your personal life being revealed to complete strangers. Unfortunately, we do not live in an ideal world. Even without any malicious attacks, thousands of reputations are ruined by negligent mistakes, sloppy programming, bad luck, and the structure of the Internet itself. These dangers manifest themselves many ways: Google's search algorithm unintentionally dredges up false information and emphasizes negative information; blog authors negligently repeat incomplete truths; researchers fail to search deeply enough to get a full picture; and technology echoes and repeats the most scandalous facts.

Google Gone Wild

Justice is blind, but search engines are blind, deaf, and dumb.

—FOLK ADAGE ADAPTED TO FIT MODERN REALITY

Almost all popular websites are automated. They are run by computer software that does not need human intervention for most actions. A bank's website uses a computer program that automatically tells you how much money is in your account without a bank employee ever lifting a finger. An e-commerce website uses a computer program to tell you what items are in stock and to process your payment without the need for a cashier to do anything. And a search engine—like Google or Microsoft Bing—uses a computer program to figure out what websites to return for your search query without a human editor reviewing the results.

The system usually works because computers are incredibly smart. When properly programmed, computers can perform literally billions of calculations in a second. Computers can store more information on a disk the size of a deck of cards than could ever fit in books in a public library. And computers can perform the most boring tasks day in and day out without ever tiring or needing a break.

But the system sometimes fails because computers are also incredibly dumb. Computers do exactly what they are told to do, no more and no less. Computers do not ask whether their instructions make sense. Computers do not consider other ways to perform the same task. A computer has no empathy or emotions, nor any sense of fairness or justice. If a computer is programmed to return the most popular links in response to a search, then it will return the most popular links even if they are obviously wrong, unfair, or harmful. And computers interpret absolutely everything completely literally; the fictional "Johnny 5" of the movie *Short Circuit* is perhaps the only computer in history that "got" a joke.[1]

Search engines like Google are run entirely by computer programs. There is no person that reviews each query into a search engine or the result that it returns. And for good reason: there are
millions upon millions of searches each day. It would be impossible
for even a team of thousands of employees to screen results for obviously offensive content, let alone for humans to perform the research required to determine what websites provided the "best" or
most truthful answers. The details of the programs that run Google's
search engine are secret, but the outlines are known: Google uses one
program, a "spider," to try to access and analyze every single page on
the Internet. This task is constantly being conducted in the background, twenty-four hours a day, seven days a week. When a user
sends a query to the Google search engine, a second computer program uses the massive database of pages that have been found by the
"spider" to figure out what websites might be relevant. Among other
factors, Google's computer program considers which pages are the
most "popular" pages related to a search term, on the basis of the
number of other websites that link to it. Other factors, like the fresh-
ness of the content and the number of times the search term appears
in the page, also play a role. For example, imagine searching for information about the former CEO of Microsoft by entering the
search term "Bill Gates" into Google. The computer program that
runs the Google search engine—which is based on a complex math-
ematical model known as an "algorithm"—would probably calculate
that the entry about Bill Gates in the free encyclopedia at
Wikipedia.org[2] is an extremely popular web page about Bill Gates: at
least 16,000 other websites link to Bill Gates's biography page on
Wikipedia.[3] On the other hand, a personal blog post that happened
to mention the name "Bill Gates" would be considered relatively
unimportant, in that it would probably be linked by very few other
sites. Such a personal blog post would be unlikely to appear in the
first page of results unless it suddenly attracted a lot of attention and
links from other parts of the Internet.

The key is that Google's process is completely automated and that it interprets "popularity" as the main measure of the importance of a page. It does not consider whether a page is truthful, accurate, or fair; instead, the computer simply asks whether the page is popular. To take a phrase from linguists, Google is "descriptive" rather than "prescriptive": the results of a Google search reflect the sites that *are* popular rather than Google's opinion of what sites *should be* popular. This moral neutrality can be good at times. Users can trust that the results returned by Google and other search engines are an accurate reflection of what exists on the Internet. The policy of neutrality has prevented partisan censorship and manipulation of search results. For most users, there are only a few instances of altered search results on Google, and each alteration is marked by a prominent notice explaining why the results were altered—usually because of copyright infringement or child pornography. Many other search engines have followed Google's example and similarly limited manual changes to their results. Neutrality about controversial issues isn't necessarily bad: it promotes vigorous political debate by exposing viewpoints that might be unpopular today but that might become popular in the future.

But this Switzerland-like neutrality can also lead to bizarre or even shocking results. Moral abstention can have profound impacts on personal reputation. Unfounded attacks may quickly rise to the top of search results because any controversy will tend to create the appearance of popularity. Google will not remove demonstrably false, libelous, or illegal search results without a court order. If a false attack on you, your business, or your family is the first result in a Google search, Google will tell you that you are out of luck. This policy has left many people feeling powerless: Google (the company) will do nothing to control the harmful actions of its search engine, under the guise of "neutrality." The slap in the face of victims is even stronger because of the massive market share of Google: Google dominates the U.S. search market and many overseas markets to the point where it is effectively the main way that information is found, anywhere in the world. The information found in Google shapes lives and reputations, and false negative information in Google can rend careers, families, and businesses. To victims of online defamation, former U.N. Secretary General Kofi Annan's words ring true: "Impartiality does not—and must not—mean neutrality in the face of evil."[4]

The Risk of Self-Reinforcing Cycles

Rankings based on popularity work well sometimes: the most important and relevant pages are often the most popular. In the Bill Gates example, the "popularity" of a page served as a valid heuristic (there's that word again) to identify a site with content that is helpful to somebody searching for information about Bill Gates. But, sometimes, things go wrong. The search engine's reliance on popularity can sometimes cause false, misleading, slanderous, and unfair pages to show up at the top of a results page. The Google algorithm has no way to know what information is true or false, fair or unfair. It performs no original research, and it does not ask for any human's opinion before returning results. If a page filled with scurrilous lies is the most "popular" page for a search term, then Google will list it as the first result in a search.

Because Google is the most popular search engine, its emphasis on the popularity of web pages can create a large problem for your reputation. If a controversial or false page is returned very high in a Google search, it is likely to be read by many users. And some of these readers might comment on the page by posting a link on their own blogs or by using a discussion site like Digg or Reddit. Google's spider will then scan these new pages commenting on the original page and take them as evidence of the original link's popularity, *even if the new discussion is about how controversial or false the original page is.* This leads to a self-reinforcing cycle of popularity: Lots of people see the page because it is at the top of a Google search, so lots of people comment on and link to the page, which makes it seem even more popular to a Google search, which promotes the page even higher up in Google's rankings . . . the cycle continues. The risk of this self-perpetuating cycle is enhanced even further because Google tends to reward blogs with high search rankings when they publish new content, even though blogs are often rushed into publication before stories can be fully researched. This "blog bonus" often causes false negative information to quickly rise to the top of a Google search.

Users who share false or misleading Web content are not always malicious or nasty. Many users just want to share what appears to be an interesting piece of news or gossip with their friends and acquaintances. These users are simply too eager to share and do not think to do their own investigation into the truth of the news. Other users are bloggers who want to be among the first to write about a story, lest they be "scooped" by other bloggers or the so-called mainstream media. These users let competitive pressure stand in the way of thorough investigation.

And yet other users repeat false or misleading information because they are blinded by a cognitive bias that makes them more likely to uncritically accept certain false information they see. People often believe stories that match their preconceptions about the way the world works. A reader who believes that "the rich" are ruthless and greedy is more likely to accept a story about a wealthy businessman's malfeasance; a reader who believes that "the poor" are responsible for their own plight is more likely to uncritically accept a story about an unmotivated welfare recipient. Politically active readers are more likely to believe (and share) a story about misdeeds by the "other side" than about their own. The existence of this type of bias is perhaps inevitable, but it has contributed greatly to the speed at which false and inaccurate information spreads. Many websites attract many people with similar biases— ranging from political sites on both ends of the spectrum to news discussion sites that are pro- or anti-copyright—which leads to further reinforcement of each user's biases because they consistently share stories that reinforce the perceptions underlying their biases.

The cycle is particularly dangerous because pages that contain false, incomplete, misleading, or scandalous information often attract the most attention; for example, a tabloid blog about a celebrity's alleged infidelity is often far more interesting than a dry biography or his "official" website. As a result, users are more likely to read and talk about controversial pages simply because of the human appetite for scandal. Google takes the resulting discussions as a sign of the scandalous page's importance and then moves the page higher up the results list. The more prominent the scandalous page becomes in a search engine, the more people will see it, discuss it, and comment on it—all of which increases the apparent popularity of the page and makes it more likely to appear even higher in a search. Once the cycle has started, it rarely breaks on its own.

In short, the self-reinforcing cycle is "Google Gone Wild." The search engine uses a completely automated method to organize the information on the Internet. But the automation also means that there is nobody to step in and fix things when they go wrong. Search engines that rely on the popularity of links can quickly spiral out of control in a way that highlights controversial and false information. And, because very few people perform their own independent research, many readers will simply repeat the same false, incomplete, misleading, or otherwise incorrect information. The resulting copies of the same incorrect data can quickly overwhelm the first page of search results, further reinforcing the false information. Once the downward spiral has begun, it usually takes deliberate intervention in order to stop the search engine gone wild.

Users Believe the "Google Truth"

By now, most people know better than to believe everything that they read, especially online. But that does not stop many Web users from giving too much weight to what they read online and from believing the information that appears at the top of a Google search. The results from Google often appear to reflect the truth, but in reality they are nothing more than the links that happen to be the most "popular," as measured by an arbitrary system of link-based counting. In other words, the "Google Truth" (the collection of links that Google suggests are true and important) often replaces the real truth because users fail to look deeper.

All too often, one event or perspective dominates the Google Truth about somebody. The Google Truth often appears to summarize a person's life (thirty, fifty, or even seventy years' worth of it) with links to one event that happened to gather a lot of comment. Or, thanks to a self-reinforcing cycle, a biased or false perspective may dominate the Google Truth. And, all too often, readers take the Google Truth seriously, as if a computer program really could figure out what is important about somebody's entire life and present it in just a handful of links.

The authoritative look of Google's search results contributes to the problem. Google's website looks like a professional arbiter of truth and accuracy. If a Google search for somebody's name—for example, "Bill Gates"—returns a page of results all repeating the same lie, then it appears that Google has at least impliedly endorsed those results as being relevant and correct. Of course, Google disclaims all responsibility for its search results, but many users still understandably think that search results have somehow been vetted or approved by Google's computers. Part of this mistaken belief comes from a natural trust of computers: Computers appear unbiased and rarely make mistakes. The fact that Google's search engine often returns correct and unbiased results makes it all the more dangerous when Google fails by returning false or misleading statements. Users become accustomed to Google's getting things right and don't think critically enough when Google gets it wrong. Because of their trust in Google, users reinforce its failings.

Even earnest, careful, and unbiased users are often stymied by the Google Truth. If false or misleading information is dominant in the first page or two of search results, then even a careful reader might never make it far enough through to find a glimmer of the truth. Even the most conscientious reader cannot spend all day trying to tease the truth out from tens or hundreds of pages that tell different tales. If false information has been so often repeated as to effectively smother the truth, then the false information will become the Google Truth.

There is yet one more problem with the Google Truth. Even if a user is able to wade through a series of false or misleading pages in order to find the truth about a subject, the existence and popularity of the false pages will give a false impression that the subject is mired in controversy. A false appearance of controversy can be just as bad as actual guilt in some professions: teachers, police officers, and babysitters could all have their careers ruined by a false impression of a controversy over their character. And the reputations of a small business can be severely harmed by a false controversy over the quality of its workmanship.

No Means to Respond

The damage done by search engines is increased by the fact that no major search engine provides any meaningful way for a victim of false information to respond to false allegations. If the Google Truth about your reputation is a complete lie, Google will simply disclaim all responsibility for its search results and suggest that you build a personal web page to correct the record. It will not remove most false information from its search index or allow you to meaningfully comment on or respond to the false results.

Search engines claim that any means of response would open them up to manipulation and spamming. But the real answer is much easier: To a search engine company, profit is more important than fairness. Even if it would be fair and just to allow victims to respond, search engine companies know that it might hurt their business in the long run. And search engine companies believe that it would be too expensive to have a live human mediate each dispute. So, the companies just pretend that the problem of false online information does not exist and leave victims of the company's services to fend for themselves.

But telling users "go make your own web page with the truth, and maybe people will find it" is really no answer at all. Controversial and false pages tend to gather more attention and links than accurate pages; the truth is usually less interesting than rumors and lies. Further, even if a victim could make her own homepage and get it into the first page of Google results, that would still not erase the damage done by false and misleading sites. Users would still have no way to know whether the victim was telling the truth, and if the lies outnumbered the truth by nine to one, then very few people would believe the truth.

So far, Google is the only major search engine to even try to offer victims of online reputation damage a chance to respond at all. Google has created an experimental feature (Google Search Wiki) that allows users to make brief comments on search results. But these comments are not displayed unless a searcher goes out of her way to enable them. And the comments suffer from the same problem as the rest of a search: anybody can comment on any result, and there is no way to screen true or false comments. Nothing about the system gives any priority to the victim and the search comments could easily be flooded by an attacker or users just repeating the same wrong information. Google also offers a "Google Profile" that allows individuals to write a short description of themselves. These profiles are experimental and have been appearing at the bottom of Google searches for personal names. Google claims that victims of online false information can use them to recover their good names. But Google Profiles are too little and too late: they appear only at the bottom of the page and are more or less useless to people with common names.

The Modern Panopticon: Google Sees All

**Economists have predicted ten of the
last three recessions.**

—COMMON ADAGE

Google knows ten of three true things about you.

—INTERNET REALITY

Without Google, much of the harmful content online would be irrelevant. The backwaters of the Internet would stay obscure. Nasty rumors would be circulated very narrowly, brief moments of anger or spite would disappear into dusty corners of the Internet, private secrets would not be widely revealed, and attackers would have no way to carry their messages to their audiences. An Internet without a search system would be like having a telephone but no phone book; it would be possible to call your friends and businesses you have already visited, but it would be very difficult to find new places or information.

But Google and other search engines are voracious for data and eager to share it. They provide more information than many people ever knew existed. They dig deep through the Internet and find all references to any person, place, or thing. And, with the best intentions, these search engines blindly categorize what they find and share the most popular results. They don't know (or care) what content is harmful, what content is private, or even what content is true—all they can tell is what content is in demand.

Search engines are by far the most common way to find information online. If there were any doubts about the popularity of Web searches, a recent survey showed that 86 percent of U.S. Web users think that searching the Internet is the best way to find information—even compared to offline data retrieval methods.[5] But there actually was an Internet before the emergence of Google and other powerful search engines. Back in the mid-1990s, "directories" were a popular way to finding information on the Internet. The Web was small enough that a team of editors could try to catalog all of the important sites into a hierarchical directory—for example, at early versions of Yahoo.com, sites about cooking were listed under the "Food" category; sites about space exploration were listed under "Science"; and all manner of official sites were listed under "Government." Because the directory was human-edited, there was a natural filter on the content that got listed. For example, personal attack sites were unlikely to be included in the directory at all, so many attack sites remained completely invisible. The few rudimentary Web-based journals of the time (the precursors of today's blogs) were listed on a journal-by-journal basis, so there was no easy way to search for the content of any individual web page or journal post. The result was that personal attacks, harmful comments, and other personal information were effectively hidden—there was simply no way to stumble across attacks against everyday people.

Search engines revolutionized the Internet. They started to take over for directories by the late 1990s, and the last death bells rang for directories in 2002, when Yahoo! replaced its directory with a search engine; the Yahoo! directory is still available, but it is no longer the default means of finding information through Yahoo!. The first major search engine was created when Digital Equipment Corporation ("DEC"), then a major manufacturer of heavy-duty computer hardware, set up a rudimentary search engine known as AltaVista in order to demonstrate the computing power of DEC computers.[6] Unlike directories, AltaVista allowed users to find any information hidden on any page on the Internet. The AltaVista search engine accomplished this by replacing human editors with the first "Web spider": a computer program that tirelessly "crawled" from link to link on the Internet, retrieving every web page it could find and taking note of what words appeared in the page's HTML code. Suddenly AltaVista unlocked the potential of the Internet: If a user searched for "Tony Blair," AltaVista would provide a list of all pages on the Internet that contained the phrase "Tony Blair," rather than just a small sampling of directory entries related to the U.K. government. A user searching for a more obscure term—perhaps a Brit looking for information about Blair's first Secretary of State for Northern Ireland, Mo Mowlam—might be out of luck in a directory, but AltaVista would return all the pages that contained Mowlam's name. AltaVista allowed users to find information that was once hidden in the depths of the Internet: a passing reference to a particular restaurant in a personal journal, a single mention of an individual's name on a government website, all reviews of a software program across all software-related websites, and so on.

Other search engines—including Google—soon followed in

Alta Vista's footsteps. Vast troves of data hidden in the depths of the Internet were quickly brought to light. Users could now search through the full text of millions of web pages rather than merely browse through a list of a few thousand websites. Today, Google and other search engines are able to index the content of literally trillions of pages on millions of websites (see Figure 6-1). Now, the most obscure information can be found through a Google search; even if a directory could provide a list of historic Red Sox rosters, it takes a Google search to find public-domain photos of 1912 third baseman Larry Gardner buried in the Library of Congress's photo-sharing project.[7]

Now search engines are becoming even more specific to particu-

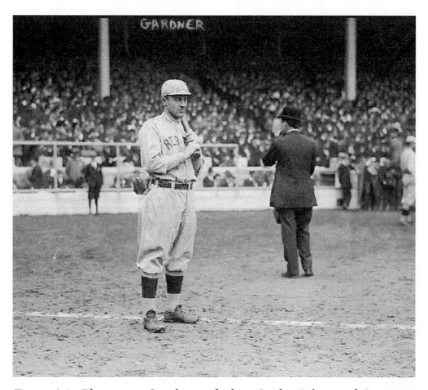

Figure 6-1. If it exists, Google can find it. Credit: Library of Congress/ Flickr.

lar needs. There are search engines designed to find information relevant to Christians,[8] search engines designed to find only blog posts,[9] and even experimental search engines designed to return results based on drawings rather than words: if you provide a drawing, it will provide a list of web pages that describe similar-looking objects.[10] But, more important to online reputation, there are now people-specific search engines that seek to locate all information about any individual. These sites—like Pipl and Spock—allow users to search for a name ("Michael Fertik") and provide all known information about them: address, phone number, photos, social networking profiles, political contributions, publications, references in government documents, and more. It is one-stop shopping for personal information, whether good or bad. The depth of information found is astounding; Pipl has been described as "so good it'll scare your pants off."[11] One user reported that she "pipled" herself and "found blog posts, comments, profiles all over the web, even a MySpace account I swore I cancelled more than a year ago."[12]

Anything Digital Can Be Searched

Search engines are getting more powerful every day. In the early days, search engines could understand the content of only simple HTML pages. Complex pages that included advanced techniques like JavaScript were difficult for search engines to understand, so the search engines often skipped them. Websites with complicated navigational systems or thousands of pages often caused the spider to stall out. Desktop documents, like Microsoft Word documents or Adobe PDF files, were out of the question.

But, today, search engines have evolved to catch up with many of the file formats that are posted online. Google and other search engines can easily read and index the contents of Microsoft Word documents, Microsoft Powerpoint presentations, Adobe Portable Document Format (PDF) files, and much more. And search engines are becoming far more adept at delving into the depths of interactive websites that may contain hundreds (or even tens of thousands) of pages that are accessible only by manipulating buttons or submitting requests for data. This newfound ability to interact with complex sites has allowed vast swaths of database data, ranging from marathon results to social networking information, to quickly be added to Google's database.

Even photos are becoming searchable in ways never before possible. Optical character recognition ("OCR") allows computers to "read" text that appears in images. OCR is quickly becoming so common that it is even included in free personal reminder services like Evernote—take a picture of something you want to remember, and the service will automatically find and index any text in the image. And OCR is being improved by well-meaning projects like reCAPTCHA—a massive automated project to prevent spam by testing whether users can successfully identify words scanned from old books (a "CAPTCHA" is a contrived acronym for a "Completely Automated Public Turing test to tell Computers and Humans Apart," more familiarly known as those funny-looking quizzes on many websites where you have to identify the letters in a smooshed image; "reCAPTCHA" is one particular project using this technology to improve the ability to scan and read old books). The result is that massive amounts of old content that may currently be available in image format—old newspapers, old magazines, old government reports, old property tract listings, and more—are going to become searchable in the next few years.

Facial recognition is more immediately dangerous for reputation, and it is also quickly advancing. Google's Picasa service allows users to "tag" people in one or two photos, and then it will automatically suggest tags in future photos on the basis of facial recognition.[13] Right now, the tags are visible only to authorized viewers, but there is no technical reason why photo recognition perfected in Picasa couldn't be expanded. And, thanks to the photo-tagging features of popular sites like Facebook and MySpace, there is a ready corpus of millions of human-edited tags to provide a starting point for such a quest. While Google is unlikely to violate its users' trust by raiding Facebook or MySpace for image tags, it would take only one less ethical site to start a trend.

If facial recognition were to become more common, the impacts on online reputation would be obvious. Right now, it is hard to find many images of individuals. They may appear in many online photos, but if the photos are not captioned (many pictures aren't) then the subjects are effectively invisible to a search. If facial recognition becomes more popular, a simple search for somebody's name will reveal tens (or hundreds) of photos of them. This is especially true for embarrassing photos of teenagers that have been spread to a wide audience. Right now, many of these images have been distributed without any identifying information; the victim of embarrassment is effectively anonymous to all but his friends. But in a world of electronic facial recognition, the identities of many people in these photos will be revealed, with obvious potential for embarrassment before potential employers, schools, and others. And, if sufficiently scandalous, a risqué or drunk image might become the first thing people see when searching for a particular person (see Figure 6-2).

Notes

1. "Whatever God wants, he keeps!" For a more full explanation, see **Go**: http://wildwest2.com/go/601.

2. Unnamed Wikipedia editors, "Bill Gates," via Wikipedia.org. **Go**: http://wildwest2.com/go/602.

3. Yahoo! Site Explorer reported 16,937 links to Bill Gates's biography page as of September 2009.

4. Kofi A. Annan, "Walking the International Tightrope," *New York Times*, January 19, 1999. **Go**: http://wildwest2.com/go/603.

5. Press Release, "Searcher Moms—A Search Behavior and Usage Study," Performics. **Go**: http://wildwest2.com/go/604.

Figure 6-2. Don't let the Internet be your digital scarlet letter. Credit: MorphoMir via Flickr.

6. Peter H. Lewis, "Digital Equipment Offers Web Browsers Its 'Super Spider,'" *New York Times*, December 18, 1995. **Go:** http://wildwest2.com/go/605.

7. Bain News Service, "Harry Hooper (left) and Larry Gardner (center), Boston AL (baseball)" 1912, via Library of Congress/Flickr.com (accessed February 1, 2009). **Go:** http://wildwest2.com/go/606.

8. SeekFind. **Go:** http://wildwest2.com/go/607.

9. Technorati. **Go:** http://wildwest2.com/go/608.

10. Retreivr, via labs.systemone.at. **Go:** http://wildwest2.com/go/609.

11. Roi Carthy, "Pipl.com: People Search Engine So Good, It Will Scare Your Pants Off," *TechCrunch* (blog), January 29, 2009. **Go:** http://wildwest2.com/go/610.

12. Commenter "Ann-Marie," "Pipl.com: People Search Engine So Good, It Will Scare Your Pants Off," *TechCrunch* (blog) (January 29, 2009, at 7:42 P.M. P.S.T.). **Go:** http://wildwest2.com/go/611.

13. Don Reisinger, "Picasa Refresh Brings Facial Recognition," *TechCruch* (blog), September 2, 2008. **Go:** http://wildwest2.com/go/612.

Why People Attack Each Other Online

Your reputation is constantly at risk from malicious attack by people you know—and even from complete strangers. Every day, thousands of innocent victims find that they have been smeared, slandered, and dragged through the mud online by one or more attackers. The motives for these attacks vary widely, ranging from petty jealousy to sociopathy. But these attacks have one thing in common: they often leave an indelible mark on the victim's search results.

Most people are subject to few malicious online attacks, but you still need to be on guard against them. It is necessary to take precautions now because malicious reputation attacks create some of the most severe, pernicious, and persistent forms of reputation damage. Even if you have not yet been a victim of a malicious attack, it is important to understand the motivations of online attackers so that you know how to prepare yourself in case of the worst. By analogy, prudent drivers wear their seatbelts every time they get in the car, even though they hope to avoid accidents. And, as described in Chapter 11, starting your preparation now can help prevent and minimize the damage caused by an online attack; if you have carefully bolstered your online profile and carefully monitor your online reputation for changes, an attacker will find it very difficult to cause major damage.

This chapter provides insight into the types of people that might launch an online reputation attack against you. If you are the victim of an anonymous online attack, this chapter may help identify who is behind it and how the person can be convinced to stop or retract the attack.

There Have Always Been Attacks on Reputation

Malicious gossip, rumor, and slander are as old as human society. Ancient texts are filled with stories of whispered conversations and false allegations. To take just one example, in the Christian Bible, Paul the Apostle uses people who spread gossip and lies as an example of the evil that can infect humankind: "They are gossips, slanderers, God-haters, haughty, arrogant, boastful, . . . faithless, heartless, ruthless."[1] The apostle Timothy similarly condemns "gossips and busybodies" who "[say] things they ought not to."[2] Recorded examples of gossip go back even further in history; the ancient Greek leader Pericles, who ruled Athens from 461 B.C. to 421 B.C., was not immune from public whispering. A popular rumor of the time alleged that he was always depicted wearing a helmet in order to hide his deformed skull.[3]

If gossip and slander are common in the offline world, then it should come as no surprise that they are also common online. Turning on a computer, sadly, does not replace negative emotions with positive ones. Nor do people instantly magically become angelic when they go online. If anything, many people who are polite face-to-face become more aggressive and harsh online. See Chapter 5 for an explanation of how anonymity can empower ill will.

There can be no complete list of motives for online attacks. Any attempt to list every possible reason why humans maliciously attack each other would necessarily be incomplete; every day, people find new reasons to do horrible things. But there are some common categories that explain the vast majority of malicious Internet reputation damage. Among them are jealousy, envy, revenge, bullying, vigilante enforcement of social norms, politics, business and greed, extortion, social gossip, and sociopathy.

The Usual Suspects: Jealousy, Envy, and Revenge

Three of the most common negative human emotions are the cause of many online reputation attacks. There are no reliable statistics about the motivations behind online attackers—nor is there likely to ever be a comprehensive study—but it is a safe bet that more than half of online smear campaigns against private individuals start with one of the "big three" motivations: jealousy, envy, and revenge.

Jealousy

Beware, my lord, of jealousy; it is the green-eyed monster which doth mock the meat it feeds on.

—IAGO IN SHAKESPEARE'S *OTHELLO*

Jealousy is the feeling of insecurity that comes with a fear of losing something. It is most strongly associated with the feelings of insecure lovers, who constantly worry that their loved one will leave them for another. Jealousy of this form is closely related to (but still distinct from) envy, which is the emotion felt by someone who desires what somebody else has.

Jealousy has always been a source of human drama. It is Shakespeare's "green eyed-monster,"[4] the "magnifier of trifles,"[5] "the jaundice of the soul,"[6] and even "that dragon which slays love under the pretence of keeping it alive."[7] Jealousy has motivated lovers to massively destructive acts and has spurred slander and lies for generations.

As far as online reputation goes, jealousy is a particularly dangerous motivation. Jealousy robs the mind of logic and replaces it with blind passion. A jealous attacker will stop at nothing to protect what he thinks is his, even if it means destroying what he intended to protect.

If you are faced with a jealous attacker, your best bet may be to avoid confrontation and work to play defense while the jealous attacker's emotions play out. Many (but not all) attacks that start with jealousy end within a few weeks when the attacker's emotions run their course.

Envy

Envy shoots at others and wounds itself.

—PROVERB

Envy is a desire for that which somebody else has. It is often associated with feelings of unfairness or rivalry. Just like jealousy, it has a long pedigree. Envy has always been considered one of the "seven deadly sins." The vice of envy was considered so serious that the poet Dante, during the Middle Ages, wrote in his famous *Divine Comedy* that the punishment in the afterlife for envy was for the envious to have their eyes sewn shut with wire, so that they could no longer see what others possess.[8] Countless modern examples abound; the classic tale of Snow White—famously collected by the Brothers Grimm and later popularized by Disney—revolves around Snow White's stepmother's envy of Snow White's beauty. Advertisements for fancy cars and other luxury goods play on our feelings of envy toward what others have. And, of course, the 2004 film *Envy* revolved around one character's envy of another's business success.

Envy is such a powerful emotion that it often causes people to try to destroy somebody else rather than attempt to improve themselves. An envious attacker will often use defamation and slander in an attempt to bring down her victim. In the pre-Internet era, this was often through whispered lies and rumors; today, it can take the form of full-fledged online barrages with permanent consequences.

An envious attacker is often snide and subtle. The duration of the attack depends on the nature of the envy: Is the attacker upset about one particular event (your winning an award or being recognized by a leader) or about your status generally (being a supervisor, being the straight-A student, or living in a nicer neighborhood)? If the attacker is upset about a particular event, her envy will usually blow over pretty quickly; play defense for a week and then you can go on the counterattack. But, if the attacker is upset about a more permanent condition, then you can expect a constant volley of small attacks until something else distracts the attacker weeks or even months later. In that case, you will want to get ahead of the attacks by building *Google walls* (described in Chapter 11) to help slow the spread of your attacker's messages. It may also be worth trying to work out the situation offline by befriending and being kind to the attacker; envy is an emotion that sometimes can be overcome by friendship if you are gentle and invite the attacker to participate in the benefits of which she is envious.

Revenge

Those who plot the destruction of others often perish in the attempt.

—Thomas More

Revenge is a desire to get even or get back at somebody for a perceived wrong. It is an attempt to make somebody else feel pain as a form of punishment or comeuppance. It is often closely related to jealousy or envy, in that those two emotions can lead to a desire to take revenge on somebody else for a perceived success or the person's wrongful acts.

Revenge is a familiar and common motive. Many movie villains (and a few movie heroes) are motivated by a quest for revenge for some perceived wrong. On the lighter side, a popular party joke involves a young boy's twenty-year quest to get revenge on a clown by telling him off—much of the humor in the joke comes from the fact that the boy's act of revenge is so much smaller than what the listener would expect in the situation. In the real world, there have been many plots to get revenge through spectacular (and often dangerous) means; all too many have ended in tragedy.

An attacker fixated on revenge is particularly dangerous because, all too often, he is willing to martyr himself to destroy his victim. Online attackers bent on revenge have devoted countless hours building attack sites and spreading hostile messages around the Internet. They have done everything from sending nasty e-mails, to creating fake photos, to attempting to hack into their victims' computers in order to simply destroy everything they can. Very little will stop an attacker fixated on revenge. Your best plan is to avoid confrontation—especially physical confrontation—and hope that the attacker's anger is short-lived. Revenge frequently motivates attackers to go beyond the pale; if your attacker does, you may want to discuss legal action with a licensed attorney.

Bullying

Solitary, poor, nasty, brutish, and short.

—THOMAS HOBBES, *LEVIATHAN* (1651), PERHAPS DESCRIBING
WHAT MIDDLE SCHOOL WOULD BE LIKE 350 YEARS LATER

Bullying is an attempt to raise oneself up by directly demeaning others; the attacker hopes to improve his social status or self-esteem by putting others down. Or, the attacker hopes to frighten the victim into giving up a particular concession: Offline, bullies are famous for stealing lunch money or homework. Online, bullies can still often intimidate victims into giving up things of value: lunch money the next day, passwords to accounts, secrets, embarrassing photos, or more. Online bullying ("cyberbullying") is unfortunately common. One study found that 43 percent of teenagers have been bullied online at least once. And, because of the anonymous nature of the Internet, almost half of the victims of online bullying do not even know the identity of their attacker.[9]

Offline bullying can take many forms: physical, harassment, emotional, or reputational. Online bullying is often limited to harassment or emotional and reputational attacks. Online bullying can be devastating to victims, especially because it often leaves a permanent record that face-to-face bullying does not. Electronic harassment can consist of flooding the victim's computer with insulting e-mails, instant messages, or other communications. It can also take the form of indirect attacks such as spreading lies and rumors among the victim's peers online or posting insulting messages on discussion areas visited by the victim and the victim's peers. This kind of bullying can spread quickly by e-mail or instant messaging or through MySpace, Facebook, and similar sites. And, just as in the offline world, the message spread by bullies is often simple: Bullies often allege that the victim is a teacher's pet, is immature (in any of a number of colorful ways), has an unrevealed sexual orientation, or is of easy virtue. Another unfortunate trend in online bullying is extortion based on a threat of revealing personal or private data—even to the point of threats to distribute revealing photos.[10]

Online bullying is particularly common among students. To an outsider, the online conduct of teenagers may seem bizarre. But, in some ways, these attacks should come as no surprise: The online conduct of teenagers is simply an extension of their offline lives. Many have compared middle or high school to *The Lord of the Flies*, a novel (and two movies) that describe the brutal social structure established by a fictional group of shipwrecked schoolchildren. Electronic bullying is also common among students because teenagers frequently lack the maturity or self-discipline to express their angers and frustrations in "adult" ways or to fully appreciate the consequences of their actions online and off. Many teens think that bullying is a necessary part of their social experience, simply because it has always happened to teenagers. If anything, teenagers are more likely to use online attack methods than adults; today's teenagers grew up with the Internet and never experienced the pre-Web world. The Internet has always been part of their social lives, and they may see it as less well supervised than their schools because most teachers and parents cannot possibly keep up with everything that teenagers do online.

When faced with a bully, students may want to tap into the school's dispute resolution procedures. Schools often have policies that provide an appropriate punishment to bullies (like picking weeds or sitting in detention) that does not create a risk of physical confrontation or resentment. Parents should be extremely careful about intervening; the social world of teenagers is extremely complicated, and well-meaning intervention might do more harm than good by making your child appear overly dependent or insufficiently assertive. However, parents should feel free to help the student develop age-appropriate and positive online content to burnish their online reputation and make sure that online bullying does not come up during college applications or job interviews by either eliminating the offensive content at its source or by surrounding it with enough positive and neutral content that it goes unnoticed. Adults faced with bullying should identify the perpetrator and take action through the workplace (assuming the bully is a co-worker) and then either ignore the online record of bullying or passively defuse it by creating new, positive content.

Vigilante Enforcement of Social Norms

The Internet is turning the whole society into a kangaroo court.

—KOREA TIMES EDITORIAL[11]

Vigilante justice was a common and distinguishing feature of the Old West frontier. In the new Wild West 2.0, vigilante justice is also common. One increasingly common form of online vigilante justice is electronic enforcement of social norms, such as digital reminders to follow customs like cleaning up after one's dog. But, with a little bit of bad luck, events that start as a gentle nudge toward following social norms can set off a chain of events that leads to mob justice and ruined reputations.

Offline, it makes sense to enforce some common social norms. Crowded urban society is made more pleasant when citizens follow many common unwritten standards of behavior. The exact norms vary from society to society, but they all define "good" or "proper" behavior in public. They are normally simple acts like letting people off the subway car before trying to board, not talking loudly on cell phones in crowded spaces, and wearing enough deodorant but not too much perfume. These norms fill the gap between pleasant society and criminal behavior—very minor wrongs cannot be criminalized, but life would be difficult if these behavioral standards were routinely violated. Even some acts that are technically illegal (but rarely enforced by the police) are enforced by social compliance; it is rare to see a police officer stop a pedestrian for littering a cigarette butt, but dropping a cigarette butt in a crowded public space is likely to trigger a lecture on waste disposal.

In offline society, the punishment for violating a social norm is approximately calibrated to the importance of the violation: observers often deploy a sharp glance, an exasperated sigh, or even a heated exchange of words. In most cases, offline rebukes for norm violations are one-off events with no permanent consequences for the violator. A sharp word disappears with its last echo, and rarely do offline rumors about breaches of social norms spread beyond a small group. But the Internet changed everything. Thanks to digital cameras and the ever-increasing quality of cell-phone cameras, norm violations can be instantly captured in a cameraphone photograph, posted online, and spread worldwide. This form of online vigilante enforcement of social norms has happened repeatedly, with massive consequences for the victims. In a widely publicized incident, a woman in South Korea allowed her small dog to defecate on a subway train. She refused to clean up the mess after being asked to do so by other patrons. A cell-phone photo of the act was posted to a discussion website, which led other members to find her real name, address, employer, and phone number. The woman was harassed by anonymous callers to the point of dropping out of college in an attempt to get away from the attention. While her act was illegal (and disgusting), it is hard to believe that the punishment fit the crime. Even assuming that the perpetrator was correctly identified and that there were not any mitigating circumstances not visible in the photos (not that anyone took time to check), it defies all conceptions of due process to believe that one violator should be randomly singled out for such severe punishment. One editorial following the incident called for "societal soul-searching to prevent a lack of ethical awareness from turning the [Internet] superpower into [a] villain."[12]

All too often, vigilante social norm enforcement starts innocently enough. The first person to notice the improper behavior may simply be honestly trying to maintain social order and not mean to harm the offender. Or the first person to post a photo online might just innocently mean to share something unusual she saw that day. But, once a story is posted online, it is out of any one person's control.

A real example can show how the Internet can take matters out of any one person's control. A humorous blogger thought he was being cute when he posted a short blog entry about a student who had approached him about buying a term paper. He gave her a bogus paper and described his trickery in his blog. The story quickly spread to major social news sites, where some readers discovered and posted the student's full name, e-mail address, and dormitory address. The blogger tried to retract the story once he realized that things were spiraling out of control, but it was already too late. The blogger was shocked to find out that hundreds of people had e-mailed the buyer's dean with information about the alleged cheater and created at least ten web pages (still available through a Google search for the student's name today) permanently archiving her misdeed. He maintains that the story is true but insists that he never intended such severe consequences for a student who suffered a temporary lapse of judgment on what was ultimately an inconsequential school assignment.[13]

It remains an open question whether such strong vigilante enforcement of social norms is beneficial. It certainly encourages social compliance. There is a very strong disincentive to misbehave if, at any moment, one faces the risk of permanent damage to one's reputation for violating a public norm. And there are many norms worthy of strong enforcement: The self-explanatory "New York Subway Masturbator" committed a contemptible act deserving of punishment and deterrence. But it is not clear that the violation of smaller norms—often taken out of context—deserve such severe sanction. The "dog poop girl" committed an indefensible act, but it is far from clear that she deserved to lose her job over it; the normal sanction for dog defecation is a citation from the sanitation department, not the loss of a job and a permanently ruined reputation. Further, overzealous norm enforcement can discourage legitimate forms of difference: Some people think that street protests are distasteful, but street protests are also an important part of our democratic dialogue as a means to air disputes. Overzealous enforcement of a perceived norm against this form of protest could chill legitimate discourse, to the harm of our society. And there is always the risk that somebody innocent will be falsely accused, that the next "dog defecator" or "subway masturbator" will be falsely identified and that the real culprits will remain unsanctioned.

If you have been the victim of overly aggressive social norm enforcement, then you have an uphill reputation challenge. No matter what you do, your top priority is to avoid fanning the flames of conflict higher. An online argument or conflict will just draw more attention to the problem. Your best bet is to quietly build some Google walls around the negative content to help slow down the spread of the story. If the story has been exaggerated in a way that is clearly and objectively false, you may *carefully* try to correct the story by trying to post or e-mail your clarification where the story appears; at all costs, remain calm and never argue with your accusers. Instead, provide cool, collected, rational, and objective factual clarifications to the record. Because vigilante norm enforcement taps into social emotions, you will have difficulty getting any allegations removed from the Internet unless you can verifiably prove that it wasn't you or that the events alleged absolutely did not happen.

Politics

First, they smear the candidate. Then they smear his party. And if that doesn't work, they smear his supporters.

—MODERN POLITICAL REALITY

Politics is infamously dirty, and one of the most common forms of dirty politics has always been to smear the other side—be it the opponent, his family, his party, his associates, or even his supporters. In the era of 24/7 news, blogs, and political chat, it is no surprise that this form of dirty politics has moved online. If anything, the Internet has made politics substantially dirtier because it creates a race to the bottom for attention and allows supporters of a candidate to smear adversaries without the candidate having to get her own hands dirty.

Political smears are knowingly false accusations designed to discredit a candidate or party. Smears targeted at a candidate can be anything from classic allegations of marital infidelity, to McCarthy-style allegations of supporting communism, to more modern smears implying that a candidate has used illegal drugs. But not all smears are limited to attacking the candidate or politician herself. Today, political smears are deployed against the candidate's family, in a form of guilt-by-association. Attackers also target a candidate's party, to make it appear that the candidate is favored only by some undesirable group (depending on the candidate and the office sought, the allegedly undesirable group may range from hippies to carpetbaggers to racists).

Attackers target the media, alleging bias or untrustworthiness. And attackers target a candidate's financial backers and vocal supporters in an attempt to intimidate them out of participating in the political process.

Gossip and smears about politicians are relatively easy to spread. There are discussion sites based around most major political parties and political positions. These sites are filled with like-minded partisans who are eager to learn more about their opponents. A smear— be it a false rumor, a faked photograph, or anything else—that starts on one of these political sites can be seen by thousands of politically active individuals in a single day and then be quickly spread by them to other websites that reach a larger audience. The content of the rumor can range from an unsourced false allegation that a candidate engaged in some misconduct, to a faked photograph, to a faked news story, to lists of names and addresses of supporters of a candidate in an effort to keep them from participating in the political process.

Recent elections demonstrate the power of the Internet. Online gossip about candidates, parties, and supporters has reached epidemic proportions. The effects of this change in politics have yet to be fully realized, but it is certain that at some point there will be a backlash against ever more intrusive personal politics. In the 2008 U.S. elections, one national candidate had her personal e-mail account hacked and its contents spread to the world (including family photos),[14] another national candidate was repeatedly accused of hiding his religion, and countless rumors swirled about other candidates. The shenanigans extended to attacks on supporters of political measures as well; in California, competing groups created "walls of shame" listing the names and addresses of donors to the opposing side during the campaign over whether to repeal the state's controversial gay marriage law; many donors reported being harassed at their businesses after the lists were made public.[15] It is widely expected that the cyberwar over gay marriage will continue through future election cycles, with supporters and detractors growing ever more heated in their efforts to intimidate the other side in the debate.

Online smears can also be used by an autocratic government to maintain control over a country's population. While this behavior has not been seen in the United States or Western Europe, there is no way to know whether governments in other parts of the world have engaged in such tactics. Government interference in online politics can be as simple as paying staffers to spread rumors and lies about the opposition and its leaders or supporters. An attack of this form can be particularly devastating if a leading opposition candidate is convincingly targeted across online and traditional media. It is often said that "*1984* was not an instruction manual," but many of the tactics in the book can be used by autocratic regimes on the Internet today.

Nationalist politics also often motivate online reputation attacks. While there have been relatively few incidents of this in the United States, online smears have played a large and important role in international relations in other countries. In Russia, for example, there is a continuing campaign to smear many Estonian politicians as Nazis.[16] Of course, the charge is groundless—many Estonians continue to despise Germany for its occupation during World War II— but that does not stop the online smear campaign. And, in the same area of the world, the nation of Georgia, formerly part of the Soviet Union, recently engaged in a shooting war with Russia over the area known as South Ossetia. During the war, both sides are alleged to have attempted to use cyberattacks to take offline the other side's communication networks.[17] And, after the war, the Russian government (or factions aligned with it) is alleged to have attacked the popular website Twitter.com in order to silence a pro-Georgia blogger.[18] Online combatants simultaneously engaged in a public relations war, each trying to outsmear the other side and to spread (often false) rumors and allegations of war crimes committed by identified opposing generals and leaders, sometimes accompanied by manipulated photos and falsified news stories.

Business and Greed

A reputation once broken may possibly be repaired, but the world will always keep their eyes on the spot where the crack was.

—JOSEPH HALL (PHILOSOPHER AND BISHOP)

Business rivalry has been a frequent cause of online reputation attacks. Competitors are the most common sources for business-related online smears. There is nothing wrong with a business competing for customers by making honest comparisons between its products, services, and prices and its competitors'. But sometimes the competition goes too far and spreads lies or attacks company employees. These attacks may be disguised as fake reviews from customers or even as fake regulatory or government warnings—such as a fake health inspector's report about a competing restaurant.

Similarly, disgruntled employees may decide to spread vicious falsehoods about a company. These attacks are particularly dangerous because the employee's knowledge of the company allows her to create a believable lie and because a disgruntled employee may often be able to weave a sympathetic story about misconduct at the company. Of course, most whistleblowers or disgruntled employees simply relay true stories about what happened. But some disgruntled employees go further and selectively leak internal documents to give a false impression of internal affairs or create false documents from whole cloth. Or a disgruntled employee may simply create lies about the company.

In a similar vein, activists for or against a particular cause may falsely smear the reputations of companies. Truthful reports from activists are (in the United States, at least) protected from legal consequences, but some activists have gone further and created lies in an attempt to smear companies whose policies they don't like. Much like whistleblowers and disgruntled employees, activists often know enough about their targets to spin a plausible story. And, also similarly, activists often receive a sympathetic hearing in the media.

Finally, internal corporate feuds can spill out into the public sphere online, often creating serious reputational harm. Conflicts over projects, pay, or promotions can lead angry employees to blog about each other or the company. Such feuding employees may leak company secrets, or may demean each other or the company as a whole. Such internal disputes have the air of dirty laundry; online, they all too often become permanent stains on a company's reputation.

If you have been smeared because of your business, see Chapter 13, which provides special advice for small business owners and professionals.

Extortion

What's a little extortion between friends?

—Bill Watterson (creator of the comic strip
Calvin and Hobbes)

Online extortion works the same way as offline extortion: an aggressor creates a list of demands and threatens to harm the victim unless the victim complies. Extortion has a long and sordid history, from modern schemes to extort money from actors by threatening to reveal personal photos[19] to the "*danegeld*" payment of 7,000 pounds of silver by Charles the Bald to Viking invaders in 845 A.D. in order convince the raiders not to pillage Paris—perhaps the first recorded protection racket.[20] But, no matter where it happens, extortion is motivated by greed or a lust for power. Greedy criminals see online extortion as a relatively nonviolent way to separate victims from their money.

Online attackers use many of the same methods as offline extortionists: threats to reveal compromising photos or information, threats to spread lies, threats to boycott a business, or threats to cause physical harm to the victim or the victim's family. And online extortionists have even created unique forms of cyberextortion, such as "cryptoviral extortion"—which is the use of a computer virus ("ransomware") to encrypt (encode) the victim's data and files so that the victim's computer is useless until the victim pays a ransom.[21] If anything, online extortion is more dangerous than traditional extortion: The ability to extort people anywhere in the world complicates law enforcement, and the Internet often provides powerful digital anonymity to criminals who might otherwise leave a trail of physical evidence (such as the typewriter flaws that inevitably appear in clichéd cops-and-robber shows). As with everything else, the power of Internet anonymity is not inherently good or bad, but it changes how people interact; it empowers people to make (good) anonymous political speech just as much as it empowers people to make (bad) anonymous criminal speech.

The Internet has also democratized extortion, just as it has democratized information. Extortion was once a shady business conducted by mobsters and drug dealers who preyed on the rich, the famous, and the desperate. But, thanks to the power of the Internet, it is much easier for almost anyone to conduct extortion or to become a victim of it. An online extortion artist can stalk victims anywhere in the world, often from the comfort of his own parents' basement.

It is only natural that online extortion attempts often put the victim's reputation at risk. Reputation can be destroyed nearly instantly from anywhere in the world, without any need for dangerous physical confrontations or any possibility of leaving physical evidence behind. Even if the allegations made by the extortionist are untrue, the victim will still have to spend hundreds of hours cleaning up his reputation and explaining why the allegations are false.

Actual examples of online extortion are plentiful. One man was arrested after stalking nearly 4,000 women, some of them underage. He is alleged to have threatened to reveal private and embarrassing photos of his victims unless they performed sexual acts during Webcam chats with him. Of course, those Webcam chats themselves became part of the extortion scheme, because he could simply threaten to reveal the most recent sultry performance unless the victim agreed to perform again. Many women complied with his demands out of fear of having their images and reputation ruined by public disclosure of intimate photos and videos.[22]

Other forms of cyberextortion threaten the victim's reputation in order to extort money. Some creative extortionists have threatened to publicize the fact that the victim visited a controversial website, often after luring or tricking the victim into visiting it. The allegations can range from claims that the victim has some extreme fetish to a claim that the victim visited sites that deal in child pornography. The truth of the allegation is somewhat irrelevant, and the extortionist offers to "help" the victim avoid disclosure of this private fact for a "modest" fee. This type of scheme falls somewhere between a protection racket and the classic offline "badger game," in which a married man is tricked into being photographed in what appears to be a compromising position with a woman (who is usually the photographer's co-conspirator).

Businesses have also been targeted in similar extortion schemes. Some less-than-ethical "review" websites offer businesses the "opportunity" to "investigate" negative reviews against them for a less-than-modest fee, often $5,000 or more. Businesses that pay up can have their reputations cleared, but businesses that refuse to pay electronic protection money will find that the negative reviews on these sites often become prominent in Google searches for the name of the business. Some lawsuits have been filed, but allegations of unethical practices continue.

An extortionist is a unique adversary in online reputation attacks. Most extortionists do not care about the identity of their victims; they simply want to find the easiest targets, extract as much as they can, and move on. And most extortion attempts are one-off transactions; if the attempt fails or becomes too difficult, most rational extortionist simply move on to another victim. There are plenty of fish in the sea for an extortionist. Thus, for most targets, it is possible to defeat an attempt simply by becoming a difficult target. But some extortionists think that they cannot back down because to do so would be to show "weakness." And other online reputation extortionists fear, ironically enough, that if they let a target get away, they will get a reputation as ineffective extortionists. They want to cultivate an image of being "tough" extortionists who cannot be intimidated out of a gig.

Reputational extortionists and blackmailers are also vulnerable in other ways. Most extortionists face a crucial problem: once they have used up their arsenal of attacks, they lose their leverage over the victim. Once a private fact has been revealed, the extortionist can no longer dangle the threat of revealing it. A reference to the Sword of Damocles is appropriate. The legend is that a large sword was dangled by a single horsehair over the head of a man, in order to instill in him an appreciation of fear. A wise man once said that what makes a Sword of Damocles effective is not that it falls but that it hangs.[23] Similarly, what makes reputation extortion an effective technique is not what is revealed but what is threatened. If a victim turns the tables by revealing the private fact before the extortionist can, then the extortionist loses his leverage. In 2009, late-night host David Letterman used this technique by preemptively revealing that he had had inappropriate relations with his staff after an extortionist threatened to disclose the same information.

If you are the victim of an extortionate scheme, use extreme caution and do not provoke a violent reaction. Carefully consider the decision to go to law enforcement. It may be worth confidentially contacting a trusted lawyer in your jurisdiction to discuss legal options and other strategies.

Social Gossip

Gossip needn't be false to be evil—there's a lot of truth that shouldn't be passed around.

—FRANK A. CLARK (AMERICAN SCREENWRITER)

Social gossip has existed as long as humans have gathered around a communal fire. Somewhere, there is probably a cave painting memorializing ancient gossip—perhaps one caveman was rumored to be less skilled at hunting than he claimed to be or was rumored to be the father of more (or fewer) children than he thought.

Perhaps human gossip is inevitable because of the power it has over groups. Gossip binds members of a community together by creating a common base of shared facts and insider knowledge. The act of gossiping allows members of the group to prove their fidelity to a social group (and their usefulness to it) by sharing tidbits of information. And sharing embarrassing secrets about others may help elevate the social status of the gossiper in relation to the acts being described. Gossiping also allows people to undermine the social standing of the victims of gossip, whether the gossiper is motivated by envy, revenge, or some other emotion.

Gossip offline can be harmful; rumors spread through social networks at incredible speed, and much gossip is hurtful or false. But the same gossip becomes even more harmful online when it leaves a permanent digital trail. Gossip on social sites like Facebook and MySpace can be shared and retransmitted with just a click. Gossip on personal blogs can be copied, is often quickly indexed by Google, and is sometimes even permanently archived by sites like Archive.org. An inappropriate rumor or even a flat lie can quickly become "Google truth" as it is spread and repeated from blog to blog. And, worse, gossip that was once contained within a small social network can become fodder for the entire Internet once it hits the wider Web.

If you have been the victim of false social gossip that has gone online, you will often be able to isolate the false content easily; most social gossip appears on only one or two websites, and gossipers do not spend as much time linking and developing their attack as do most intentional attackers. If you can prove the gossip false with objectively verifiable concrete facts, then it may be worth setting the record straight by e-mailing a gentle and calm message explaining the problem to the sites where the false information is hosted.

Sociopathy and Inexplicable Motivations

We all experience many freakish and unexpected events.

—Actor Viggo Mortensen

Not all intentional attacks can be easily explained. Sometimes, pure antipathy or sociopathy spurs people to attack each other, online or offline. For example, the horrific actions taken by many serial killers cannot be explained through anything other than pure antisocial motivations. Most online attacks are far less dramatic, but many online attacks still defy explanation other than a pure desire to hurt others. While rare, these attacks are extremely dangerous because the attacker is unlikely to respond to reason or to relent out of human compassion. Other attacks may simply occur because the attacker does not realize that he is hurting the victim; from a computer terminal hundreds of miles away, it may all seem like a harmless prank.

The vast majority of Internet users are sane and compassionate people. But a few shocking incidents show how far the worst-of-the-worst can slip. And, unfortunately, every Internet user needs to be aware of the worst possible behavior online. Stories of innocent—or at most careless—reputations being ruined are common online. Internet pranksters don't always realize that their victims feel real pain. Sometimes the pranks are tasteless but relatively harmless, like gaming Google so that a swastika symbol (卐) appeared as the "hottest" Google search for a day. But other pranks go too far, like publicly and permanently humiliating an insecure or autistic teenager who has a publicly visible journal on LiveJournal and then permanently memorializing the attack on websites dedicated to documenting that kind of prank. These attackers are particularly damaging because they are unpredictable and often work by a different set of social rules—and because their attacks are often so tabloid in nature that they draw more attention.

The good news is that, as described in Chapters 10–13, you can help repair the damage from any kind of online reputation attack, and you can also take steps to help ensure that the damage does not spread further.

Notes

1. Romans 1:29 (International Standard Version). **Go**: http://wildwest2.com/go/701.

2. 1 Timothy 5:13 (International Standard Version). **Go**: http://wildwest2.com/go/702.

3. Plutarch, *The Lives of the Noble Grecians and Romans*, trans. John Dryden.. Available free online through Project Gutenberg. **Go**: http://wildwest2.com/go/703

4. Iago in Shakespeare's *Othello*, III, iii.

5. Johann Christoph Friedrich von Schiller, *Fiesco*, I, 1.

6. John Dryden, "The Hind and the Panther," in *John Dryden: The Major Works*, ed. Keith Walker (New York: Oxford University Press, 1987).

7. Havelock Ellis, *100 Little Essays of Love and Virtue* (1922). Available free online through Project Gutenberg. **Go**: http://wildwest2.com/go/704.

8. Dante, "Purgatory," in *The Divine Comedy* (1321): Terrace 2, Cantos 12–14. Available free online through Project Gutenberg. **Go**: http://wildwest2.com/go/705.

9. Cynthia G. Wagner, "Beating the Cyberbullies; Targets of Taunting Need Help Turning the Tables on Tormentors," *The Futurist*, September 1, 2008. **Go**: http://wildwest2.com/go/706.

10. Ibid.

11. *Korea Times*, "Internet Witch-Hunts" (editorial), June 9, 2005. **Go**: http://wildwest2.com/go/707.

12. Ibid.

13. **Go**: http://wildwest2.com/go/708.

14. M. J. Stephey, "Sarah Palin's E-Mail Hacked," *Time*, September 17, 2008. **Go**: http://wildwest2.com/go/709.

15. Martin Wisckol, "Prop. 8 Leaders Accuse Foes of Harassment, Intimidation," *Orange County* (CA) *Register*, November 14, 2008. **Go**: http://wildwest2.com/go/710.

16. "The Truth about eSStonia [*sic*]," *The Economist*, August 16, 2007. **Go**: http://wildwest2.com/go/711.

17. "Russian and Georgian Websites Fall Victim to a War Being Fought Online as Well as in the Field," Reporters Without Borders (press release), August 13, 2008. **Go**: http://wildwest2.com/go/712.

18. **Go**: http://wildwest2.com/go/713.

19. "Politician Charged in Travolta Extortion," *PopEater* (blog), January 23, 2009. **Go**: http://wildwest2.com/go/714.

20. Michael Moïssey et al., *The Cambridge Economic History of Europe: Trade and Industry in the Middle Ages* (New York: Cambridge University Press, 1987): 803–804. **Go**: http://wildwest2.com/go/715.

21. "Kaspersky Lab Announces the Launch of Stop Gpcode, an International Initiative against the Blackmailer Virus," Kapersky Lab (press release), June 5, 2008. **Go**: http://wildwest2.com/go/716. John E. Dunn, "Police 'Find' Author of Notorious Virus," *TechWorld*, September 8, 2008. **Go**: http://wildwest2.com/go/717.

22. Kim Zetter, "U.S. Military Contractor Allegedly Hacked Teens to Extort Nude Photos from Them," *Wired*, March 19, 2009. **Go**: http://wildwest2.com/go/718.

23. For example, *Arnett v. Kennedy*, 416 U.S. 230, 232 (1974) (Marshall, J., dissenting).

CHAPTER

8.0

Types of Internet Attacks

To defend against online attack, one must understand the methods used by attackers. There are as many kinds of online attacks as there are malicious attackers, but attacks can be roughly categorized by the *content* of the attack and the *means by which the attack is spread*. These are the same categories that professionals use when analyzing and defusing online reputation attacks.

Be aware: we describe a variety of methods through which reputations are attacked, but this section is not a how-to manual for online reputation attacks. Those who seek to attack others online will find nothing that is not already available in the metaphoric dark alleyways of the Internet. Instead, we offer this section as a guide for those who seek to understand online attacks or prevent their spread. If you are reading this in the hope of learning how to attack others, we kindly ask that you put the book down now before wasting any more of your own time.

Content Versus Method

An online attack can be broken down into two important components: the content of the attack, and the method of its distribution.

The content of the attack is the "what"—what the attacker says or does to make the victim look bad. All too often, the content relates back to the classics: "sex, lies, and videotape."

The method of distribution is what the Centers for Disease Control would call the "vector," or the means by which the attack is spread. Attackers can use e-mail, search engines, viral content, and other means to spread their smears.

Of course, one attacker might utilize several different attacks, each with its own content and distribution method. Or one particular smear—a lie, or privacy breach, or manipulated photo—may be distributed by several methods. By examining the unique content and distribution methods of each attack, you can learn how to defeat them.

The Content of an Attack

The Simple Lie

The most common online attack is simple: the attacker spreads a damaging lie about the victim. A flat lie of this type is considered to be libel under many state laws. The subject of the lie can be anything from a playground insult to an accusation of infidelity. Some classic attacks are common online: attackers often claim that the victim is sexually promiscuous, has committed an act of marital infidelity, or has a sexually transmitted disease.

A purported "dating advice" website called DontDateHimGirl.com provides some useful statistics about the ways people attack each other. The site claims to be a guide to help women avoid dating cheaters, liars, and cads. Users of the site can post "reviews" of the men they have dated. The reviewer remains anonymous, but the men are described by full name, location, and sometimes photograph. Some of the reviews are likely true. But, at least one person has sued the site, alleging that the anonymous reviews were not only entirely false but posted by people whom he had never met.[1] To determine what kind of allegations capture the most attention, we searched more than 50,000 reviews that were posted. Of these, more than 19,000 call the man a "cheater" or a "cheat," more than 8,500 claim that the purportedly single man is married, more than 2,300 allege that the man has an STD, almost 1,000 claim the man has a disease generally, and more than 300 claim the main has AIDS. The prevalence of these particular allegations shows the power of these attacks. By comparison, only 100 reviews call the man a "slob," and only 700 reviews call the man "lazy." In life, there are probably more slobs than cheaters, but, among angry ex-lovers and unrequited suitors, it is 190 times more popular to call your ex- a "cheat" than a "slob."

Another typical lie is that the victim has committed some socially unacceptable act. A lie like "Joe is an axe murderer" is too obvious—nobody will believe it. Instead, attackers of this kind focus on plausible smears that may play into a stereotype of the victim or a fear shared by the audience. A sample accusation of this kind is that a teacher or day care worker abuses children. This kind of attack predates the Internet. In the 1980s, there was a panic over so-called "satanic ritual abuse." Talk shows and news programs were filled with reports that thousands of children were being sexually abused by cult members, with some reports going as far as to allege human sacrifice and cannibalism.[2] Gossip magazines featured lurid tales of alleged abuse committed against celebrities when they were younger.[3] Thousands of child care workers were accused of being members of Satan-worshipping cults that abused children as part of their sacred rites. Some of the accused were jailed, many lost their jobs, and hundreds lost standing in their communities.

While it is impossible to know the truth behind every allegation, many high-profile accusations were discredited,[4] and one study of 12,000 accusations of satanic ritual abuse revealed none that could be corroborated.[5] But the complete absence of hard evidence did not stop the accusations from ruining lives and careers.[6] The story demonstrates that accusations that are hard to disprove can spread dangerously quickly without anyone stopping to closely evaluate the evidence—especially when the accusations tap into other common fears.

The Half-Truth

True or partially true statements can also be the subject of an online attack if they are misleading—for example, because they have been taken out of context. Attacks of this kind are often legally actionable as libel or under a theory called "false light," but an online attack can be harmful even if it does not trigger legal liability.

A simple example of the importance of context is the statement "Jim took a knife and cut Tim's stomach open." If you envision a bar brawl, then Jim seems guilty. But if Jim is a surgeon trying to save Tim's life, then Jim seems to be a good Samaritan. The only thing that changed was context. Another classic half-truth is elegant in its simplicity: a disgruntled sailor wrote in the ship's log "captain sober today."[7] The statement was entirely true—the captain was sober that day—but the statement leaves a clear (and false) impression that the captain's sobriety was noteworthy for its rarity.

This kind of attack can be particularly damaging because anybody who investigates it will be able to verify some of the facts underlying the story. As they say, the best lie always has a kernel of truth. Rumors based on a kernel of truth can spread very rapidly: in 1954, an urban legend in Seattle claimed that a powerful new radio transmitter was dangerous to human health. The proof, some said, was that the radio waves had dug tiny pits into thousands of windshields across the Seattle area.[8] The story caused a panic as people inspected their windshields and found hundreds of tiny pits. As it turns out, the transmitter had nothing to do with the pits; they were simply the result of normal wear-and-tear on glass windshields and usually went completely unnoticed. But the tiny kernel of truth allowed the panic to grow out of control.

The Manipulated Photo
There are some things you just can't un-see.

—COMMON INTERNET SAYING

Manipulated photographs can be used as a form of online attack. Photographs are a particularly powerful medium of attack because images are considered trustworthy and because photos tap into subconscious visual associations. One study of the Tiananmen Square incident in 1989 showed just how suggestive doctored photos can be. The iconic image of one man standing in front of a tank shows him standing alone—but when volunteers were shown a manipulated picture of the showdown that added large crowds, the volunteers (falsely) remembered reports of mass violence.[9]

Photo manipulation is almost as old as photography itself. Some scholars believe that an iconic 1860s photograph of Abraham Lincoln is actually a composite of Lincoln's head placed on the body of prominent politician John Calhoun.[10] The digital revolution has democratized photo manipulation and made image manipulation easier than ever. Digital photography has made it possible to instantly share personal photos with friends and relatives around the world. But, thanks to modern software, many users now have the ability to perform manipulations that once took sophisticated darkroom equipment. In reference to the popular Photoshop® digital editing software, manipulated images are often referred to as "photoshopped" images or "photoshops"—despite the attempts of Adobe's lawyers to prevent the use of "Photoshop" as a generic term for photo manipulation.

Sometimes the manipulation is obvious, such as placing a caption or speech bubble on a photo. Any lie can be the subject of the caption or speech bubble. False quotations can also be attributed with this method. Despite its simplicity, this can be a damaging attack if carried out well.

Another powerful form of manipulation is to add or subtract

something from a photograph. Politics has long been a fertile field for this form of manipulation: During the Soviet era, image editors removed a number of disfavored Communist Party officials from photos with Stalin. Americans did the exact opposite: In 1950, a close race for the U.S. senate seat for Maryland was affected when Senator Joseph McCarthy's staff faked a photograph by *adding* a Communist Party official to a photo of a rival politician. The photo was widely distributed before being revealed as a forgery, and many people believe that the false association with communism contributed to the rival's defeat.[11]

Attacks through photo forgery may be especially dangerous because they can be hard to detect. A manipulated photo released by the government of Iran shows how easy it is to pass off a photographic fraud. In mid-2008, Iran conducted a missile test, but only three of its four missiles actually fired. Iran digitally painted over the failed launcher with a copy of a successful missile launch and sent the photo to newspapers. Many Western newspapers, including the *Los Angeles Times* and the *Chicago Tribune*, ran the forged photo on their front pages.[12] A close examination revealed the manipulation (identical smoke trails, a ghostly shadow, and redundancies in the clouds), but not until the newspapers had already been printed.

Another example shows the democratization of photo forgery. In 2004, an individual political activist combined an old photograph of Senator John Kerry—then running for president—with an old image of Jane Fonda rallying against the Vietnam War. The manipulated photo appeared to show Kerry sitting just three feet away from Fonda. It was quickly circulated as "evidence" of Kerry's alleged lack of patriotism. In reality, Kerry was never that close to Fonda, but the visual association with Fonda's unpopular tactics may have influenced many voters. Some voters never found out that the image was faked, others didn't believe the correction, and yet others subconsciously associated Kerry and Fonda as a result of the image even after learning that it was fake.[13] In the words of the photographer of one of the original (legitimate) images, "People just see it, and it creates this impression that it really happened."[14]

The problems of photo manipulation are a preview of what is going to happen soon to video. Technology is only a short step away from democratizing digital video manipulation. Special effects software like Adobe's After Effects® package now provides video editing power once reserved for Hollywood studios. Creative home moviemakers have used this software to make almost-believable special-effects videos purporting to show San Francisco being invaded by a *Star Wars* fleet.[15] The video quality is as good as that in the original *Star Wars* movies, and some scenes are crisp enough to look real when viewed online. Soon, manipulating digital video will be almost as easy as manipulating digital photography. We must prepare for a new era in which neither photo nor video can be believed.

The Breach of Privacy

Another sadly common form of online reputation attack occurs through breach of the victim's privacy. Whether accidental or intentional, all privacy breaches cause a uniquely personal harm to the victim. Often, the victim's deepest secrets or most intimate moments are revealed to the world. This can be intensely embarrassing, to the point of causing the victim to withdraw from social contact and retreat into isolation.

The subject of a privacy breach can be anything personal or embarrassing. One common form today involves sex and videotape: a jilted ex-lover posts provocative private photos or videos of the victim on the Internet. Some may even go so far as to post a "sex tape" showing the victim engaged in intimate relations. This attack is so common that there is even a name for it: "revenge porn."[16]

One of the first incidents of online "revenge porn" probably happened sometime around 2000. That was the heyday of file-sharing networks like Kaazaa and Napster, which allowed users (mostly college students) to share multimedia files with each other. It all started when a female student at a major U.S. public university filmed some very intimate videos for her long-distance boyfriend. Although it has never been proven, many people believe that the boyfriend then placed the files in his "shared files" folder during an argument, which made the videos accessible over the file-sharing network. Soon, the videos were being copied from campus to campus and were saved by tens of thousands of people. The woman was mortified, to the point of being afraid to search Google for her own name.[17] To this day, the videos can still be found online. More recently, in Italy, one man was sentenced to two years in jail for creating a website that showed his ex-girlfriend in pornographic photographs, along with her phone number.[18] He had also sent more than 15,000 e-mails containing indecent pictures of his ex-, all done without her consent, of course.

Privacy breaches are not limited to intimate photos and videos. Public revelations about private facts like sexual preference can also cause immense embarrassment. Some people choose not to reveal their sexual orientation to the world, whether because they live in a conservative place or because they work for an employer who is not tolerant. An attacker may injure the victim by "outing" him: revealing the victim's sexual orientation without his consent. Recently, several politicians have been "outed" by online activist communities. Any other private fact of this nature can be used as an attack, including HIV status, status as a crime victim, sexual history, or anything else intensely personal.

Harassment and Hoaxes

Some attackers harness the Internet to harass their victims. These attacks rely on the anonymity of the Internet, the social distance created by it, and the fact that many readers never do any serious fact-checking of their own.

One form of online harassment uses the power of a large group to overload the victim's communications. The goal is to flood a victim's e-mail, phone, fax, or postal mailbox with so much material that they lose the ability to communicate. The massive audience of the Internet makes this attack possible: the attacker simply fabricates a reason why many people should call, fax, or e-mail the victim and then spreads that fabrication as far as possible.

One of the first online attacks of this kind happened in the wake of the 1995 bombing of the Murrah Federal Building in Oklahoma City.[19] The attacker used an AOL message board (a precursor to Internet forums) to spread a fake advertisement for t-shirts related to the bombings. The fake advertisement claimed that the shirts bore shockingly offensive slogans like "Visit Oklahoma . . . it's a blast!" and "Finally a day care center that keeps the kids quiet—Oklahoma 1995." Readers were instructed to call "Ken" at a phone number in Seattle if they wanted to order a shirt. Of course, there were no shirts for sale, and the phone number listed was that of Ken Zeran, an innocent victim who had nothing to do with the fake advertisement. Hundreds of people called Zeran to tell them how they felt about the shirts. The advertisement (and Ken's phone number) was quickly copied across the fledgling Internet, and an Oklahoma radio DJ even read it aloud to his listeners. Soon, Zeran's phone was ringing off the hook with angry callers and death threats. The prankster who created the malicious advertisement has never been publicly identified.

This kind of attack continues today. In 2008, a video of a vicious fight among nine teenage girls was posted to the popular video-sharing site Youtube.com. In the "comments" section, an anonymous user posted the name, home address, and phone number of several of the pugilists. Another anonymous user posted the phone number and home address of "Darlene Ashley" and claimed that Ashley was the mother of one of the aggressors shown in the video.[20] In reality, Ashley has no children and had no connection to the incident whatsoever. But hundreds of callers simply assumed the comment was correct and deluged her with messages like "we're now coming to get you, you have nowhere to run." Some even challenged her to fights: "So you like to beat up on girls, huh? You want to meet somewhere in Florida? I'll teach you a lesson." Ashley stopped answering her phone after she received other threatening messages.

Another similar attack does not even require a controversial issue. The attack is carried out by simply listing the victim's phone number as the way to receive technical support for a popular product or as a means to reach a popular celebrity. One group of pranksters listed their own phone number as being that of basketball legend LeBron James.[21] Within twenty-four hours, they received over 200 calls from fans. Had they used a different number (and other pranksters certainly have), they could have caused chaos.

SWATing

One of the most dangerous online attacks is a practice called "SWATing." This frightening tactic is still very rare, but there have been several well-publicized incidents. The term "SWATing" comes from the acronym for the heavily armed "SWAT" units found in many police departments. The goal of a "SWATing" attack is to cause the police to break down the victim's door on the basis of a false report of a standoff or burglary in progress.

Anonymous attackers used to be able to "SWAT" by taking advantage of a security weakness in antiquated 911 systems: Until recently, many police emergency call centers relied on the same caller-ID systems used by households. It was thus possible to use Web-based phone services to call the victim's local 911 from anywhere in the world but to use "caller-ID spoofing" to make it appear that the call came from the victim's home phone number. The attacker would then pretend to be the victim, claim to be calling from the victim's house (which the 911 dispatcher would verify on the basis of the fake caller-ID information), and describe some dire emergency: One attacker claimed that there were armed robbers in the victim's house; another claimed that the victim was holding hostages at gunpoint. In each case, the 911 dispatcher sent armed police to the victim's house in search of the emergency. In one particularly brazen attack, the attacker went further and tried to trick the victim into believing that he was being burglarized, in the hope of triggering a violent confrontation between the police and the victim.[22]

Fortunately, many 911 systems have been upgraded to avoid this problem, and several attackers have been caught. One attacker was recently sentenced to five years in jail, and there are other trials pending.[23]

Spreading the Attack

Of course, a reputation attack of any kind is harmless if it is hidden; shouting insults into the wind does nothing but strain the attacker's voice. There are as many ways to spread a smear as there are smears, but the categories described in this section represent some of the most common methods of attack. They all rely on either getting a message to as *large* an audience as possible (in order to make many people aware of the smear) or to as *targeted* an audience as possible (in order to make the victim's friends, family, employers, or co-workers aware of the smear). Attackers frequently mix-and-match means of spreading a harmful message in order to gain both a wide and a targeted audience.

Hosting the Attack

The most fundamental question for most online smears is how the attacker makes it visible at all.

Sometimes an attacker will create an entire website or blog dedicated to smearing the victim. It costs just a few dollars to register a domain name ("JoeSmithSucks.com"); in addition, many blogging sites (like BlogSpot or LiveJournal) provide their services completely free. The attacker can put any kind of content on her own site—including photos, videos, text, and more. But, creating an attack site of any kind does not guarantee that anybody will see it. The Internet can be a very lonely place. If the Internet were a Western movie, many websites would be ghost towns, complete with tumbleweed slowly rolling across Main Street. There are hundreds of millions of

Internet users, but almost none will randomly stumble across a particular attack site unless there is a reason to find it.

Other times, an attacker will use a discussion forum or social site to spread his attacks. This can be done by writing an attack in a message or by using social features of the site. Social sites are often very easy to use and provide advantages for an attacker: the site comes pre-stocked with an audience and with functions such as "forward to friends" links and comment functionality. But, using these sites limits an attacker to only the types of content allowed on the site (e.g., only videos on YouTube or only photos on Flickr), and there is always the chance that the site owner will remove offensive or attacking content.

Many attackers use hybrids of the these methods: Attackers who build their own websites or blogs may try to drive traffic to the attack site by creating a link directly through social sites, community websites, e-mail lists, and other places.

Targeted Social Spreading

Sometimes, an online reputation attacker tries to spread the smear to a targeted audience, often the close friends and peers of the victim. One of the easiest ways to do so is by taking advantage of an online community. The most basic version of this attack uses social networking sites like Facebook, MySpace, and Bebo. These social sites are designed to allow groups of users to interact. For example, Facebook allows friends to send messages to each other and allows all users to post short messages in regional and academic-based communities and to display messages on their close friends' "wall" (basically, a bulletin board for each user). Similarly, MySpace allows friends to post "comments" on each others' profiles and to send short messages to one another. An attacker who uses any of these sites can spread a smear by simply posting a comment on the victim's profile or wall or by posting the smear on the profiles and walls of mutual friends. The result is that the smear is visible to mutual friends. This behavior is common among high-school-age users of the sites and frequently exacerbates disagreements that started in the classroom.

But, attacks using these sites are somewhat limited. These sites attempt to eliminate anonymous attacks by forcing users to register with their real names. Enforcement of the real-name requirement is imperfect, but the majority of users are identifiable. And each of the sites is designed to be somewhat privacy protective: MySpace requires users to register and log in before they can view most photos, and Facebook shows very little information to unregistered users. Offensive comments may be seen by friends and peers, but often only temporarily. And most comments made within Facebook or MySpace are not currently indexed by Google, limiting the reach of the attack (at least for now).

In order to avoid the privacy-protective features of social networking sites, many attackers launch their attack from other websites used by the friends and peers of the victim. These websites often have fewer privacy protections than the social networking sites, and some are even designed to empower anonymous online smears. These sites are usually targeted at a particular community of which the victim is a member—perhaps a discussion site for the victim's college classmates, an unofficial gossip board for the employees of a particular large company, or an unfiltered message board targeted at aspiring doctors or lawyers. These discussion sites often allow an anonymous attack to reach a wide swath of the victim's peers and colleagues.

For example, the now-defunct site JuicyCampus.com marketed itself as a gossip hub for college students, complete with subsites for almost every U.S. college. The site's homepage bragged that the site was "totally anonymous—no registration, login, or e-mail verification required." Students were encouraged to anonymously submit short tidbits of gossip, which were then displayed to other students. Predictably enough, the site became home to vast amounts of scandal and innuendo. One typical JuicyCampus post claimed that "[name] is the biggest fag/dick in [dorm]. agree?" Another typical post listed eight women "guaranteed to [have sex] on the first night," described by full name and residence. Another series of posts attempted to identify the "ugliest" and "sluttiest" girls on campus. In the interest of gender equality, some popular posts also described the "biggest manwhores on campus" and tried to identify men "on the downlow" (i.e., who were secretly homosexual).

Googlestuffing

The fastest way to hurt a man is now through Google.

—MODERN REALITY

The attacks we have described rely on reaching the peers and colleagues of the victim directly. But Google is so powerful that it can do a lot of an attacker's work for her.

Search engines like Google, Yahoo!, Microsoft Bing, and others possess immense power. Most Web users look for information by starting with a search engine. If a Web user wants to know more about you or your company, the odds are quite high that she will start by entering your name (or the name of your business) into a search engine.

Attackers know the power of search engines and try to harm their victims by inserting false or misleading information into the results of a search for the victim's name. In many ways, search is a perfect way to spread a smear: search engines reach a massive audience, and the attack is targeted precisely at people who are looking for information about the victim.

Attackers hope to cause the search engine to return a link either to an attack site or to another site that has a copy of the attack (like a forum discussion about the victim). To be effective, an attack of this kind must appear near the top of the search results for the victim's name so that many users see the attack. The attacker would like nothing better than to cause the entire first page of search results to be smear sites, a practice we call *Googlestuffing*. But there is no way for attackers to directly insert their sites into the search results; each search engine has its own secret means of calculating which sites will be ranked the highest, and there is no way to override it.

Instead, attackers try to trick search engines into ranking their attack very highly. If the attacker has set up her own attack website, the attacker may try to "optimize" the site by filling it with carefully selected links and by making repetitive use of the victim's name. These tricks are intended to make a search engine think that the site is highly relevant to a search for the victim's name.

Even if an attacker isn't completely successful at bringing her own attacks to the top of a search, she can still cause damage by a modified form of Googlestuffing: She can simply try to increase the prominence of false or misleading content created by others. This form of Googlestuffing can be just as effective as creating his own attack, especially because it is often easier to bring older content to the top of a Google result than it is to have that effect on newer content.

Googlebombing

A spirited attacker may also try to manipulate search engines in other ways. In many ways, a practice called *Googlebombing* is the opposite of Googlestuffing. The goal is to use a search engine to spread a smear to people who *aren't* looking for information about a particular person or company. For example, the most famous early Googlebomb was intended as a smear of then-President George W. Bush. By carefully manipulating links, pranksters were able to trick Google into returning a link to the president's official biography to anyone who searched for the term "miserable failure." The point was obvious; Web searchers who weren't looking for information about Bush still got a message about President Bush's popularity.

This kind of attack is less targeted than Googlestuffing, in that it reaches people who aren't looking for information about the victim (and might not even know the victim). But, because tens of millions of Google searches are performed each day, a Googlebomb attack can spread a smear to thousands of viewers. Even if it is not targeted, it can still do a lot of damage.

E-Mobbing

If one person can create a devastating personal attack, a crowd can do much more. Creative attackers have found many ways to encourage a crowd to do the attacker's dirty work. Attackers have motivated crowds by using social norms, politics, and appeals to the crowd's sense of mob justice. All too often, the crowd rushes to judgment, regardless of the actual innocence or guilt of the condemned party. As explained by one expert, "Collectives tend to be mean, to designate official enemies, to be violent, and to discourage creative, rigorous thought. . . . We might be genetically wired to be vulnerable to the lure of the mob."[24]

The result is often an *e-mob* or *e-lynching*. Because Google and many other search engines effectively view links as "votes" on the truthfulness or importance of a statement, a crowd that has rushed to judgment may cause vast reputation damage when its smears become self-sustaining.

By provoking a group's sense of right and wrong, an attacker can encourage the mob to smear or harass a victim. Attacks of this sort invoke the proverbial *online justice squad* (sometimes better known as the *electronic lynch mob*) by spreading an allegation that the victim has gotten away with some particularly offensive act. The community's moral outrage is kindled by the allegation that the victim will escape without punishment, especially if there are issues of privilege or class. This emotion can often overcome normal social restraint and the common desire to stay out of controversies. By manipulating these emotions, a careful attacker can turn a peaceful community into a bloodthirsty mob that seeks to punish the victim for his alleged transgression.

If the allegation is sufficiently offensive and the crowd sufficiently receptive, the crowd will take over the attacker's dirty work by spreading the allegations further or prying into the victim's privacy.

The speed of the crowd's response can be amazing: within days, an allegation on one website can be copied and spread to hundreds of other sites, where it can be viewed by hundreds of thousands of others. The wider the allegation is distributed, the faster it spreads. Meanwhile, the original attacker can sit back and watch the show without ever having to get his hands dirty.

Often, these mobs start within a small community away from the victim. Juvenile discussion sites like "4chan" or politically active sites like Reddit.com launch many attacks. These sites permit or encourage attacks on outsiders and may quickly become an echo chamber as users reinforce each others' sense of outrage. Without outside members to invoke reason or encourage peaceful conflict resolution, the outrage builds until community members begin to take destructive actions toward the victim.

These types of electronic mobs are not unique to the Western world. China recently experienced its own misdirected justice mob. In 2008, a rich woman in a gray car slapped an old woman on foot, allegedly for daring to ask why the driver was setting up what appeared to be a false humanitarian relief tent. A small protest immediately occurred and the gray car was overturned. The appearance of haughtiness by a rich woman fanned moral outrage in thousands of Chinese citizens. One bystander took a photo of the car's license plate, which read "Sichuan B D37332." The photo was posted online, and somebody else provided the alleged registration information for the owner of the car. The car was registered to one Fan Xiaohua, and the posting contained the alleged phone number and home address of the offender. But the phone number posted was that of a different Fan Xiaohua who lived in a different city. By the time somebody posted a correction, it was already too late. The wrong information had spread far and wide, leading to widespread harassment of the wrong Fan Xiaohua and vast smearing of her reputation. The mistakenly blamed Fan said, "Nowadays, I don't dare answer the mobile phone because it could be someone calling up to curse me out."[25] One editorial condemned the practice: "Internet violence usually begins as

moral condemnation. So some netizens conferred the right to use violence upon themselves out of a sense of serving justice. . . . When
the netizens get together to use violence, they also go in under the
twin covers of group anonymity and personal anonymity."[26]

Viral Content

An attacker does not have to tap into a community's sense of justice
or outrage to spread an attack. Some forms of attack are self-
perpetuating because of their humor or whimsy. This so-called viral
content is often quickly copied around the Internet. Much like a nu-
clear chain reaction, each iteration makes the content available to
other users who themselves copy, download, or e-mail it to yet others. Viral content can quickly be replicated across the Internet and
end up copied across completely unrelated sites.

A benign example of viral content is the now-passé "FAIL"
meme. The meme involves photos that contain some obvious error or
inconsistency—such as a news report with the words "horse killed"
written over a photo of a deer[27] or a security camera pointed directly
at a wall[28]—tagged with the word "FAIL" in large block letters. The
humor is obvious: somebody forgot to think before doing his job.
These isolated nuggets of content are easily understood and easily
copied from one website to another.

But some viral content is malicious, and even nonmalicious viral
content can harm the reputation of the people depicted. One "FAIL"
image purports to show a fake driver's license confiscated by the police; the image is funny because the license has a photo of a couple
rather than of one person. Unfortunately, the image leaves the name,
address, birth date, and driver's license number fully legible. If any of
that information is real (or belongs to somebody else), then the holder
of the license is vulnerable to harassment and reputation attacks.[29]
Another well-distributed "FAIL" image shows a contestant on the
once-popular game show "Who Wants to Be a Millionaire." In the image, it appears that the contestant has answered the question "Which
is larger?" by stating that an elephant is larger than the moon. Of

course, the photo has been manipulated: in the original, the contestant correctly answered a question about the everyday name for the trachea with the word "windpipe."[30] The entire question and answer in the manipulated image are fake. Nonetheless, the victim looks like an idiot in the photo, and most viewers never bother to check the facts.

Other forms of manipulated photos are equally effective as viral smears so long as they are self-contained and easy to replicate. One recent viral smear involved politics and the 2008 election. An image circulated on the Internet, purporting to be from a political debate on the Fox News Channel. A caption showed the heading "Obama/Biden–Osama Bin Laden—Coincidence?" This image triggered a sense of outrage that a news organization would publish such smears, and it was quickly spread around the Internet as evidence of bias in media coverage of the 2008 election. Of course, the image was again a forgery: the original caption broadcast by Fox simply identified the speaker as "Dan Griswold–Cato Institute," with no mention of "Obama" or "Osama." Instead, an unknown prankster had simply added the offensive caption himself.[31] The reputations of commentator Dan Griswold and the news network both suffered.

Pay to Play

A dedicated attacker—whether motivated by business or by personal reasons—can leverage the power of money to promote a smear. Most online advertising programs are designed for use by profit-making businesses that wish to advertise products and services. But many programs allow anybody to place an advertisement. The democratization of advertising has been a boon for owners of small- and medium-size businesses, who can now reach hundreds of thousands of potential customers. But it also allows others to spread attacks and smears through paid online advertising.

Contextual search advertising is one of the most powerful ways to quickly advance an online reputation attack. If you have used Google to search the Internet, you have most likely seen contextual search advertising: the advertisements that appear at the top of a

Google search and on the right side of the page that are context-specific ads related to the search you performed. Anyone can place a text advertisement nearly instantaneously, usually for just pennies per click. By placing an advertisement, an attacker can reach every person who searches for information about the victim or the victim's business. Those curious enough to click are directed to the attacker's site, and even those that don't click still see the text of the advertisement.

There are some restrictions on the sites that can be promoted—for example, the Google AdWords program refuses to run advertisements against "protected groups" singled out on the basis of race, religion, and similar characteristics. Nor can the text of ads themselves "include accusations or attacks relating to an individual's personal life."[32] But those restrictions have been evaded by ads that instruct viewers to click to "learn the truth about" an individual on an attack website; just like "captain sober today" creates a distinct implication, so too does "learn the whole truth about John Doe." If you have been the victim of an attack that is promoted through Ad-Words, you should immediately contact Google and attempt to get the advertisements removed.

Some other online advertising programs are less careful than Google AdWords about the content of the advertisements they accept. The BlogAds network runs advertisements across many popular social and political-commentary websites. But the network has been accused of not enforcing quality standards and of creating a "race to the bottom" by allowing individual sites to determine whether to accept an offensive advertisement. An unscrupulous attacker can easily find a sufficiently unscrupulous site to host his attack advertisement.

Hybrid Attacks: False Flags and Trolling

There are a few unique attack types that combine an attack and a distribution method. These usually rely on trickery of some kind and almost always rely on the anonymity of the Internet.

One of the most common hybrid attacks is the "false-flag" attack, sometimes also known as a "joe job" when performed by e-mail. In this attack, the attacker impersonates the victim, often on a discussion forum or community message board. The attacker, using the victim's name, proceeds to make offensive, immature, unintelligent, or outrageous comments. This form of attack is possible because many websites fail to verify the identity of people who post comments. Some simply allow users to post their comments under any pseudonym. It is a simple matter for an attacker to use a victim's real name as his pseudonym so that the resulting comment appears to have been written by the victim—many people will simply assume that a post under the username "JohnDoe1951" was actually written by the person named John Doe. On forums where it is not possible to use the victim's name as an online pseudonym, then the victim can use a pseudonym that hints at the victim's identity ("MicrosoftCEO") or just include the victim's name and e-mail address in the body of the comment as a fake "signature."

Of course, "false-flag" attacks are by no means limited to posting comments on website forums. One writer made a name for himself by creating an entire blog impersonating Steve Jobs, the CEO and co-founder of Apple Computers. The impersonator's blog was filled with biting cynicism about Apple's customers and designers. The author was able to maintain his anonymity for a year before being revealed.[33] Luckily for the real Steve Jobs, the URL of the blog gave away the fact that it was not written by the real Jobs: http://fakesteve.blogspot.com. But many impersonators don't use obviously fake names: Aerosmith's Steve Tyler sued one anonymous individual who set up a fake blog under Tyler's name.[34] Another fake blog, purporting to be that of Levi Johnston, the boyfriend of the daughter of the 2008 Republican vice presidential candidate Sarah Palin, was set up as soon as the story broke about the daughter's pregnancy.[35] The blog purported to show that Johnston was in favor of abortion.

Other fake sites impersonate entire groups. Two very nonreligious college students created the website for a fake fundamentalist

Baptist church[36]; over time, the site has evolved so that the parody is obvious, but it initially fooled many users into thinking that there was a real Baptist church espousing ridiculous and heretical viewpoints.[37] Even as late as 2005, the site was still fooling professional writers into thinking that the church was sincere. An author on the normally well-respected Web magazine *Salon* referenced "the doomsday predictions of . . . the Landover Baptist Church[,] who believes that the tsunami was God's punishment to heathen Indonesia for its disbelief in Jesus" without any nod toward the fact that the site is a parody.[38] Satiric sites like that for Landover Baptist can be an important part of social dialogue in a free society, but they also demonstrate the gullibility of many Web users.

False-flag attacks are particularly dangerous because it is often difficult or impossible for the victim to repudiate the offensive content. Simply posting "that wasn't me" does not help—the attacker can create other comments that appear to revoke the repudiation. Replying often draws more attention to the original content, making the damage worse. And a repudiation might not even ever be seen: because some websites list their comments in order by the date they were submitted, a late repudiation may show up far down the page and thus be practically invisible. Some reputable websites have an editor in charge of comments who is empowered to remove false-flag comments, but they are often overwhelmed or slow to respond. Other websites, under the false guise of "free speech," leave it up to users to deal with anonymous impersonators. Unsurprisingly, many victims feel completely helpless when faced with an anonymous impersonator and an irresponsible website.

Attacks of this kind have long been recognized as particularly damaging, even before the Internet made them so easy. Under the international laws of war, enemy soldiers who wore false uniforms of the International Red Cross or carried with them insignia suggesting that they represented that organization could be executed as war criminals, even though the international laws of war normally require that enemy soldiers be kept alive, treated humanely, and released at the end of hostility.

"Trolling" can also be used as another form of social attack that intertwines the medium and the message. The definition of "trolling" varies by context, but one of the most effective forms of "trolling" is to make extreme but believable offensive or controversial statements in an attempt to bait readers into reacting. Experienced users of Web forums tend to be discerning and are able to identify trolls. But, forums populated by users who are more familiar with "real-world" discussions (where trolling is a rare practice) tend to fall victim to trolls more easily.

To use trolling as a form of online attack, the attacker just has to bait the victim into making angry or offensive statements. The attacker can do this in any way that lures the victim into an angry or emotional statement. Sometimes an online attacker will just attack the victim directly, in the hope of prompting the victim into an angry defense. For example, anonymously attacking the victim's credentials, education, parenting skills, or other attributes may be sufficient to trigger an angry response. An angry, over-the-top response makes the victim look bad; the victim may appear to lack emotional control or may seem vindictive. To make matters worse, sometimes the attacker can remove or edit the initial triggering comment, making it appear that the victim is shouting into the wind or vastly overreacting. Or the attacker can try to bait the victim into revealing personal information, by challenging a specific credential such as the victim's education, salary, IQ, or the cost of the victim's home. The attacker can then use the personal information against the victim directly or make the victim appear to be a braggart. The possibilities are limited only by the depraved creativity of attackers.

Some creative forms of online attack rely on third-party sites that accept and relay any information provided to them. For example, in the United States, political campaigns are required to disclose the names of their significant donors. Attackers have used this system to smear both candidates and individuals. One group of political activists attempted to donate to President Barack Obama's political campaign under parodic names, including "Osama bin Laden," "Saddam Hussein," and "Bill Ayers" (the 1960s radical to whom some of Obama's opponents tried to link him).[39] These contributions were widely reported and would likely have appeared in public fundraising databases (such as Opensecrets.org) had they not been manually intercepted as a result of the publicity. It is equally possible to make political contributions in the name of an unwilling victim. By making the campaign in the name of an unwilling donor, it is possible to associate a victim with political causes she may disagree with or one that she would be embarrassed to be caught supporting. In one recent example, online campaign finance records show that news blogger Matt Drudge donated $2,300 to the 2002 Republican campaign. The donation has been used to suggest that he is biased in favor of conservative news stories. But, while Drudge admits to voting for Republicans, he claims that the donation was "a fraud" done by somebody else "in my name."[40]

Impersonation will always be a danger as long as the technology underlying the Internet allows (and even encourages) anonymity. Websites have no way to reliably identify users, and users have no way to identify each other. The result is a mismatch of impersonators, anonymous users, and earnest citizens trying to be heard above the din. If you want to avoid impersonation, you must claim your online identity before anybody else does, as described in Chapter 11.

Notes

1. The lawsuit was eventually dismissed on procedural grounds, without determining whether the statements were lies.

2. A day care worker was accused of performing an amputation on one child and of turning another child into a mouse. The prosecutor pressed charges, despite the fact that both children were found fully intact and in human form. The day care worker spent seven years in prison before the New Jersey

Supreme Court threw out the case. *State v. Michaels*, N.J. Supreme Court (June 23, 2004). **Go:** http://wildwest2.com/go/801. For more coverage, see **Go:** http://wildwest2.com/go/802 and **Go:** http://wildwest2.com/go/803.

3. Leon Jaroff and Jeanne McDowell, "Lies of the Mind," *Time*, November 23, 1993. **Go:** http://wildwest2.com/go/804.

4. Ibid. **Go:** http://wildwest2.com/go/805.

5. Timothy Moore, "Satanic Ritual Abuse," *Encyclopedia of Psychology* (Farmington Hills, Mich.: Gale Group, 2001), via findarticles.com. **Go:** http://wildwest2.com/go/806.

6. See, for example, the haunting documentary *Capturing the Friedmans*, which tells the story of a family torn apart by doubtful accusations of ritual abuse. **Go:** http://wildwest2.com/go/807.

7. Dale Turner, "Kind Words Can Be the Greatest Gift," *Seattle Times*, October 17, 1992. **Go:** http://wildwest2.com/go/808.

8. Alan J. Stein, "Windshield Pitting Incidents in Washington Reach Fever Pitch on April 15, 1954," *HistoryLink* (undated). **Go:** http://wildwest2.com/go/809.

9. Laura Rico, "Memory Can Be Manipulated by Photos, Study Finds," University of California (press release), November 19, 2007. **Go:** http://wildwest2.com/go/810.

10. Hany Farid, "Photo Tampering throughout History" (undated), via dartmouth.edu. **Go:** http://wildwest2.com/go/811.

11. Museum of Hoaxes, "The Tydings Affair." **Go:** http://wildwest2.com/go/812.

12. Mike Nizza and Patrick J. Lyons, "In an Iranian Image, a Missile Too Many," *The Lede* (blog), July 10, 2008, via nytimes.com. **Go:** http://wildwest2.com/go/813.

13. Snopes.com, "Photograph Shows Senator John Kerry and Jane Fonda Sharing a Speaker's Platform at an Anti-war Rally," March 1, 2004. **Go:** http://wildwest2.com/go/814.

14. Carla Marinucci, "Doctored Kerry Photo Brings Anger, Threat of Suit," *San Francisco Chronicle*, February 20, 2004. **Go:** http://wildwest2.com/go/815.

15. User: Swarby, "Death Star over San Francisco" (video), via Youtube.com. **Go:** http://wildwest2.com/go/816.

16. Richard Morgan, "Revenge Porn," *Details*, via men.style.com. **Go:** http://wildwest2.com/go/817.

17. Emily Nussbaum, "Say Everything," *New York*, February 12, 2007. **Go:** http://wildwest2.com/go/818.

18. Reuters, "Man Jailed for Posting Porn Pics of Ex-girlfriend," *New Zealand Herald*, March 5, 2008. **Go:** http://wildwest2.com/go/819.

19. There is an excellent description of the facts in *Zeran v. America Online, Inc.*, 129 F.3d 327 (4th Cir. 1997). **Go:** http://wildwest2.com/go/820.

20. Ray Reyes and Billy Townsend, "YouTube Adds to Melee in Videotaped Beating Case," *Tampa Tribune*, April 10, 2008. **Go:** http://wildwest2.com/go/821.

21. Mitchell Blatt, "The LeBron James Phone Number Prank," *Juiced Sports* (blog), July 26, 2007. **Go:** http://wildwest2.com/go/822.

22. Jason Trahan, "Dangers Prank Calls Draw SWAT Teams to Unsuspecting Homes," *Dallas Morning News*, December 23, 2007, via khou.com (accessed February 1, 2009). **Go:** http://wildwest2.com/go/823.

23. Jason Trahan, "Teen Wouldn't Quit His Hacking Ways, FBI Says," *Dallas Morning News*, August 31, 2008. **Go:** http://wildwest2.com/go/824.

24. CNN, "From Flash Mob to Lynch Mob," June 4, 2007. **Go:** http://wildwest2.com/go/825.

25. ZonaEuropa, "The Case of Fan Xiaohua," May 29, 2008. **Go:** http://wildwest2.com/go/826.

26. Ibid.

27. Image at **Go:** http://wildwest2.com/go/827.

28. Image at **Go:** http://wildwest2.com/go/828.

29. See the original thread at **Go:** http://wildwest2.com/go/829.

30. Snopes, "Dumbo and Dumber," Snopes.com, October 30, 2007. **Go:** http://wildwest2.com/go/830.

31. David Mays, "Faked Fox News Image" (blog), September 7, 2008. **Go:** http://wildwest2.com/go/831.

32. Google, "Advertising Policies" (company document). **Go:** http://wildwest2.com/go/938.

33. Brad Stone, "'Fake Steve' Blogger Comes Clean," *New York Times*, August 6, 2007. **Go:** http://wildwest2.com/go/832.

34. Eric Krangel, "Aerosmith's Steven Tyler to Blog-Impersonators: Dream On!" *Silicon Alley Insider*, September 30, 2008. **Go:** http://wildwest2.com/go/833.

35. View the original fake blog at **Go**: http://wildwest2.com/go/834.

36. View the original fake blog at **Go**: http://wildwest2.com/go/835.

37. Joshua Griffin, "Parody Site Isn't All That Funny," *Jedi Council* (blog), June 2, 1999, via theforce.net. **Go**: http://wildwest2.com/go/836.

38. Scott Thill, "Writing in the Margins," *Salon*, January 31, 2005. **Go**: http://wildwest2.com/go/837.

39. Scott W. Johnson, "Dubious Donations," *New York Post*, October 27, 2008. **Go**: http://wildwest2.com/go/838.

40. Noah Shachtman, "Matt Drudge, GOP Scourge?" *Salon*, October 1, 2003. **Go**: http://wildwest2.com/go/839.

CHAPTER

How to Measure Damage to Your Internet Reputation

There was once a popular fantasy that the online world was a free-for-all where there were no rules and nobody got hurt. This fantasy relied on a belief that everything that happened online was artificial or "not real" because it all happened through a computer in what seemed to be a virtual world. As a result, many Internet users thought of the Internet as the Disney cartoon version of Pinocchio's Pleasure Island: a place where antisocial and forbidden behavior could be carried out without any consequences. But the fantasy that the "virtual world" does not affect the "real world" is simply not true: the online world is part of the "real" world. Real people and real lives are affected by the Internet every day. Billions of dollars of commerce moves online. People use the Internet to make real decisions with real consequences.

Some forms of Internet attack are particularly damaging: hard-to-disprove allegations that are spread to friends and family can make a victim feel helpless, sometimes to the point of withdrawing from social contact entirely. But, luckily, not all incorrect Internet content is damaging. Some attacks are never seen by their intended targets; virtual tumbleweed rolls across the attack sites as they sit abandoned. And some false content may be found but ignored—if it is obviously false, appears untrustworthy, or looks like it refers to someone else.

The following sections walk you through the process that professionals use to measure the impact of false online content on your reputation. Note that the source of the false content (whether the content was created intentionally or by mistake) does not matter very much at this stage. To a victim of false online content, it may not matter whether the content was innocent, accidental, or intentional.

Types of Harm Caused by Online Content

The first step to measuring the harm caused by Internet content is to determine what types of injuries are being inflicted by the content. Some types of false Internet content harm personal, social, and professional relationships. Some cause social and professional embarrassment. Still other types harm business interests. And yet other types harm privacy interests or damage users' right to quiet enjoyment or exploration of the Internet, perhaps causing them to retreat from social interaction and exploration.

Direct Harms to Reputation

This section discusses some of the most common ways that this type of content can impact your reputation. Think about the ways that a piece of false or malicious online content could impact your reputation; the more categories of damage that it triggers, the worse it is.

Personal Reputation

The most common harm caused by false or misleading online content is harm to your reputation among friends, colleagues, and others. There are always at least two impacts of this type of content.

First, it directly diminishes your standing in the community every time somebody reads the false content. Second, it indirectly diminishes your reputation because the false content often prevents people from finding positive truths about you.

Social Reputation

Your social reputation is your standing among friends, acquaintances, and the community at large. False or malicious online content has damaged your social reputation if it makes your friends whisper behind your back, your neighbors gossip about you, and acquaintances look at you askance. Your social reputation affects your everyday life in the community. It determines what your closest neighbors think about you. It determines whether friends and acquaintances trust you. It determines what social gatherings you are invited to and what people think of you once you get there.

Often, false rumors spread quickly through communities. One neighbor tells a friend, who tells another, who tells another, until the whole network believes the false content (or at least thinks it might be true). The content itself can be anything that would change the perception of the victim in the community. It can be a false statement of fact ("Bob has a DUI conviction" or "Bob was accused of molestation" or even just "Bob wastes electricity") a false statement about the victim's beliefs ("Saritha is a Republican/Democrat/Socialist/Nazi/anarchist/etc."), a false statement about involvement in some controversy ("Jose and his neighbor are feuding like children"), or anything else. Even things that some people might think are helpful can be hurtful: Telling the world that Chuck denies the allegations against him often just draws more attention to the original allegations.

Professional Reputation

Your professional reputation is your reputation among co-workers, employers, and professional colleagues. It defines whether people will hire you, fire you, trust you with new projects, give you new assignments, or advance in your field.

In many professional fields, your reputation is everything. If false or malicious online content casts a shadow over your ability, judgment, or qualifications, then you will lose business or career advancement. Many people will not take time to investigate the online allegations; they may think that there are plenty of fish in the sea and that it is simply not worth taking a risk on someone with a tainted reputation. The result is likely a drop-off in job opportunities, opportunities for advancement, and the like. People may even begin to avoid you at the corporate water cooler in the interest of avoiding any association with scandal.

The content of a smear that impacts your professional reputation can be anything that impugns your professional judgment ("Joe tried to steal from the till"), your qualifications ("Tyrone didn't actually get the degree listed on his résumé" or "Tyrone was fired from his last job"), or your interpersonal skills ("Tia sexually harassed her secretary") or simply content that suggests that you have failed in previous endeavors.

Social or Professional Embarrassment

Any misleading or malicious online content can cause personal or professional embarrassment, even if it is not a direct attack on reputation. A wise author has sold hundreds of thousands of copies of a children's book called *Everybody Poops*.[1] But that doesn't mean that we would be any less embarrassed if someone were to publicize a photo of us in the act of doing so (or picking our nose, or any other common-but-personal act).

In the digital era, all kinds of online content can trigger this kind of personal or professional embarrassment. Photos of drunken mistakes, tales of youthful indiscretions, and other common-but-best-forgotten information can cause personal or professional embarrassment. The content can cause harm even if it is true; most people don't have their personal mistakes trumpeted to the world, and a dedicated online attacker can paint an entirely false picture of her victim just by highlighting true (but usually fleeting) stories.

Harms to Privacy

Beyond reputation, there is an interest in privacy for the sake of privacy. There are some things that you would rather keep personal even if they are not embarrassing or reputation-damaging by themselves. It might not damage your reputation to disclose many personal and private bits of information—including personal information like medical conditions, your HIV/AIDS status, and any hereditary health conditions—but they also might be things you want to keep private.

Or, to take a more digital-age example, your search history (the list of all search terms you entered in a search engine like Google) may be extremely private, even if it is not directly embarrassing or reputation-damaging. But that very kind of information was released by America Online in a massive privacy breach; the company released the search histories of 650,000 users in an attempt to provide anonymous information about searches to researchers. But, the information was disclosed in a manner that allowed many of the supposedly anonymous users to be identified by name.[2] Their complete search histories—personal foibles and all—were on display for the world to see. Digital voyeurs reveled in the data, investigating individual users for the fun of it and tracking down what appeared to be the most unusual searches.

Of course, harms to privacy often turn into harms to reputation. Even if it is wrong to do so, many people will draw negative inferences from many personal and private facts. If it were revealed that you were searching for information about herpes, many friends and acquaintances would question whether you were sexually promiscuous. Such a leap is far from justified—the Internet empowers curiosity fulfillment just as much as it provides personal medical advice—but it would be taken, nonetheless.

Harms to Quiet Enjoyment

Some false or malicious Internet content prevents you from quietly living your own life without interference from others. An innocent-looking blog that lists your e-mail address might not embarrass you—it is just an e-mail address—but it might make you vulnerable to spam. Similarly, a site that lists your political contributions might not be news to anybody who knows you, but if it lists your full name and address (as many political contribution sites do), it creates a risk of harassment and unwanted efforts by scam artists to separate you from your money. After all, if you were willing to give $500 (or even $2,000) to a political candidate, a scam artist might think that you have enough money to be worth targeting with an in-person visit. Or, a display of your photograph on a site describing members of a controversial political or social group might open you (and your family) up to in-person harassment.

Other threats to your peaceful enjoyment of life are more uniquely digital. If somebody registers your name as a username on many sites, just to stop you from using them, this makes it more difficult to enjoy your online experience. If somebody places a false fraud alert on your credit file, this makes it more difficult to obtain credit. As long as the Internet remains a popular social medium, attackers will create new ways to harass and intimidate in this way.

Harms to Online Exploration

There are even online harms that are unique to the Internet. The Internet has been a boon for social exploration by giving users the chance to try new personalities and interests online, often under the protective cover of a pseudonym. Users get to try new political and social positions or just play devil's advocate without fear of personal repercussions. For example, someone who lives in a very conservative area may want to learn more about alternative sexual orientations and to discuss his personal situation with others. Thanks to the anonymity of the Internet, many users are able to look beyond the parochial confines of their small town and discover information about life in the big city. But, if a malicious user threatens to expose the "real-world" identities of users who are trying to learn more about themselves and their identity, users will be far less likely to explore.

Audience Reached

After considering the types of harm that a piece of content can cause, the next most important thing to a victim of online reputation damage is measuring the audience reached. After all, a piece of potentially harmful content that nobody views is relatively harmless in effect: It does not matter to your reputation that a computer somewhere is storing a digital representation of some harmful information, because the information affects your reputation only when a human views it. On the other hand, a smear or attack that reaches thousands (or even hundreds of thousands) of people can be devastating to your reputation and leave you working to rebuild your good name from the ground up.

At the same time, the composition of the audience matters. If an online smear is seen mostly by people who (for example) live in a different country from the victim, the victim will not suffer as much direct harm: It is unlikely that the victim was going to interact with anyone in that audience, anyway, so there is little direct social or professional harm. The victim still might be embarrassed, but he is unlikely to lose social status or a job opportunity. On the other hand, if the false negative content is seen by people very close to the victim— her friends, family, and co-workers, for example—it can be profoundly damaging even if it is seen only by a handful of people. Because the people who see the negative information are the people who interact with the victim every day, false material that reaches a targeted audience can be very damaging.

Mathematically, what we call the *Libel Index* captures the relationship between harm and audience:

Potential harm = Audience size × closeness of audience

In other words, the potential harm that a piece of negative Internet content can cause is roughly equal to the size of the audience multiplied by the closeness of the audience to the victim. An extremely large audience can be damaging if it shares *some* relationship with the victim, but a large audience made up entirely of complete strangers is not necessarily acutely damaging. On the other hand, false negative content that reaches a targeted audience can be very damaging, even if the audience is not very large.

Measuring the Audience: Search Engines

To understand the audience, think about who might find a piece of negative content and how. Is the information easily found in a Google search for the victim's name or business? Is it being spread to discussion sites or chat forums? Is it being e-mailed or otherwise proactively pushed? Is it spreading virally?

Search engines are one of the most powerful ways that false or misleading information is spread. Negative information that shows up near the top of a Google search for the victim's name can be particularly damaging because it will be seen by people who are looking for information about the victim. On the other hand, negative information that shows up near the top of a Google search for keywords that appear completely unrelated to the victim might reach a large audience, but the audience is unlikely to be targeted: a lot of people who don't know the victim might see it, but most of the people who do know the victim won't happen to search for those magic keywords. Search terms that are somewhere in the middle—related to the victim, but only loosely—will have an intermediate impact; some people who know the victim are likely to see the content, and so are some people who don't (see Figure 9-1).

For content that appears in a search engine search, take note of where the content appears in the search results. The vast majority of users only look at the first three search results in an average web query.[3] If a negative result appears in the first three results, it will be vastly more powerful than if it appears near the bottom of the first

Search Term	Audience Size	Audience Relevance	Libel Index
Joe Smith	**Small** There are unlikely to be very many people searching for your name unless you share a name with somebody else.	**Very High** People who are searching for your name in a search engine are likely to be searching for you, but they might also be searching for somebody with a similar name.	**High** If negative content appears for a search for your name, then it will probably reach a targeted audience that could be very dangerous.
Joe Smith Springfield	**Very Small** Very few people will be searching for you with such specificity.	**Extremely High** It is almost certain that somebody searching for your name and an identifying characteristic (such as your town) is trying to find information about you.	**Very High** If a search for your name plus some identifying information dredges up negative information, it is almost certain that somebody close to you will see it.
flowers	**Extremely Large** Tens of thousands of people all around the world use search engines to search for "flowers" every day.	**Low** The vast majority of people who search for "flowers" online are probably in different states and have never heard of you.	**Medium** If negative information about you appears in such a generic search term, it will be seen by a very large audience. Most of the audience will never meet you and never interact with you. But, some people in your community still might see it.
flowers in Springfield	**Somewhat Small** Fewer people search for flowers in your community.	**High** People searching for flowers in your community are probably people who you will interact with.	**Medium-High** Many of your friends and social colleagues will never search this way, but many of your potential customers will.
"the meanest person on earth"	**Medium** This is the type of search that could spread as a joke worldwide but that will generally spread only within those communities of people who are "in" on Internet jokes; most everyday users will never think to try it.	**Very Low** The search term appears to have nothing to do with you, so it is very unlikely that your friends, family, customers, or co-workers will happen to type this search into a search engine.	**Medium** This is an example of a Googlebomb: it is a search term that appears unrelated to you but one that would harm your reputation if any information about you were to appear in the results. This type of search can spread as a joke to thousands of people, but you will never interact with most of them.

Figure 9-1. How Much Do Search Terms Matter? People use a variety of search terms to find information. Some people are looking for information specifically about you, and others happen to stumble upon you. This chart demonstrates the importance of various search terms.

page or even on a subsequent page. If there is positive or neutral content about you in the first three links, any negative content further down the page will have a significantly smaller impact (see Figure 9-2).

Figure 9-2. Search Positions. Many search engines display 10 results on the first page. But most users have screens that are smaller than a full page of search results. Accordingly results after the sixth or seventh result are hidden below the bottom of the page and are not visible without scrolling. These results are called "below the fold" (in reference to the fold on a newspaper) and are not seen by many searchers. Information here (positive or negative) will make less of an impact than information in the first few results. Only about 7.5% of users click on any of the results after the sixth result.
Illustration: David Thompson.
Icons: Public domain via Wikimedia Commons.

Also think about the appearance of the content in a search result. How tempting is the link? Is it obviously about you? Content that has a compelling headline ("Joe Smith is a liar and a cheat" or even just "Learn the truth about Joe Smith") is likely to attract far more clicks and readers than content with a boring or obscure headline ("Regarding falsity of recent reports"), even if the exact same false information is repeated across both sites. Compare the prominence of the negative information to the prominence of positive and neutral information; if there is positive or neutral information with a compelling headline, it may draw many clicks away from the false or misleading negative information.

Measuring the Audience: Blogs, Forums, and Others

If the content is being distributed by a blog, discussion forum, or other social site, think about the users of that site. How many people use or visit the site? A personal blog is unlikely to attract many readers unless it is written by an online celebrity like Cory Doctorow, while a national gossip blog (e.g., TMZ or Gawker) is bound to attract hundreds of thousands of readers per day. Tools like Alexa.com allow you to estimate how popular a site is.

Think about whether the audience of the site includes people you are likely to know and interact with. For example, a neighborhood "microblog" may not attract many readers, but it is certain to reach people near you. If you are an aspiring professional, a discussion board dedicated to your field is likely to reach people with whom you will interact. And if you run a small business, a blog dedicated to consumer issues will likely reach some of your customers. On the other hand, national discussion forums dedicated to sports, jokes, and breaking news tend to attract a very generalist audience; there is nothing unique to you about most of these forums. Content on that kind of site may reach many thousands of people, but you are likely to know and interact with only a handful of them.

Measuring the Audience: Overall Concerns

Content that is obviously false or a joke will have less impact than content that appears reliable. But, remember that sarcasm doesn't carry very well online, so many people might believe false or negative content to be earnest even if it is "obviously" a joke to you.

If you share a name with somebody else, consider whether other people will confuse information about you and information about the other person. You will probably be able to figure out what content refers to you and what refers to your "doppelnamer." But, many other people will not be able to tell which content refers to which person. Remember that confusion over names works both ways; readers might write off negative information that is actually about you if they (falsely) believe that it is about somebody else with the same name, but they might also think that negative information about somebody else is about you. See how much other context surrounds any negative information, and try to figure out if a casual reader would be able to determine if it is about you or somebody else. Hints like your city, occupation, university, and other information might make the difference between your being confused with somebody else and not.

In the end, measuring the harm caused by online content comes down to an intuitive feel: How many people see it, how well do you know those people, and how bad does the content look?

Notes

1. Taro Gomi, *Everybody Poops* (Kane/Miller 1993). **Go:** http://wildwest2.com/go/901.

2. Holly Jackson, "Leaked AOL Search Logs Take Center Stage in New Play," *CNET*, June 13, 2008. **Go:** http://wildwest2.com/go/902.

3. "The Short Attention Span of Web Searchers: Most Never Read Past 3 Results," *ReputationDefenderBlog*, June 16, 2008. **Go:** http://wildwest2.com/go/903.

10.0

Your Reputation Road Map and Online Reputation Audit

This chapter describes how to create your own *reputation road map* and how to use that reputation road map to perform an *online reputation audit*. The examples are based on the techniques the professionals use to help individuals improve their online reputations, but business owners and professionals will also benefit from the lessons in this chapter. Chapter 12 has special information for businesses and professionals.

The road map to online reputation success can be broken down into a few simple steps. First, determine who might be looking for information about you. Second, identify your goals. Evaluating your goals will help you determine whether you want to use the Internet to advance your career, to present a positive image to friends and colleagues, or to just protect your privacy online. Third, perform an online reputation audit. You can check your own online reputation by using a variety of sources to figure out what other people see when they look for you online.

Later chapters describe more advanced steps. Chapter 11 teaches you how to protect yourself by carefully supplementing your total online profile with appropriate and truthful positive content. Chapter 11 also teaches you how to support existing positive content about you, which may act as a buffer against unfair attacks and other harmful content.

This progression from goal-setting through research, improvement, and monitoring makes intuitive sense. You can't reach your goals until you know what those goals are. You can't plot a path to success unless you know where you are standing today. You can't defend your reputation unless you know when and how it is being attacked. And, as far as online reputation goes, your best defense is often a good offense.

Why Take Control?

Be yourself, take control of your life.

—EMMA BUNTON (SINGER)

Be yourself, take control of your reputation.

—MODERN INTERNET ADVICE

Some people may question the need to actively manage their online reputation. They may ask, "Why does it matter if there is negative stuff online?" The answer is that you make an impression online, whether you like it or not. And, unfortunately, your online first impression is often your *only* first impression. As explained in Chapter

2, the Internet is the instant universal research source, used by everyone from journalists to nosy neighbors. If there is negative content
online, it is almost certain that somebody will find it and use it
against you.

Other people just think nobody would have a reason to attack
them online. But online reputation damage is caused by more than
just intentional attack; many reputations are harmed or destroyed
when "the machine" spins out of control, as described in Chapter 6.
And, as explained in Chapter 7, anyone with social or business interactions is subject to online attack by jealous competitors, bitter ex-
lovers, and anyone else who has a motive to spread gossip offline. Even
the most virtuous people are subject to online attack; some websites
are frequented by disaffected youth who often inflict malicious
pranks (or even outright attacks) on innocent victims simply for the
sake of inflicting pain. If anything, the earnest innocent are at the
most risk from vicious attack by angst-ridden Web dwellers because
they approach the Internet with such different cultural expectations.

Some people object to online image management because they
think that it is wrong to obscure negative information online; these
people believe that somebody searching for them online will be able
to properly weigh all the information that can be found—positive
and negative—and then reach the correct judgment. But these people wrongly assume that Web searchers will take the time to carefully
weigh false negative information against true positive information
and then manage to correctly identify which is true. In reality, Web
users form their first impressions with just a glance and without
bothering to look further. But, even more important, it is very difficult to refute some kinds of false negative information: How do you
disprove allegations that you had an affair, or smears alleging that
you have low morals, or a lie charging that you misused an official
position? It is near impossible. The law does not tolerate falsehoods
offline; there is no reason why you should tolerate falsehoods online.

Other people may claim that it is unfair or misleading to improve
your online image beyond cleaning up absolute falsehoods. But that

argument does not reflect the reality of the Web. One way to think about online reputation management is to think about getting dressed before leaving the house. We all wake up with morning breath and with our hair matted to our heads. We go through our morning ritual of getting cleaned up and dressed before leaving the house because we want to present a positive image of ourselves to the world. Putting on some clothes and washing your face is a socially accepted way to improve how people see you; nobody considers it deceptive to look in the mirror and pick the food out from between your teeth or to put some cream on a blemish. Online image management is the same— it is a form of putting clothes on your online image.

Another way to look at it is that when you apply for a job, you put your best foot forward. It is immoral (and possibly illegal) to lie on a résumé, but it is prudent to describe your accomplishments in a positive light. These days, your online résumé is part of your professional image, whether you like it or not. Employers, potential business partners, and even social contacts will look you up in Google. If you want to be successful and respected, you need to make sure that they find positive and truthful information that accurately reflects the positive side of your character.

Checking Up on Your Online Reputation

There are several steps to take as you begin to look into how you look online.

Step 1: Know Your Audience

All the world's a stage,

And all the men and women merely players:

They have their exits and their entrances;

And one man in his time plays many parts.

—WILLIAM SHAKESPEARE, *As You Like It*

In the Internet era, we are all micro-celebrities. Everyone can find information about anyone. Instead of the infamous Big Brother of *1984* watching over everyone, there are 500 million Little Brothers all looking at one another.[1] Whether you like it or not, you have an audience.

The first step toward online reputation success is recognizing your audience. For example, if you are a student applying to college or graduate school, then the odds are good that at least one admissions officer will look online to learn about your school, look for any news articles about you, and maybe even check Facebook for evidence of your judgment around alcohol and cameras.[2] The admissions office is one part of your audience. And the admissions office is a tough crowd: If you claim to have been volunteering in Africa over spring break, an admissions officer will quickly notice if your Facebook profile features pictures of your spring break trip to party in South Padre Island. Instead, you want to present a social profile that shows you in noncontroversial age-appropriate pursuits (at a football game, a dance recital, or an athletics competition) and perhaps *briefly* mentions your involvement in other activities. You do not want a page showing you in an inebriated state or comments from friends reflecting the same. Nor do you want an obvious résumé that has clearly been made just for the purpose of admissions offices: Your friends and the admissions office would see right through it.

If you are a Romeo or a Juliet looking for love (online or off), it is a good bet that the people you meet will be searching sites like Facebook and MySpace for more information about you. Your audience includes all of your potential romantic partners and their friends. You would be wise to make sure that the image of you that can be found in Facebook matches the image you are trying to present on your dates. If you hope to come across as a responsible member of the community, it might be worth getting rid of those drunk photos. On the other hand, if you want to come across as a hip club-goer, you might want to make sure there are photos of yourself enjoying the nightlife. And no matter what image you try to present to your dates, you need to be especially careful to make sure there are no negative comments about you on social networking sites or on attack sites like DontDateHimGirl.com that specialize in bringing down would-be lovers. A negative comment by a bitter ex- can ruin your dating prospects; with so many fish in the sea, a potential date might just decide to move on. On the other hand, some tasteful (and we mean tasteful!) content on social networking sites can confirm that you're a safe person whom others would want to date.

For people changing jobs, a hiring manager may search for evidence of project success (or failure) in online trade journals and through field-specific discussion websites. Hiring managers may even check networking sites like LinkedIn to test the depth of a candidate's digital Rolodex™. Your audience includes everyone who might play a part in deciding whether you get hired. Of course, most jobseekers want to convey a mature image; to take one example, a political speechwriter may have lost an opportunity for the job of a lifetime in the White House thanks to an alcohol-soaked photo on Facebook.[3] For many professionals, your image is your business. Your audience is all of your potential clients, who will search Google for information about your services, try to find reviews by other clients, and look for any disciplinary or legal action against you. This applies to professionals of every stripe, from consultants, to doctors and lawyers, to master craftsmen, to handymen. Professionals have special requirements and will benefit from specific advice in Chapter 13, in addition to the foundation provided by this chapter.

And everyone has an interest in avoiding being a victim of online harassment and groundless attack. The whole world is thus part of everyone's audience. Online smears (by a known attacker or even by a complete stranger) can poison social relationships and destroy your image in the local community. Proactive protection, careful monitoring, and rapid response can limit the harm caused by this kind of incident.

As you begin your effort to control your online image, it's wise to take the following two steps:

1. *Create a list of your goals.* The first step in putting together a list of your goals is to list the most important roles you play in your everyday life. You may be a neighbor, an employee, a school parent, a family member, a professional, and more. Think about all of the important roles that you play. Brainstorm as many ideas as possible; it might be useful to think about what you have learned in prior chapters, or to look at the list of sample goals in Figure 10-1. Keep brainstorming more roles in the back of your head; you never know when you might realize that you play another important role. Just as Archimedes had his (literal) "eureka!" moment while sitting in the bathtub, reputation inspiration might strike you at any time.

You can create your list on a piece of paper or through word processing software like Microsoft Word. Sample templates are available at http://wildwest2.com/templates/.

2. *Identify the people related to each goal.* Next, think about *who* might be searching for information about you in each role that you play. For example, if you are a PTA parent, other parents might look for in-

Figure 10-1. Starting Your Reputation Road Map.

The first step toward creating your own reputation road map is to identify all of the important roles that you play in your community. You might be a parent, a friend, a supervisor, and an online dater. Or you might be a student, an employee, and a local sports star. Whatever you do, you will have unique needs that can be addressed by first identifying your audiences. Some sample roles are listed here, but you are likely to have different ones.

Roles You Play				
Parent				
Friend				
Employee				
Student				
Online dater				
Everyday person				

formation—and so might school board members, teachers, or other children. If you are a professional, your customers might be looking for information about you—and so might your competitors. And don't forget that random people might search for information about you for the sake of identity theft or harassment. Take your list of roles and brainstorm a list of people who may be searching, as shown in Figure 10-2. Go ahead and take some time to think and brain-

Figure 10-2. Who Might Be Looking for You?

The next step in creating your reputation road map is to figure out what kinds of people might be looking for information about you. Think beyond just friends and co-workers; might competitors be looking for information about you in order to learn more about your company—or even to lure you away?

Roles You Play	People Who Might Be Looking			
Parent	Neighborhood parents Teachers PTA members			
Friend	Friends Friends of friends Acquaintances			
Employee	Co-workers Supervisors Rivals Competitors			
Student	Teachers Parents Classmates Rivals College admissions officers			
Online dater	Potential dates Their friends Your nosy co-workers or friends			
Everyday person	Identity thieves Stalkers Disaffected youth looking for people to mock			

storm. You will need the list you create in this section in order to pro-
ceed to the next step.

Step 2: Put Yourself in Their Shoes

Now that you know what roles you play and who might be searching
for you, think about what information you want them to find about
you. How will they make decisions about you? How would they react
to positive or negative information? How much research are they likely
to do? For example, a nosy neighbor might have hours to spend dig-
ging deep into the Internet to try to find dirt about you, but a college
admissions officer is unlikely to have time to perform more than just a
cursory search. A potential date might not care about that photo of
you holding a beer while driving a bass boat, but an employer might,
especially if you are seeking a safety-related job.

Use the list of roles you created in Figures 10-1 and 10-2 to put
yourself in the shoes of each person who might be searching for you.
First, think about what methods they will use to look for information
about you. Almost everyone uses Google and other search engines, so go
ahead and count that. But think about other methods, as well. If you are
a jobseeker, employers might use LinkedIn to find information about
your career. If you are young, peers might use MySpace and Facebook to
search for your social networking profile. If you work in a professional
field, customers might turn to field-specific directories, like those for
doctors and lawyers. And, finally, think about whether any of your information is in a place where it might be found by identity thieves,
pranksters, or others who might wish you ill. Jot down each information
source that you can think of. An example is given in Figure 10-3.

Next, think about what terms a searcher might use to find information about you. A searcher might use your name ("Joe Smith"), or
your name with additional terms related to a specific accomplishment
or project ("Joe Smith lumberyard"), or just terms related to a specific
achievement or project ("Springfield lumberyard owners"), or just
terms looking for dirt ("Joe Smith gossip"). Brainstorm all the ways
you might be found. An example is given in Figure 10-4.

Figure 10-3. Think about Information Sources.

It is a given that almost anybody looking for information about you might use Google or other search engines. But think about other ways that people could find information about you. Are there blogs or discussion sites relevant to your location, job, hobbies, or interests? Might you appear on any "review" sites that describe companies, contractors, daters, and others? Make your own personal list.

Roles You Play	People Who Might Be Looking	Sources They Might Use		
Parent	Neighborhood parents Teachers PTA members	**Google and other search engines** **People search directories** **Neighborhood blogs** **Local newspapers** **School directories**		
Friend	Friends Friends of friends Acquaintances	**Google and other search engines** **People search directories** **Local blogs** **Social networking sites** **Discussion sites regarding shared interests (e.g., sports, hobbies)**		
Employee	Co-workers Supervisors Rivals Competitors	**Google and other search engines** **People search directories** **Professional networking sites** **Discussion sites regarding your work (e.g., doctors, contractors, auto mechanics)**		
Student	Teachers Parents Classmates Rivals College admissions officers	**Google and other search engines** **People search directories** **Campus blogs** **Campus gossip sites** **Social networking sites** **Major or field-specific discussion sites**		
Online dater	Potential dates Their friends Your nosy co-workers or friends	**Google and other search engines** **People search directories** **Dating "review" sites** **Social networking sites**		
Everyday person	Identity thieves Stalkers Disaffected youth looking for people to mock	**Google and other search engines** **People search directories** **Data brokers**		

Figure 10-4. List Search Terms

Next, think about what search terms people in each role might use to find information about you. These are just some rough suggestions. Think in detail about
the ways that people could find you.

Roles You Play	People Who Might Be Looking	Sources They Might Use	Search Terms They Might Use	
Parent	Neighborhood parents Teachers PTA members	Google and other search engines People search directories Neighborhood blogs Local newspapers School directories	**Your name** **Your name plus other identifying information (e.g., city, job)** **"Parent at [your school]"** **"[school] PTA"** **"local real estate"**	
Friend	Friends Friends of friends Acquaintances	Google and other search engines People search directories Local blogs Social networking sites Discussion sites regarding shared interests (e.g., sports, hobbies)	**Your name** **Your name plus other identifying information (e.g., city, job)**	
Employee	Co-workers Supervisors Rivals Competitors	Google and other search engines People search directories Professional networking sites Discussion sites regarding your work (e.g., doctors, contractors, auto mechanics)	**Your name** **Your name plus other identifying information (e.g., city, job)** **Your name plus job description**	
Student	Teachers Parents Classmates Rivals College admissions officers	Google and other search engines People search directories Campus blogs Campus gossip sites Social networking sites Major or field-specific discussion sites	**Your name** **Your name plus other identifying information (e.g., city, job)** **Pranks and Googlebombs**	
Online dater	Potential dates Their friends Your nosy co-workers or friends	Google and other search engines People search directories Dating "review" sites Social networking sites	**Your name** **Your name plus other identifying information (e.g., city, job)**	
Everyday person	Identity thieves Stalkers Disaffected youth looking for people to mock	Google and other search engines People search directories Data brokers	**Your name** **Terms looking for vulnerabilities ("passwords" or "vacation dates")**	

As you are working, think about which search terms overlap between different groups. For example, almost anyone (including friends, business associates, and employers) might search for information about you by entering your name into a search engine. When you notice these overlaps, think about how the information that appears first will affect several groups and is thus especially important. You want to be sure that any content that appears is appropriate for all of the groups. In contrast, search terms that might be relevant only to one group (like "Michael Fertik business" for business associates) might be noticed less frequently, but it is important that these targeted searches find relevant information.

Finally, think about whether any of your goals may require special treatment. If any of your roles might subject you to online attack, you should note that now. For example, if you are a controversial public figure or if you have publicly taken a position that is contrary to the "Internet common wisdom," you run a much higher risk of online attack. Jot down any notes. An example is given in Figure 10-5.

Step 3: Perform an Online Reputation Audit

**You can't get where you're going unless
you know where you stand.**

—TRUE ANYWHERE IN LIFE

Now that you understand how people will search for information about you, you need to know what they can find about you today: You need to perform an *online reputation audit.* An online reputation audit is a comprehensive evaluation of your total online profile. It can reveal existing strengths and weaknesses and help guide you toward a reputation development plan. The steps listed here are intended to be used as guidelines; you should always customize your own online reputation audit according to your unique circumstances.

An online reputation audit is simple in theory: search using the

Figure 10-5. Wrap It Up with Your Personal Notes.

It is a given that almost anybody looking for information about you might use Google or other search engines. But think about other ways that people could find information about you. Are there blogs or discussion sites relevant to your location, job, hobbies, or interests? Might you appear on any "review" sites that describe companies, contractors, daters, and others? Make your own personal list.

Roles You Play	People Who Might Be Looking	Sources They Might Use	Search Terms They Might Use	Special Notes
Parent	Neighborhood parents Teachers PTA members	Google and other search engines People search directories Neighborhood blogs Local newspapers School directories	Your name Your name plus other identifying information (e.g., city, job) "Parent at [your school]" "[school] PTA" "local real estate"	**Be aware of PTA politics and risk of them getting personal; what happens online stays online**
Friend	Friends Friends of friends Acquaintances	Google and other search engines People search directories Local blogs Social networking sites Discussion sites regarding shared interests (e.g., sports, hobbies)	Your name Your name plus other identifying information (e.g., city, job)	**No need to work to create an excessively cheery impression for friends; just make sure there's nothing negative**
Employee	Co-workers Supervisors Rivals Competitors	Google and other search engines People search directories Professional networking sites Discussion sites regarding your work (e.g., doctors, contractors, auto mechanics)	Your name Your name plus other identifying information (e.g., city, job) Your name plus job description Your name	**Check employer policies about blogging, trade secrets, etc.**
Student	Teachers Parents Classmates Rivals College admissions officers	Google and other search engines People search directories Campus blogs Campus gossip sites Social networking sites Major or field-specific discussion sites	Your name Your name plus other identifying information (e.g., city, job) Pranks and Googlebombs	**Be vigilant to remove alcohol-addled photos from social networking sites Peers will generally support pro-school blogging but will quickly identify pro-self blogging**
Online dater	Potential dates Their friends Your nosy co-workers or friends	Google and other search engines People search directories Dating "review" sites Social networking sites	Your name Your name plus other identifying information (e.g., city, job)	**Limit online information available to prevent bad dates from becoming stalkers**
Everyday person	Identity thieves Stalkers Disaffected youth looking for people to mock	Google and other search engines People search directories Data brokers	Your name Terms looking for vulnerabilities ("passwords" or "vacation dates")	**Anything out-of-touch or excessively self-promotional may set off a bad reaction among disaffected youth**

list of places and keywords created in your reputation road map and note what you find.

Some questions to ask at each step are these: Is the content found relevant or irrelevant—is it about you or about somebody else? Is the content positive or negative? Is it true, false, or somewhere in between? How new or old is the information? Many search engines privilege very new information and very old sites, reasoning that new sites are news and that old sites are reliable and stable sources of information.

Consider the type of site the information appears on. Is it on a personal blog, a newspaper, a government-run site, or something else? This matters because personal blogs tend to be transient in search engine rankings; they're here one day and gone the next.

As you work, refine your search on the basis of what you find. You want to be aware of everything out there, even if some of it is not very visible right now. If you find something damaging, you should focus your search in on related keywords to determine if there is more of the same type of information out there. For example, if a search for your name reveals an allegation of a DUI arrest, you should also search for your name plus "DUI" and other related keywords in order to determine if there are other web pages that repeat the same allegations. Even if these sites are not very visible now, you need to be aware of them because they could bubble up in a search result later. Dangerous information is often like an iceberg: what you see at the top of a Google search is often the tip of what is available online, and the information that is hidden under the surface now can rise up and damage your reputation later.

When you are searching, take a moment to consider typos and alternate spellings. Some people are also likely to commit various misspellings of your name or interests ("Mike Fertick" or "Wild West 3"). This is a common problem. When the singer Britney Spears was at the peak of her popularity, Google reported that users frequently searched for terms like "Brittney," "Brittany," "Speers," and more. The singer Bruce Springsteen is still often mistaken for a nice Jewish boy named "Bruce Spring*stein*." And even Google itself is subject to typos like "Googgle." While misspellings of your name are relatively rare, it is still worth rerunning the most important searches with some of the more obvious misspellings in order to determine if you are being slandered under a misspelled name.

How to Perform Your Search

In this section, we suggest some common sites to search, along with a few tips for each source. Your needs will vary according to the reputation road map you developed earlier.

Google

Google has delivered more information to more people than any other single source in history.

—Simple fact

Pay special attention to Google. It is by far the most-used search engine around the world. Google has delivered more information to more people than any single source in history, and it is one of the first and most important places people look for information about you, no matter who you are and what you do.

If you use Gmail or another Google service, then log out before you start to search in order to avoid biasing your results via the "search personalization" feature that displays different search results to different people on the basis of their pattern of use. You want to see what the average user sees, rather than results customized for your particular interests.

Run a series of comprehensive searches on Google. Google's main search page can be found at http://www.google.com. Start by searching for just your name or your business name. Try it with and without quotation marks. Because Google is so important, look beyond just the first page; skim at least the first three pages of results for any signs of trouble.

As you are searching, you may notice that the Google search box will suggest searches to you while you type. Not every search term triggers a suggestion, but, if you do see a search suggestion, it is a great hint as to what other people are searching for. If any of the suggested searches are relevant to you, run them! Often, for businesses, they are very good suggestions of what people are looking for, like "ReputationDefender coupons" or "ReputationDefender free trial." For individuals, they often give hints as to what information people want to know, such as "Joe Biden quotes" or "Joe Biden photo."

Next, try a quick Google Image Search using the same variations on your core search terms. Google Image Search can be accessed at http://images.google.com or by clicking on the "Images" button from the Google search page. It is often worthwhile to search within "Google Groups" if you have been online for many years or have any reason to believe that very tech-savvy people may be discussing you, your company, or your product. Google Groups is a mixture of Usenet (an old discussion system that predated the graphical World Wide Web) and Google-specific discussion areas. Google Groups can be found at http://groups.google.com or through the Google services menu. There may be much spam and irrelevant material, but sometimes revealing discussions can be found.

Other Popular General-Purpose Search Engines

Repeat this search-and-refine process for other popular search engines. At the time of writing, Yahoo! Search, Microsoft Bing, and Ask.com were the most popular publicly accessible search engines after Google.

Yahoo!'s search engine can be found at http://www.yahoo.com.

Run the most important searches that you ran using Google's search engine, and note the results. Microsoft Bing can be found at http://www.bing.com. Microsoft has been trying very hard to promote the site, so it may be very important in the future. It frequently has very different results from other search engines, and it may help you discover hidden or otherwise unnoticed negative content. The same goes for Ask.com's search engine, which can be found at (surprise) http://www.ask.com.

People-Specific Search Engines

Search engines that are designed to find information about individuals are becoming increasingly important. Many general-purpose search engines have trouble finding information about individual people. For example, a search in Google for "David Thompson" tends to find information about the "David Thompson Health Region" in Canada, rather than information about that author, and Google has trouble distinguishing between one of the authors and the David Thompson who played professional basketball.

Google has launched its own people-centric search at http://profiles.google.com. In theory, it contains information about people who have signed up for the service, but it is worth searching to see if anything can be found about you. Several other companies have also attempted to fill the gap by providing search engines targeted exclusively at describing real human beings. These search engines are a trend to watch when managing your online image.

Depending on your goals, it may be a good thing if you don't find anything under your name in these people-specific search engines. If you would prefer that your private information be kept private, then there is nothing wrong with being obscure or even completely non-existent on the Web. On the other hand, if you would like people to think of you as well known or be able to easily get in touch with you, then you may have to help these search engines along by seeding them with positive and accurate content.

Spock.com (now owned by Intelius) was one of the earliest people-related search engines. It pulls data from a variety of sources, including MySpace, Facebook, and the "open" Internet to attempt to create profiles of individuals. However, it is prone to overinclusiveness in its attempt to gather data; its computers sometimes don't realize that two pages that mention the same name are really writing about two different people.

Spock aggregates a massive amount of data. It attempts to identify friends, photos of you, your year of birth, and much other information. All of the information used by Spock.com is publicly available *somewhere*, but the website uses powerful analytic tools to put it all in one place. Because it gathers information from such a wide variety of sources, it is able to present a variety of facts about you. Just as the best lies all contain a kernel of truth, the correct information reflected in a Spock.com profile gives false credibility to any inaccurate information that is also shown.

You can find the Spock people search engine at http://www.spock.com. Make sure to try variations on your name.

One of the leading personal search engines is Pipl, found at http://www.pipl.com. Pipl allows searching for people by name, e-mail address, or even website username. Make sure you try all three options. Another popular people-based search engine is Wink. It can be found at http://www.wink.com. It suffers from many of the same problems of under- and overinclusiveness as Spock. Similarly, the tool PeekYou gets hundreds of thousands of viewers per month at http://www.peekyou.com and appears to suffer from vast overinclusiveness; many profiles have information in them that actually pertains to somebody else with the same or similar name. PeekYou allows users to make "suggestions" that profiles be updated to remove inaccurate information but does not guarantee that these suggestions will be implemented. More sites are springing up in this category, so keep your eyes open for others and visit WildWest2.com for updates.

Personal Data Finders

Some sites focus exclusively on providing an address, phone number, e-mail address, and other personal information about everyone who has a telephone or a utility bill. While they do not provide a lot of information about your reputation directly, they do provide fodder for identity thieves, harassers, stalkers, and others.

In many cases, it may be best to try to eliminate as much of this information as possible. Many of the more heinous forms of online attack involve using real-world information to scare or threaten people directly or even to flood your mailbox with junk postal mail. By making that information more difficult to find, you can provide a layer of protection for yourself and your family.

Free Data Finders

There are hundreds of sites that can be used to search for basic personal information about you. Many draw from the same data sources, often as "teasers" to drive people toward the expensive pay-per-use data search services.

One of the most popular free data search sites takes its name from the phonebook: Whitepages.com. It is available at http://www.whitepages.com. It is one of the 100 most popular websites in the United States.[4] By searching for your name, you can quickly determine how easy it would be for somebody else to find you, your address and telephone number, and other information.

A fast-growing site to find information is 123people, available at http://www.123people.com. It is a hybrid between a people-centric search engine and a data finder. It aims to provide both contact information and any Web results, although it is often both over- and underinclusive.

Yahoo! also offers a unique search product that combines its Web search with a customized people-search product. At http://people.yahoo.com, you can find a powerful search system that will attempt to find information both on the Web and in phone databases.

There are hundreds of other sites that replicate information similar to what may be found in these listings; such websites often get their information by buying access to massive personal information databases. Visit http://www.wildwest2.com/privacy for a list of some of these databases.

Paid Data Finders

There are also sites that charge between $5 and $50 to find a vast array of information that you may have thought impossible to find. Some even boast about their ability to find unlisted phone numbers and addresses for just a few dollars. Often, these sites are backed by the massive databases run by companies like Experian, Transunion, and Equifax and by the massive data aggregation systems run by companies like ChoicePoint.

Some smaller companies are even less reputable than the sites backed by the large data brokers. The company LocateCell, which has since been shut down by the combined efforts of the U.S. Federal Communications Commission and a state attorney general, offered a very special package: for $110, anyone could buy a list showing every call placed or received by a target cell phone.[5] While this business is now gone, it shows the extent to which information that once seemed private can become instantly accessible worldwide—at least for the right price.

Fortunately, fewer people will use the paid sites to find information about you than will avail themselves of free sites. Anyone willing to invest the money it would take to order personal information through one of these sites could probably have found the information in other ways. Ultimately, some of these sites provide information for beneficial purposes such as job screening and identity verification, rather than for malicious purposes. Unless you have a reason to believe that somebody is willing to spend $5 to $50 to get your personal information, it is not necessary to search paid systems, although it is worth noting that some reputation management firms have special deals that allow them to check databases that would otherwise be inaccessible to the general public.

User-Created Content: Encyclopedias, Complaint Boards, and Forums

Many sites are based on so-called user-created content. These sites allow Internet users to share their thoughts with the world. They range from mass-edited encyclopedias, to group blogs, to sites that collect complaints about businesses, to thinly veiled attack sites, to forums that work like massive party lines and allow open discussion of many topics. They often appear high in the rankings of search engines because they contain vast amounts of original content.

These sites can be particularly dangerous because the owners of these sites generally believe that they are under no legal obligation to remove harmful content. Site owners in the United States have successfully used Section 230 of the Communications Decency Act as a shield against any liability for libelous or harmful content that was created by Internet users. This remains a rapidly evolving area of the law, and future legislators may fix the Section 230 loophole.

It is worth searching a few of these sites if they are relevant to you or your profession, even if there is no indication of trouble in a Google search. Content may be lurking in these sites, ready to bubble up into a Google results page at any moment. Or you may find the first indications of a future problem, such as by learning that a bitter ex- has started to post about you.

No matter what, it is worth a quick search of Wikipedia for your name or the name of your business. Wikipedia, available at http://www.wikipedia.org, is a free collaboratively edited encyclopedia.[6] Anyone can edit any article, and anyone can create new articles. Pages on Wikipedia tend to be very highly ranked in Google search results, largely because so many other websites link to Wikipedia. The vast majority of readers will find no relevant information about them on Wikipedia, but every now and then a malicious editor will slip an inappropriate reference or an unsubstantiated attack into the site. These attacks can usually be resolved easily through the Wikipedia editing and dispute resolution processes, described in Chapter 12. To search, simply go to the "Advanced" Wikipedia search page accessible through **Go**: http://wildwest2.com/go/1009, enter your name in quotation marks, and check all of the boxes for searching. That will provide you the most full look into all the content on Wikipedia.

You should also take a moment to check "complaint" sites. These sites specialize in giving anonymous Internet users a place to vent their complaints about subjects ranging from philandering boyfriends to bad businesses (more on businesses in Chapter 13). Because most of the sites allow anonymous complaints, it is easy for a malicious user to create fake or inaccurate complaints. For example, if you are male, it is worth checking the site DontDateHim-Girl.com to see if you have been "reviewed" as a good or bad dater. These sites are particularly harmful to reputation, and once they pop up in a Google search, they often lead to self-reinforcing cycles of negativity.

Social Sites

There are many websites that allow users to interact socially. These sites often allow users to post any kind of content they want. And these sites often are unable to monitor or control what users create, largely because users create more content than the site owners are willing to review.

First, check purely social sites. These sites exist solely to allow users to connect socially to one another. The easiest to search is My-Space. MySpace was one of the first social networking sites to hit it big, and continues to attract an audience skewed toward teenagers. Each user has a "profile page" she can use to display almost any kind of content, and users may also comment on each others' content. Users can spread smears and attacks in the form of comments or "posts" on profile pages or through blogs on the site. If you believe that you may be subject to rumor or attack online, especially by teenagers or youth (for example, if you are a teacher or interact with students), then it is worth closely searching MySpace to see what people are saying about you. Several people have even reported that they have discovered fake

MySpace profile pages created about them, often with insulting or embarrassing fake content. To search, go to www.myspace.com and search for your name (with and without quotation marks), using the search box provided. Be sure to select both the "people" and the "MySpace" search options; that will allow you to search for profile pages that use your name and also any other content that references your name.

Facebook is a social networking site that got its start in the college market. Accordingly, users of Facebook skew slightly older than those on MySpace, and they range from high school students through working professionals. At press time, it was very difficult to search Facebook without creating an account. This is obviously good and bad; it makes it more difficult to monitor, but it also makes it difficult for mischievous or slanderous users to harm you, because their smears will not be easily found by people who don't also use Facebook. If you are willing to create an account, you can create a basic account under your real name, set all of your privacy settings to their highest level (which will make it impossible for other people to find your real profile), and then search using the search tool for logged-in users. If you do not want to make a profile, then find the Facebook search page from www.facebook.com (usually titled something along the lines of "Find Friends") and search for your own name to determine if there are any fake profiles set up under your name. You will not be able to determine if any other slanderous or malicious content has been created.

Social media sites, like blog sites and short-message sites, are also worth a quick search. Users can create and share almost any form of content with a wide audience by using these sites. While many blogs and short-message sites appear in Google's main Web database, it is often easier to find some blog content by using specialized blog and short-message search services.

One of the hottest short-message sites is Twitter. It allows users to create and share stream-of-consciousness messages less than 140 characters long. Celebrities have started to use Twitter to spread quick updates on their everyday lives to their fans, and many normal people share updates on a daily (or even hourly) basis. These short posts can be searched by visiting the search page at http://search.twitter.com. Try searching for your name with and without quotes. Often, these short messages include links to other websites; if you find something that appears to be about you, be sure to find out more about any links that are included.

It is also worth checking to see if your name is mentioned on any blogging sites. One easy way to check is to look at blog search engines, rather than trying to check every blog out there. After all, if a blog is not popular enough to be listed in a blog search engine, then it probably will not do a lot of damage to your reputation. One of the easiest tools to search many blogs at once is Google Blog Search. You can visit the Google Blog Search tool at http://blogsearch .google.com. Just enter your name with and without quotes, and Google Blog Search will search thousands of popular (and not-so-popular) blogs for references to your name. Another popular blog search tool is provided by the site Technorati.com. By visiting the site at http://www.technorati.com, you will be able to enter your name and search for references across thousands of the most popular blogs on the Internet.

Now that you have completed your online reputation road map and an online reputation audit, you can take the next steps toward proactively managing your reputation. Chapter 11 describes how to take control of your online reputation. If you run a business, see Chapter 13 for information about how to optimize your business.

When to Call in the Professionals

Performing an online reputation audit is tough work. There are hundreds of websites that can be searched, and the list is constantly changing. It takes many hours to perform a proper online reputation audit, and possibly longer if you have a popular name or a long history online. Many popular sites, such as Facebook, can be searched effectively only if you have registered to use the site. And each site has its own tips and tricks for searching. While this book gives you many of the secrets of effectively performing an online reputation audit, it is impossible for most people to stay abreast of all of the trends in online reputation management.

For many readers, it will make sense to call in the professionals at this step. A professional reputation management company may be able to perform a reputation audit both more quickly and more completely than you could on your own. This form of electronic outsourcing has a long pedigree: Tim Ferriss, author of the *New York Times* bestselling book *The 4-Hour Workweek*,[7] recommends freeing up twenty or more hours of relaxation time every month by outsourcing every task that doesn't require your physical presence. Ferriss focuses on the idea of an everyday "virtual assistant" for routine e-mails and calls, but the concept can easily be extended to hiring a professional to do your reputation management. If you really want to follow Ferriss's advice to its logical extreme, hire a virtual assistant and instruct the virtual assistant to sign you up for a reputation management service.[8]

Just as with anything else, be careful when selecting a company to perform an online reputation audit for you. There are many fly-by-night companies that claim to perform online reputation services but that in reality provide very little and have limited or no customer service. Choose a company with a long history in reputation management, with known people at the helm who care about customer service. Of course, the authors would recommend their own company, ReputationDefender (www.reputationdefender.com), but please do your own research. In the meantime, check out the special offer for Wild West 2.0 readers at http://www.WildWest2.com/specialoffer/.

Notes

1. George Orwell, *Nineteen Eighty-Four* (1949). **Go**: http://wildwest2.com/go/1001.

2. "Admissions Officers Peek at Applicants' Facebook Profiles," *The Wired Campus* (blog), September 19, 2008, via chronicle.com. **Go**: http://www.wildwest2.com/go/1002.

3. CNN, "Obama Speechwriter Favreau Learns the Perils of Facebook," December 6, 2008. **Go**: http://wildwest2.com/go/1003.

4. Compete.com rankings, September 2007 through September 2008.

5. Office of the Missouri Attorney General, "Locatecell.com Must Stop Selling Cell Phone Records of Missourians, under Court Order Obtained by Nixon" (press release), February 16, 2006. **Go**: http://wildwest2.com/go/1005.

6. See also Paul Boutin, "Galaxy Quest," *Slate*, May 3, 2005. **Go**: http://wildwest2.com/go/1006.

7. Tim Ferriss, *The 4-Hour Workweek* (New York: Crown, 2007). **Go**: http://wildwest2.com/go/1004.

8. In the interest of full disclosure, Ferriss has a relationship with ReputationDefender.com, the professional reputation management firm that employs the authors.

11.0

Getting Proactive:
The Best Defense Is
a Good Offense

You need to proactively protect your online reputation. On the rough and tumble digital frontier, law enforcement can't protect you from malicious attacks, and good intentions can't protect you from computer errors or "the machine" spinning out of control. Active self-defense is the only way to protect your online reputation from accidental damage and malicious attacks.

An analogy may explain why it is necessary to proactively protect yourself against reputation damage. In the physical world, many people take precautions to protect themselves from physical attacks—by locking their doors or installing burglar alarms, for example. And many people also take precautions to protect themselves from accidental physical damage—they buy insurance on their cars and carefully protect their valuables. Your online reputation can be just as valuable as your most expensive possession, but there is no way to buy the same kind of insurance for it. And, on the frontiers of the digital Wild West, law enforcement often cannot protect you from harm. The best thing you can do is to protect yourself by carefully claiming your identity and building a shield against false and malicious content. We call this process building "Google insurance"—by investing today in positive online content, you can insure yourself against the harmful effects of negative or false online content in the future.

The amount and depth of further proactive management you do will depend on your goals. If you want to be well known online, it will be critical for you to work to make sure that positive information about you can easily be found, in addition to claiming your identity and establishing defenses. If, however, all you want is digital peace and quiet, you can do your best to make that happen by claiming your identity and setting up active defenses to help guard against attack.

Claim Your Online Identity

**Somebody is going to claim your online identity.
It might as well be you.**

—THE AUTHORS

No matter who you are and what you do, you need to claim your online identity today (see Figure 11-1). Claiming your online identity helps to protect you from online impersonation and serves as the first line of defense against online attack. Your online identity is made up of all the online content that *appears* to belong to you or come from you. For example, your profile on a social networking site is part of your online identity because it appears that you control it. A blog that appears to be written by you is also part of your online identity because it looks like content that you created. To claim your online identity, you simply need to take control of websites and usernames that

Assume that you are Bill Gates, the CEO of the software manufacturer Microsoft Corp. These are possible examples of your online identity:

- Web sites
  - ○ A website at billgates.com, williamgates.com, or similar
  - ○ A website at MicrosoftCEO.com or even MicroCEO.com

- Communications media
  - ○ A blog at billgates.blogspot.com or billgates.livejournal.com
  - ○ A blog at MicrosoftCEO.blogspot.com or MicroCEO.livejournal.com
  - ○ A Twitter microblog at BillGates.twitter.com
  - ○ A Twitter microblog at MicrosoftCEO.twitter.com

- Social media
  - ○ A Facebook account claiming to be "Bill Gates"
  - ○ A MySpace account under the username "billgates"
  - ○ A LinkedIn account claiming to be "Bill Gates"

- Search media
  - ○ A Google Profile under the username "billgates" or listed under the name "Bill Gates"

Figure 11-1. What Is Online Identity?

appear to be related to you. You do not need to reveal any information about yourself or create any content; you simply need to claim identities, URLs, and usernames that refer to you by name.

Claiming your online identity helps to protect you from online impersonation. Many websites do very little (or nothing at all) to protect against online impersonation; most websites do not verify that people are who they claim to be. As a result, anybody could set up a fake blog under your name, create a fake social networking profile with your photo, or even register a domain in your name. People visiting these sites would see your name on them but have no way to know that it is not really you. Some sites might provide a means for you to complain after you have already been impersonated, but by then it is already too late—you will be stuck pleading with customer service for days or weeks while the impersonator damages your good name.

Impersonation is one of the most dangerous threats because it is often very believable and often causes results that appear very high on the list of results in Google and other search engines. By claiming your online identity, you can make it harder for other people to impersonate you: they will simply lack the tools they need to convincingly pretend to be you. You will also be able to more easily rebut any attempts at impersonation by establishing your own credible online identity; if you already have an online identity, many people will not believe an obvious fake, and you will be able to use your existing online identity to debunk rumors that come from the impersonator.

Claiming your online identity is also the first step toward defending against many other forms of online reputation damage. If you are ever attacked, you will be able to use your ownership of your online identity to help clean up your online résumé and to help improve your total online profile. Websites that make up your online identity are often very visible in search results and can be used to push aside false or misleading content. Being proactive now—before there is a problem—makes your defenses even more powerful because Google (and many other search engines) often take a long time to update: if you claim your online identity now, Google will be aware of it when you need to use it. If you wait until you are already under attack, then you may have to wait days (or even weeks) for search engines to discover your content.

How to Claim Your Online Identity

Claiming your online identity is simple in concept but somewhat time-consuming in execution. The goal is to make sure that you control your name on popular websites, mainly by claiming usernames, URLs, and identities as a placeholder against misuse and as a first fortification against attack. You do not need to upload any content today or say anything more than you want to. If you ever are attacked, then you will then be able to activate these websites to help in your defenses. Be sure to write down your usernames and passwords for these sites in a secure place, or use a service like NameGrab.com that keeps track of social usernames for you.

Types of Web Sites

There are two relevant kinds of websites in your effort to protect your identity. Many social sites identify users by their full names. On these sites, many people can share the same name. Your goal is to claim your name today so that you will have an established profile in case of future attack. Many other sites identify users by a username or pseudonym (like "appleCEO1" or "superbloggirl"). Only one person can use a username. On these sites, you want to claim usernames that resemble your name so that other people can't use them and so that you can use them to your advantage in improving your online résumé.

Real-Name Sites

On many social networking sites, such as Facebook and LinkedIn,—users are identified primarily by their full names. Users might choose a "username" when registering or logging in, but their username is not displayed prominently. On these sites, you want to create an identity so that you can establish that your true identity was there first—and claim your space before somebody else with the same name does! And, establishing an identity early may help make a profile more visible in a search engine if you ever need it.

Here are some sites that you should consider:

▶ *Facebook.* Facebook is the "granddaddy" of personal social networking. It is the largest and most popular social networking site, with millions of active users. Set up a profile under your full name on Facebook, even if you do not want to use any of the social networking features. This sounds counterintuitive in some ways, but it will allow you to be prepared in case you ever need to use it. You do not need to provide a photograph, but you should enter your location (country, city, and state). If you want, go ahead and set your privacy settings to "maximum" so that no information about you is visible to the outside world.

▶ *LinkedIn.* LinkedIn is the most powerful business social networking site. It is used by millions of people who seek to connect professionally or change jobs. If you work in a professional field, you need to make sure to claim your LinkedIn profile. Just as with Facebook, you should enter your real name and location. You may then choose to provide as much (or as little) information about yourself as you wish to reveal. Providing more information will generally build a stronger defense against online reputation attack, in that LinkedIn pages are often visible on Google and may provide a buffer against any negative or false information.

Other User-Created Content Sites

On many popular websites, users are identified by "usernames" instead of by their full names. Or users may be identified by both a username and a real name. On these sites, you want to make sure to have claimed any usernames that resemble your real name. These usernames are often viewed by Google and other search engines as highly relevant information to a search, so a profile with the username "SteveJobs1955" might appear near the top of a search for "Steve Jobs."

To claim your identity on these sites, simply visit the most popular user-created content sites and try to register your name as a username, or use a professional name-acquisition service like NameGrab to do it yourself. Provide as much (or as little) personal information about yourself as you want; it is not necessary to provide complete (or even necessarily accurate) information at this stage. Repeat the process with other names similar to your name; for example, if your name is Steve Jobs (the CEO of Apple), you might want to consider checking the usernames "SteveJobs," "StevenJobs," "StevePaulJobs," "AppleSteve," or even "SteveJobs1995."

If your name has already been taken, don't worry. Many common user names have already been taken at popular websites, simply because there are tens of millions of Internet users. To the extent possible, check whether the person using the username appears to be a legitimate user who happens to share a name—if so, there is nothing you can do, so there is no reason to worry. Instead, try to register a similar username (like "SteveJobsApple" instead of "SteveJobs"), and move on.

Here are a few of the most popular sites worth considering. There are always new popular sites, so pay attention to trends online to try to find the most relevant ones.

▶ *Google Profiles.* Google Profiles is one of the most rapidly changing profile services on the Internet. Google Profiles allows users to create a short "profile" page that describes themselves, possibly including photos. Because it is affiliated with Google, it has tremendous power. Profiles are based on a user's Google username, then displayed at a matching URL. For example, the profile of somebody with the Gmail address stevejobs@gmail.com will appear at http://www.google.com/profiles/stevejobs. The profile will also appear in a Google search for that user's name. Because Google's services are so popular, it is almost impossible to register any common names as usernames—they have all already been taken. But try to register something close and set up a Google profile. You don't need to provide any information beyond your name and maybe location; if you ever need to defend against attack, you can add more information later.

▶ *Twitter.* Twitter is an extremely popular "microblogging" site that allows users to post short (140 characters or less) messages about their life. Many celebrities use the site to provide a steady stream of updates to their fans. Users are identified by usernames (like "AppleCEO" or "SteveJobs") that each user chooses. As a result, there have been many reported incidents of impersonation through Twitter. You need to protect yourself by claiming your name (and any variants of it) as a username now.

▶ *Livejournal, Blogger,* and *WordPress.* These are all popular blogging sites that allow users to set up a free basic blog under a username or pseudonym. The username is used as part of the URL for each service: for example, the username "SteveJobs" might result in a blog accessible at http://stevejobs.wordpress.com. Because a blog at http://stevejobs.wordpress.com would appear to be written by Steve Jobs, you need to claim your name as a username now to protect yourself from impersonation. And, if you are ever attacked, a blog with your name in the URL (the way that "Steve" and "Jobs" appear in the URL http://stevejobs.wordpress.com) is likely to rank highly in search engine results. Check each service, and register your name as a username. You may also want to consider variations on your name. You don't need to start an active blog; just upload a test post to create a placeholder.

▶ *Wikipedia.* Wikipedia is a massive free online encyclopedia. It can be edited by anyone, which creates a constant risk of vandalism and reputation attacks. It may be worth registering your name as a username (*not* creating an article about yourself, which is generally prohibited by Wikipedia's rules) so that other editors will not be able to impersonate you and so that you will have a basis to contest false information on the site that you find in the future.

For a long list of other websites that may allow you to claim your identity by registering your name as a username, visit the official Wild West 2.0 website: http://www.wildwest2.com/usernames. It lists more than 30 sites that have publicly visible usernames and profiles. You do not need to register at all of those sites, but it is worth skimming the list to see if there are any relevant to your career or profession.

Domain Names
The last piece of online identity that you need to claim is the domain name that matches your name. For example, if your name is Steve Jobs, you want to control the domain name SteveJobs.com so that

nobody else can set up a site at that URL. And, if you ever need it, a domain name that contains your name will usually rank very highly in search engine results: a personal site at (for example) SteveJobs.com will provide a very strong defense against reputation attack against the CEO of Apple.

It is possible to register a domain name for around $10 per year through any popular domain name registrar, such as GoDaddy.com. You do not need any technical knowledge to register a domain name. You also do not need to set up a site in order to claim your identity, although setting up a site can be part of an active defense strategy (described later).

Look for your name as a domain name: SteveJobs.com. If that is taken, then check to see if it is in use by simply typing it into your Web browser; the odds are good that you share a name with somebody who simply got to it first. Don't worry—try other combinations by checking your full name, your name with a middle initial, or a nickname. If they are all taken, you will not be able to claim them, but neither will an imposter. If any are available, you may want to consider registering them.

More Significant Fortifications

Generally the one who first occupies the battlefield awaiting the enemy is at ease.

—Sun Tzu

Claiming your online identity is the first step toward effectively managing your reputation, but it is not the last. The more proactive steps you take today, the better your reputation will be protected from future threats. The logic is simple: the more positive and neutral information there is about you online, the harder it will be to find false or negative information about you. This is especially true if the existing content appears very "important" and established to search engines; any new false or misleading information will be less likely to displace the existing content in your online résumé.

Building positive and neutral content now—before there is a problem with false or negative content—is necessary to minimize future problems. It often takes days (or even weeks or months) for new content to appear in search results. If you wait until bad content is already visible before acting, it will already be too late. You will have to wait for your new positive or neutral content to start to displace the negative or false content. And, some search engines consider older content to be more authoritative than newer content; if you have already bolstered positive or neutral content in advance, it may appear stronger to search engines—and, by building strong positive content today, you help prevent future false negative content from rising in search engine results.

How Much Active Defense?
Everyone reading this book should invest some time into proactive reputation defense, before anything goes wrong. As described in Chapter 6, reputations can be ruined by simple mistakes online or by computers gone out of control (or, as we like to call it, "Google Gone Wild"). The more you invest now, the better "Google insurance" you will have.

People who are vulnerable to attack need to invest particularly heavily in proactive defense, before it is too late and an attack has already started. Politicians (even at the level of a homeowner's association board) are subject to attack by their opponents or dissatisfied constituents. People who advocate controversial or unpopular public positions are subject to attack by people who disagree with them. Active supporters of political campaigns (on either side of the aisle) are likely to be attacked by opposing partisans. Community activists (no matter what the issue) inevitably anger those who favor the status quo. Landlords, teachers, and other people who exercise positions of authority are subject to attack by the people they supervise. And anyone who has a bitter ex-, jealous co-workers, or other relationships described in Chapter 7 faces a substantial risk of online attack.

The Need for Positive Content

Some people require more Internet exposure than others. If you want to be a motivational speaker, a politician, or a celebrity, then you need a massive Google trail of results. For you, "image is everything." The first few items in your online résumé will create a frame through which almost every searcher will view you. To take an example, if the first few search results for your name are a debate about whether you are the best motivational speaker in your field, then most readers will automatically assume the frame that you are a good speaker. In contrast, if the first few pages debate whether an allegation of misconduct is true, then readers will look at all other pages through the lens of potential misconduct. It is vital that you present truthful positive information at the top of a search so that you can set the right kind of frame. If you want online fame, then you will also have to make sure that your total online profile is deep: it is all but guaranteed that Internet users will search far and wide online to learn more about you and maybe even to try to dig up some embarrassing photos or questionable quotes.

Even if you just want to be famous within a small group—as the best house DJ in Miami, the best neo-Fluxus painter in Seattle, the best classic-car restorer in the Midwest, or the best cosmetic dermatologist in Houston—your online image is everything. It is absolutely crucial that relevant positive content appear at the top of a Google search for your name or for your specialty. Internet users have figured out how to gauge celebrity on the basis of the Google results for a search term. If a search for your name returns only one or two relevant results, you will appear to be relatively unknown in your field.

On the other hand, if all you want is privacy and anonymity, don't close this book yet. Even if you don't want to use the Internet to advance yourself, you still have to protect your image from online attack. However, the challenge is very different: If you just seek privacy, it may be desirable for any information about you to be hidden behind people with similar or identical names. For you, detailed awareness and constant monitoring will be crucial to your success. You will still need to work hard at protecting and monitoring your online reputation, but the goals of the monitoring will be very different.

Of course, if you have been attacked online, the decision about putting information online has already been made for you. You may be able to remove some malicious content, but it is not always possible to remove it all. At a minimum, you will need to make sure that there is enough positive or neutral content out there to overwhelm the online smear.

For those in the middle, who seek neither fame nor complete obscurity, a moderate strategy is appropriate. It is not crucial that the first result of a Google search for your name be a glowing review, but it is still important to control the general tenor of an online search for your name. And it is still important that you build a solid defense against online attack, lest you become the next victim of online attack.

How to Perform Active Defense

If you want to truly own your Google results, then there must be enough positive and neutral content about yourself to completely block out any false or misleading information that might come along later. This is the ultimate form of "Google insurance." You can accomplish this goal in three ways:

1. Creating positive and neutral content about yourself, and working to make sure that it is recognized by search engines as relevant and important by carefully linking to it

2. Encouraging other people to create positive or neutral content about you

3. Bolstering the visibility of existing positive and neutral content about you

Create Your Own Content

The first form of active defense is to create your own content to serve as a buffer against false, misleading, or negative search results. By building positive content now, you will create a *Google wall* that helps to keep false negative content out of the top Google search results. You may use any means to create your own positive or neutral content so long as it is truthful and likely to be found by a search engine.

Positive content, as the name suggests, paints you in a good light. Information about your career, accomplishments, and achievements counts as positive content. So does content that makes you appear social, outgoing, and friendly—such as smiling photographs with friends or powerful people.

Neutral content is content that doesn't affect your reputation directly. A website that simply lists your name as part of a directory is a form of neutral content: it does not make you look good or bad. Neutral content can be an extremely effective part of online reputation defense, even though it does not directly improve your reputation. Instead, neutral content can be used to make false negative information more difficult to find. For example, if the first page of results for a search for your name returns all neutral content, then very few people will see negative content on subsequent pages. Neutral content is also beneficial in that it usually does not appear self-promotional or otherwise questionable; it simply fills up your online résumé with unobjectionable material that serves as a buffer against negative content.

When creating positive and neutral content, it is important to think about how it will be considered by search engines. Most search engines—including Google—use a variety of factors to determine the order in which to display search results. These factors include the popularity of the web page and the website (as measured by the number of incoming links) and the number of times that a search term (your name) appears in the text of the website. Further, most search engines will not prominently display more than one or two pages from any website in a search: if there are 100 relevant pages about you on one website, only one or two will be displayed.

The most effective strategy to build positive and neutral content is thus often to build content across a variety of sites and to link these sites as much as possible. For example, it might make sense to create a personal blog on your own domain (if your name is Steve Jobs, then at www.stevejobs.com) that contains your name prominently in the title. Then, create a profile on a networking site like LinkedIn and link to your personal blog from your LinkedIn profile. Then create a Google Profile and link to your blog and LinkedIn profiles from it. Then create a second, placeholder blog at a private blogging site and link from it to any or all of the above. The details will vary greatly according to your exact situation. Figure 11-2 shows how a hypothetical person might set up a series of links that

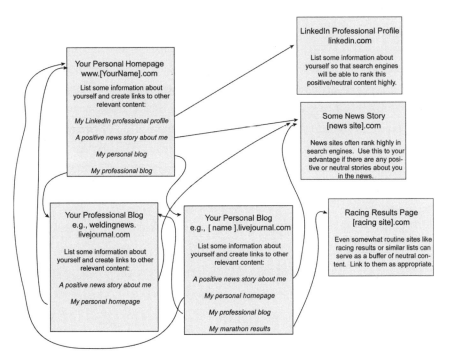

Figure 11-2. Link-Building to Success. Use several different sites to carefully link to positive and neutral online content in order to help maintain its popularity in search engines. This content can bolster your online reputation or serve as a buffer against false and misleading negative information.

would help ensure that favorable information shows up near the top of a Google search.

Be careful when creating your own online content. Do not lie or exaggerate under any circumstances; when the truth eventually comes out, the damage will be significant. Boastfulness is also an invitation for trouble; an online résumé that is too positive will stand out as unusual. Instead, write simple truthful content that reflects your interests and achievements without bragging or excess pride. Be creative when generating new content: think about all of your interactions and how you could use them to create new content.

Some of the easiest methods of creating positive and neutral content are listed here:

▶ *Blogging.* As part of claiming your identity, you should have claimed your name as a username at some of the major blog sites. Set up a blog and periodically update it with new content—maybe once or twice a week. If your name is prominently displayed in the title (for example, "The Official Blog of Steve Jobs") and you periodically update it with new and relevant content, it is likely to become a secure and important part of your online résumé. Be creative when deciding what to blog about: You can blog about your family, your neighborhood, your profession, your favorite sports team, or anything else. Just be sure that the content comes across as appropriate and well written.

▶ *Twittering.* Similarly, Twitter allows "microblogging," short, 140-character updates that are designed to be easier and faster to create and to read than a full blog. Use the service to provide periodic updates and to link to other positive and neutral content.

▶ *Profile Sites.* There are several free and paid services, such as Naymz and PeoplePond, that allow users to create a short personal profile and to link to other relevant sites. Use these services to link to other positive and neutral content.

▶ *Other User-Created Content Sites.* Sites like Flickr, Webshots, and YouTube allow users to create and share photos and videos. These sites also allow users to comment on content, to create short profiles, and to socialize with each other. You can use these sites to your advantage by uploading relevant and positive content (photos or videos) and prominently including your name in the subject or description. Take care to not be overly aggressive or self-promotional, but use the sites to your advantage.

▶ *Professional Directories.* Many professions offer free online directories of members or similar sites for professional networking. For example, professors and other academics can use the free "Social Science Research Network" (SSRN) to create short profiles and to share working papers. These sites are often ranked very highly in search engine results because they contain a large amount of relevant content and are very heavily linked. If there is a directory appropriate and relevant to your profession, use it.

Get Others to Help

One way to substantially boost your efforts is to get somebody else to help. Other people often have access to different websites and a different perspective.

If you have already been a victim of online reputation damage (accidentally or maliciously), reach out to friends and co-workers to explain the problem. It is likely that you know sombody who keeps an active blog or other website and will be able to assist you by linking to positive and neutral content about you. By linking to that positive and neutral content, that person will make it appear stronger and more "popular" and thus more likely to displace any negative content in your online résumé.

Even if you have not been a victim of online reputation damage yet, you can still reach out to others and preemptively improve your Google insurance. There are thousands of local and microbloggers who write about the happenings in local neighborhoods, small professions, and other very narrow topics. If you reach out with a relevant story or comment, you may be able to get yourself quoted by the author of one of these blogs. Any article with your quotes in it becomes relevant positive or neutral content that you can then use to fill out your online résumé.

If you are a professional or a small business owner, this might be a good chance to increase your PR exposure. Try to get mentioned by name and become a go-to source for reporters who write about your area or industry. Practice providing useful quips and interesting story leads; these can make you a resource for reporters.

Bolster Existing Positive or Neutral Content

When false or malicious information starts to spread online, it often shoots to the top of a Google search. From there, its popularity becomes self-sustaining because many people see it and link to it. But it is possible to defuse this danger in advance: If there are a number of well-established and popular positive or neutral sites at the top of a Google search, then the new false information is less likely to make it all the way to the top. By strengthening existing positive and neutral content, you can help make sure that false information fizzles out before it can harm you. This is one of the most powerful forms of Google insurance.

You can boost existing content by linking to it and encouraging others to link to it. Don't get out of control—Google's algorithm can detect attempts to force content by overly aggressive linking—but place legitimate and relevant links to existing content in your various blogs and profiles.

There also may be plenty of existing content about you online that is not very visible: Often, this includes old news articles that mention you—from business news to a bake sale to a marathon to a church bulletin. You can bolster the strength of this content and make it part of your online defense. When you conducted your online reputation audit, you may have discovered a number of hidden gems: websites that mention your name positively but that do not currently appear on the first page of Google results. By linking to some of this content, you can help elevate it and strengthen it as a form of defense.

Use Common Names to Your Advantage

If you have a relatively uncommon name, like one of the authors, you will have a chance to shape the totality of Google results to fit the image you want to create. But, having a relatively rare name also means that negative content about you will be more visible, and it may be harder to protect your privacy. If you have a very common name (or share a name with a celebrity), as does the other author, then you will have less control over the first few results for your name, but you will also be more protected from negative content because negative content about you will often be hidden by content about other people. For example, if you are named "Mike Jordan" but you are not the former basketball player with a similar name (also known as "his airness"), the odds are good that it will be difficult to find any negative information about you in a Google search.

If you do share a name with someone famous (or just with a lot of other people), you can protect your privacy by carefully and delicately bolstering existing content about the other people. Any false or negative information about you will get lost in the shuffle, without you having to disclose any information about yourself in the process. Privacy-through-obscurity is an effective strategy in a world with so many people who share the same small number of names.

Calling In the Professionals

It is often difficult and time consuming to create properly balanced and well-linked content online. Some content can be created without any technical knowledge, but other content takes an understanding of at least HTML and possibly other technologies.

Thus, for many people, it makes sense to call in the professionals when building positive and neutral content in order to create Google insurance. Professionals have built thousands of websites and know exactly how to optimize them to rank the highest in Google and other search engines. They often know the right tone to strike and the right balance of links to create. And professionals often have an arsenal of deals with specialized websites that allow rapid improvement in search results.

Just as with many other specialized tasks (ranging from oil changes for city dwellers to haircuts everywhere), sometimes it makes sense to call in a professional who does the job every day. The authors, of course, recommend the MyEdge service by ReputationDefender, but please perform your own research and check the special offers currently available to readers at http://wildwest2.com/specialoffer/.

Recovering from Online Smears: Restoring Your Reputation After the Damage Has Been Done

You may feel shock, anger, and revulsion if you have found false information about you online. Many people experience these emotions when they discover lies, false innuendo, and slander online, especially if the falsehoods appear prominently in a Google search. Discovering false information about you online can feel like learning that peers are gossiping behind your back or that your online résumé has been covered in hurtful graffiti. These feelings can be magnified if the false information is prominent enough that it may be misleading friends, co-workers, acquaintances, and others. You may also experience feelings of powerlessness because there is often no immediately obvious way to complain about a website bearing false information and no button to press to instantly fix it. And your feelings may be intensified even further if the false information was put online by an anonymous user; you may think, "How dare some coward hide behind a cloak of anonymity when slinging lies and misinformation?"

These reactions are all perfectly normal. It can be a shock to discover hurtful false information for the first time, whether it was placed online intentionally or accidentally. It often hurts doubly because so many users still believe the "Google of Eden" myth—the false impression that all Google results are pure, pristine, unbiased, truthful, and accurate—almost as if Google were a gift from the heavens. In reality, Google's algorithm was written by humans, who are necessarily imperfect. The algorithm depends on collecting input from websites and blogs, many of which are biased or false. And the algorithm is further corrupted by the self-reinforcing nature of false Web content. Finding false information about you presented through Google is probably the fastest way to be dissuaded of the myth of the Google of Eden (see Figure 12-1). If you have a strong emotional reaction upon discovering false online content, then talk about your feelings with friends and family before proceeding; it is important to recognize how you feel and to work through your emotions before beginning the hard work of repairing your reputation.

Once you have had time to process the initial shock, it is time to start the hard work of repairing your reputation. The good news is that your online reputation can be improved through careful application of a few simple principles. The bad news is that reputation repair takes time and effort, and sometimes a lot of both; it may take a few weeks and a handful of hours to fix a minor problem, but it may take several months and hundreds of hours of effort to repair the worst of the damage following a serious attack.

The process of online reputation repair can be broken down into three steps: understanding the problem, making a plan, and imple-

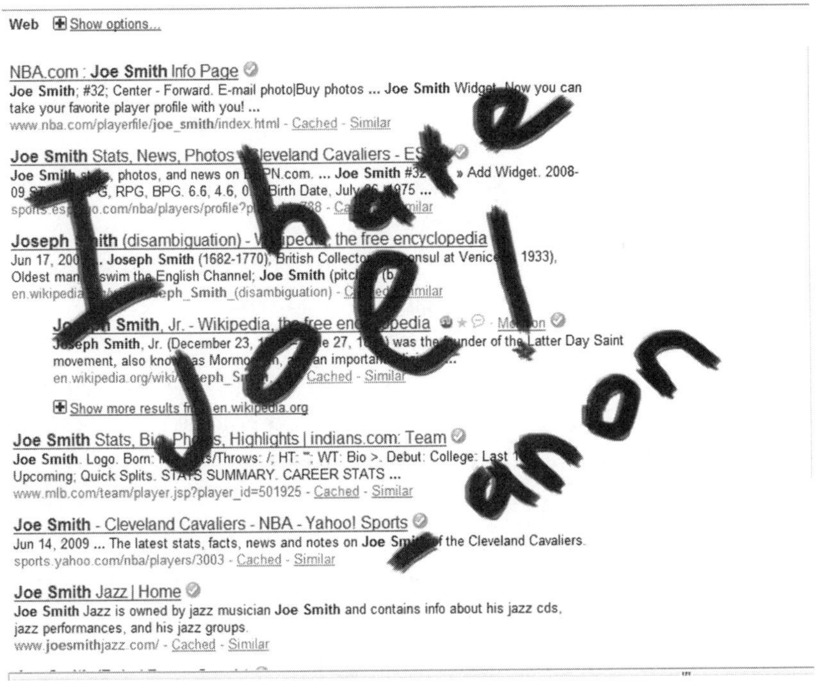

Figure 12-1. Discovering false information about you on the Web can feel like discovering hateful graffiti on your online résumé.

menting your plan. These steps are flexible; you will always be finding new information, and you will almost always have to adjust your plan.

Step 1: Understand What Happened

As a cartoon hero once said, "Knowing is half the battle."[1] Your first goal is to determine the extent of the reputation damage and to identify its original source. Understanding the extent and the source of the false negative information will help you formulate a plan to deal with it: You would need to create different plans for an intentional and widespread attack and for an isolated accidental error.

Assess the Damage

The first task is to assess the damage to your online reputation. You need to know how visible the damage is and how far the damaging content has spread.

You must know how visible the damage is in order to prioritize your online reputation repair efforts, to understand how much work needs to be done, and to develop an overall strategy. If your online résumé has been completely trashed by an anonymous attack, you may need to immediately start an intense recovery plan. On the other hand, if your online résumé is still intact and the damage appears only deep in your total online profile, then you may have time to act slowly and work more cautiously so as to not accidentally make the damaging content more visible.

Determining how far the damaging content has spread will help you to find any content that is lurking under the surface that could damage your reputation in the future. It is common knowledge (at least among boat captains) that it is possible to see only about 10 percent of an iceberg above the surface of the water. The other 90 percent of the iceberg is lurking underneath the surface. The part of the iceberg hidden underwater is at least as dangerous to ships as the part that is visible.

Online reputation damage is like an iceberg (see Figure 12-2). Many people will see the content that is "on the surface" (part of your online résumé) today. But there is a good chance that there is other negative content that is not visible right now. This negative content is not harmful at the moment, but it could become harmful later: Google might index the content in the future, or it might become more visible thanks to a change in the Google algorithm, or it might inspire a copycat attacker to smear your reputation further. You need to track down as much of this content as you can. You may be able to neutralize some of this "iceberg content" before it can do any damage. And even if you can't neutralize it all, you can build Google walls around it.

Figure 12-2. Online reputation damage is like an iceberg; there is always material that is not visible but that could still sink you. Credit: Rita Willaert.

The best way to measure the scale of the online reputation damage is to perform an online reputation audit, as described in Chapter 10, so that you are aware of your image as a whole; you may identify some new trouble spots that you were not yet aware of, or you may find out that your reputation as a whole is still generally okay. Then, home in deeper on the false negative content you found. Dig deeper through the Google search results for your name and any identifying information (as described in the online reputation audit) than any other person would; your goal is to find information that may not be very visible right now but that might become visible later. In the process of doing this, you may find other copies of the false negative content. To do this review, you will need to carefully examine at least the first three pages of Google search results (the first thirty results)—that is as deep as the vast majority of Google users look for content. Then, quickly skim through the next seven pages of results, so that you have examined a total of ten pages (for a total of 100 Google results) per search term. If the Google search result page informs you that it is omitting results similar to the ones it has already displayed, be sure to show those results so that you find duplicate copies of the same negative information. If the Google search result page informs you that there are more results from the same domain, then also be sure to display those and check if there are more copies of the same falsehoods.

Once you have dug deep, use what you have learned to go broad. You are likely to have discovered themes running through the negative information you have found—or maybe even the exact same attack repeated several times. Use these themes to create new searches to try to find more similar information. Integrate keywords and information from the negative information you have found, and repeatedly search for more copies of the same negative information. You may even want to search for direct quotes from the smears that you have found—sometimes you will discover websites that have automatically copied and distributed a smear around the Web.

For example, if you found a website comment that falsely claimed that you had committed a DUI, you would want to expand your search to look for keywords related to drinking and driving. If your initial search was for your name (call it "Joe Smith" who lives in a town called "Springfield"), your new searches might be "Joe Smith DUI," "Joe Smith drinking," "Joe Smith intoxicated," "Joe Smith traffic," "Joe Smith trial," and "Joe Smith convicted." You may also want to consider trying searches for part of your name or for other identifying information in combination with the negative comment "Smith DUI," "Smith DUI Springfield," "Springfield DUI."

Next, repeat your search across the other major search engines. Check Microsoft's Bing search engine and the main Yahoo search engine. If you have discovered any manipulated or misidentified photographs relevant to your search, you should also search for images related to your name or identifying information using Google Image Search and the Flickr.com photo search tool.

Finally, check some of the major archive providers to determine if there are automatic copies of the false information. To check the Internet Archive, click on the "Wayback Machine" link at Archive.org and then enter the URL of the site where you found the offensive content. To check Google Cache, go to Google's homepage at Google.com and enter the URL of the offensive content as a search (you must perform this search from the Google homepage rather than from a search bar; some Google search utilities are designed to go to the URL rather than search for information about it). If Google returns a result, look for a button under the result that says "cached." If there is such a button, click on it, and note whether the smear appears in the cached copy. Don't worry about solving the problem yet, and don't try to make any changes; your only goal at this stage is to gather information.

When you find false negative information, you should take note of more information than you would in a normal online reputation audit. First, take note of whether the negative content you find appears to be an "original" or whether it appears to be an automatic copy of information found somewhere else. Try to see if the content was intentionally posted or whether it was generated automatically by a computer (for example, the difference between a human-created narrative and a computer-generated "tag" on a Spock profile). Take note of whether the content has a date associated with it—is it a forum post or a blog comment that has a "posted on" date? If so, is the date recent or several months (or years) old? Is there any identifying information about who (if anybody) might have created the false negative content? A pseudonym is not perfectly identifying (and might even be an intentional red herring), but it is still worth observing it at this stage.

Figure Out How It All Got Started

The next important task is to try to identify the original source of the false information. In particular, it is important to understand whether you are facing a malicious attack, an innocent human error, or a computer out of control. Professionals use significantly different strategies for dealing with intentional attacks and with accidental mistakes. For example, if you are faced with a truly innocent human error, it is often possible to correct the record by simply going to the source and calmly explaining the situation. For errors that originate with a computer out of control, sometimes a human will be able to stop the machine—but other times no human will take responsibility and you will need to alter the machine's input in order to make its output to reflect the truth. On the other hand, serious malicious attacks may call for either an overwhelming counterattack or a careful strategy designed to avoid prodding the attacker into furthering his attack.

Many times, the websites that are relaying the false information will provide very strong hints as to whether the false information is an accidental mistake or part of an intentional attack. One very common source of accidental mistakes is "name collision"—an overlap of names between you and somebody else. If a nasty person has the same name as you, there is a risk of confusion that is nobody's fault but that could require a lot of cleaning up. This is an especially common problem for people with very popular names (sorry to all the Smiths, Joneses, Browns, and Millers out there—especially if you have a common first name). But the problem of identical names is real for people with unusual names, too; the risk of an accidental overlap is smaller, but the damage can be greater because viewers more likely to be confused (everyone knows that there are many Joe Smiths in the world, but not everyone realizes that there might be more than one Broogan Lina). To take a quick example of overlapping names, a professor at a major state university has the same name as an online defamation suspect at the same university. Some bloggers and reporters began to confuse the professor with the suspect, creating the risk of a self-reinforcing cycle—once one blog confused the two people, other bloggers simply repeated the same mistake after reading it on the first erroneous blog. But, through some hard work and quick action, the professor made sure that most news stories clarified the difference, and his personal online content further clarifies that there are two people sharing the same name at the university—and that he isn't suspect. His response to this problem would have been very different if he had discovered an intentional attack accusing him of online defamation.

On the other hand, sometimes it will be obvious that you are the victim of an intentional online attack; for example, a fabricated story about your doing some horrible act is usually strong evidence that somebody is out to get you. Real stories of intentional attacks of this form abound: business owners falsely accused of operating scams, teachers falsely accused of abuse, parents falsely accused of meddling, students falsely accused of cheating (or sleeping) their way to the top, and more. The tone of these sites often tells you something about the anger level of the person who wrote it; some attacks come in the form of simple comments in passing, but others are extensive rants repeated over and over again.

In the remainder of cases, it may be difficult to know at first glance whether negative content was intentionally fabricated or was posted accidentally. For example, an old-style Googlebomb—like the way that searching Google for "miserable failure" led to the official site of the White House—may be accidental (a glitch in the Google algorithm) or intentional (a plot by activists to make a political statement).

When you are faced with a smear (either accidental or intentional) that is repeated across many sites, you should always try to identify on which site (or sites) the smear was launched. In many ways, an online smear is like a virus: it starts in one place and then is spread person-to-person and site-to-site as users move around the Internet. In studying real viruses, epidemiologists call the first identified infection the "index case." Identifying the index case allows the scientists to start to figure out how the infection moved and to predict how the infection will spread in the future. The same is true of online smears; identifying the index case will help you to understand how it is being spread around the Internet and thus help you to stop its spread. When you are searching, try to find the instance of the smear with the earliest date. This is almost always a good candidate to be the first incidence. You can also look to see if other sites are all linking back toward one site, which itself does not link back further; that site again might be the earliest. If the smear looks like it may have originated on a social reference site like Wikipedia, then check the history of the offensive page—many sites (including Wikipedia) keep very detailed logs of every edit to an article; all you need to do is find the first edit that adds the offensive material.

Finding the first site can affect the many forms of automatic re-production that replicate smears and scams across the Internet. For example, many encyclopedia sites (and also some "link spam" sites) automatically copy their information from Wikipedia; if you can fix Wikipedia, you can fix a slew of other sites that automatically copy it. To fix Wikipedia, you will often have to identify and correct any sources that Wikipedia is using as a source, but fixing Wikipedia is often worth it because it will abruptly stop many self-reinforcing loops and save you a lot of headaches.

Step 2: Make a Plan

Now that you understand the status of your online reputation, you can start to develop a plan to repair it. The process of planning your reputation recovery begins with the same kind of reputation road map described in Chapter 10. However, you will supplement the road map with specific information relevant to the attack you have suffered. This will transform your reputation road map into a recov-ery road map.

To develop your recovery road map, start with the same exercise described in Chapter 10: Identify each audience that might be search-ing for you, identify the means each audience might use to search for you, and take note of particular keywords it might use to find you.

Then, note how the false negative information affects those goals. Is it visible to all audiences or just to some? Is it very prominent in some searches but less visible in others?

Next, create a set of recovery goals so that you can prioritize your reputation repair efforts. If you have been the victim of multiple smears (or even one smear spread across many sites), what negative content is creating the largest problem for you—is there one attack that is most visible? What audience is most important to you? What audience is most affected by the smear?

When prioritizing, also consider possible responses to the smear. It is very easy to debunk some smears: for example, it is very easy to debunk a rumor that somebody did not graduate from college (just upload some graduation photos) or is deceased (don't laugh, it has happened to celebrities and private individuals alike). In those cases, it may be a sufficient response to make sure that the debunking is more prominent in a search than the false allegation. That is a relatively easy task to achieve. In contrast, some smears are difficult (if not impossible) to disprove: for example, it is often impossible to disprove a false allegation of infidelity. In those cases, you may have to build a Google wall around the negative content in order to make it less prominent or try to remove it at its source.

Be realistic when making your goals. Because of the nature of the Internet, it can be impossible to remove all evidence of a smear. Often, the best you can do is to make it practically invisible by replacing it in a Google search with positive content—very few people look past the first page of Google, so you can effectively hide false negative information by banishing it to the depths of a Google search. Remember that some sites—especially news sites and the most important blogs—tend to show up very well in a Google search; it may be impossible to completely exile these sites from the first ten Google results, or it may take much more concerted effort. And, if you are facing an intentional attack, always remember that the attacker may post new offensive content, especially if you counterattack her directly.

Step 3: Implement Your Plan

Now it is time to put your plan in action. No matter what, you will want to use the same general tools described in Chapter 11 to claim your online identity and to start to build positive content that will be visible in Google. These tools will help you displace any kind of negative content and help build positive information that will drown out the echoes of any negative content that survives your counterattack.

Steps for Responding to Accidental Content

The social Internet works like a giant machine that has been assembled by thousands of people working from opposite sides of the world without any coordination. Usually, the parts work together well, and the right information is delivered to the right places. But, every now and then the machine goes spectacularly wrong, and completely false information is copied from one site to another in a self-reinforcing cycle. User profiles are created, tagged, and distributed without human intervention or quality assurance. A fact that is obviously wrong can be accepted by a machine without question and copied onward ad infinitum.

When this happens to you, your best bet is often to try to find a human being responsible for one of the broken parts and to try to put the brakes on the machine. The best way to do so is to try to identify the path through which the false information is spreading. If you can find one site that is at a crucial juncture in the cycle, fixing that site may stop the cycle and stop the information from spreading.

Often, automated sites have a button or a link that says something along the lines of "flag this page for review" or "mark as offensive." Using these buttons is often a good start, especially if clicking the button gives you access to a form or an e-mail template that allows you to explain the problem. When you explain the problem, speak as calmly and rationally as possible. Explain the situation in a way that would help an outsider with no familiarity with you or the problem. Give all of the details that are necessary to solve the problem: the

URL of the page with a problem, your name, the exact problem, and so on. Support your request with links to verifiable information that agrees with your version of events. Avoid blaming the webmaster, avoid making extreme allegations about how the false information got started, and avoid calling anybody lazy or negligent. Instead, explain how the information is false, and try to work positively to fix it.

You may be shocked, outraged, angry, and offended to find false information about you online. These feelings are legitimate. However, you must control them when you are working to fix your online reputation. This is especially true when you are contacting other people to recruit their assistance in solving your online reputation crisis. Think about the problem from their perspective: they don't know you, they may not know anything about the problem, and they almost certainly receive many requests to fix things every day. Many webmasters and site administrators are reasonable and are happy to work with the rare person who carefully explains the situation, explains why the content is false, and makes a clear request.

On the other hand, if you e-mail a webmaster using an angry or accusatory tone, then she may just choose to ignore you—or she may even make the problem worse by highlighting the problematic content. In other words, the old adage applies to online reputation as much as to anything else: you get more positive results online with honey than with vinegar.

See the sample letter on the next page.

Unfortunately, many sites do not make it easy to get in touch with a human being; one of the main attributes of online sites is that they don't require constant staff presence (unlike a retail store, which must have a handful of staff around anytime it is open). If you encounter a site that makes it hard to contact an administrator, try to find the e-mail address of a human who might be responsible: Look in any "about us" pages or even through investor documents if available. If you still haven't had any luck, try a generic e-mail address such as "administrator@," "webmaster@," "info@," "help@," or "admin@" plus the domain (e.g., "administrator@wildwest2.com"). If

Dear Webmaster,

I appreciate the time you've spent building PeopleTagger.com. I was browsing your site, and I noticed that it looks like there has been an error. At http://peopletagger.com/JoeSmith/ there is a computer-generated profile of me, Joe Smith. However, it looks like the algorithm has combined two different people. I am the Joe Smith that lives in Reno, NV, and I work in the finance industry. You can see my work profile and photo at http://megacorp.com/bios/JoeSmith.html to verify. But the PeopleTagger algorithm appears to have added information about a different Joe Smith who lives in Las Vegas and was convicted of casino robbery. A quick glance at the mug shot of that Joe Smith, available at http://vegassun.com/news/2004/2/24/casino_robbery.html, will make clear that he and I are different people. I was hoping that you could correct the profile at PeopleTagger to reflect the existence of two Joe Smiths in Nevada. Again, I really appreciate your help and your hard work on the site and I'd be happy to provide any more information you need.

Sincerely,

Joe Smith

those addresses fail, try using a domain name lookup tool like Whois.net to see if the website has provided an e-mail address with its domain name registration. Or search Google for a customer service name or telephone number; for example, many websites listed the customer service phone number for Amazon.com long before Amazon.com made it publicly available.

If you still cannot find a human being to talk to, or if a human cannot (or will not) fix the problem, then you're on your own. To the extent possible, try to figure out where the website is drawing its data, and try to put correct (or positive) data in that stream: for example, if a personal profile site has an incorrect description of you, you may be able to fix that by claiming your online identity. Otherwise, you'll just have to build a Google wall around the false negative content.

Steps for Responding to an Attacker

Malicious attacks present unique dangers, but also unique opportunities for resolution. The first step is to think about the seriousness of the attack you are facing. Some malicious attacks are just one-off events triggered by an attacker's need to vent frustrations or by a juvenile desire to create mischief; these types of attacks often fade away quickly and can be easily resolved. But other attackers are dedicated and persistent, with a deep-seated grudge toward their victims. These attackers are particularly dangerous because they may continue to spread their smears no matter what you do or say—and they may become even bolder if they know that you are fighting back.

Identify Your Attacker

If possible, you should identify your attacker. Knowing your attacker will give you insight into his methods and the risk of future attacks. Sometimes, you will be able to work the problem out with your attacker offline; often, online attacks start with relatively trivial offline insults that can easily be worked out face-to-face. Other times, your attacker may fear retribution once identified and may give up his campaign to smear you.

Sometimes the identity of your attacker will be obvious: If a blogger working under his real name takes out a grudge on you, then it will be a simple matter to identify the blogger. But, other times, the identity of your attacker will be less obvious: If you are attacked through a forum post under a pseudonym (e.g., "Auburn1234"), it might not immediately make clear who your attacker is.

Even if your attacker is not working under his real name, you can still put clues together to identify the person. Some attackers reveal themselves by repeating information that only a handful of people know; if only two people were present at a meeting and the details of that meeting are revealed online, you'll have a pretty good clue as to the identity of your attacker. Or, if an attacker posts photos of your house, then the angle of the photo (from a neighbor's yard) or some subtle details (is there a reflection of the photographer's car?) might give it away. Even the pseudonyms chosen by your attacker might be a clue: the (fictional) example of "Auburn1234" might be a giveaway if you know a potential enemy who grew up in Georgia.

That said, be very careful not to fall for red herrings. A technically savvy attacker might try to impersonate somebody else in order to throw you off the trail or to try to smear two enemies at once. This tactic is as old as war itself: For thousands of years, governments have tried to neutralize two threats at once by inciting war between them.

If the online clues still don't add up to an identity, you still might be able to find the real name of your attacker through legal process. Attackers inevitably leave digital fingerprints on their work. One of the most important digital fingerprints is the attacker's IP address, which is often stored by the websites that the attacker visits. However, for reasons described later in this chapter, the legal process is time-consuming and expensive and may not be worthwhile in all cases.

Choose Your Strategy

You are faced with three options when responding to an attacker: fighting back directly (e.g., by responding directly to defamatory messages), trying to resolve the conflict offline (e.g., through negotiation or through legal action), or trying to isolate the negative content indirectly (e.g., by building Google walls around the negative content). Fighting back and offline conflict resolution both offer a chance of completely repairing your online reputation, but they also create a risk that the attacker will dig in deeper and increase her efforts to attack. In some ways, fighting back against an attacker is a lot like a military conflict: As succinctly framed by President Clinton, fighting a conflict is a good idea only if the conflict can be won and if you possess superior firepower that can destroy the enemy (rather than just inspiring the enemy to fight back harder).[2]

There is no generalized guide to making this decision; each situation is unique and requires careful consideration. Start by considering who your attacker is: If you know the attacker, consider his personality, his motivations, and what attack resources he has access to (e.g., whether he is a member of a large online community that might support further attacks). If you are being attacked by a group, you may want to be extremely cautious about doing anything that might anger the group: Even if you are legally and morally right, a group may be so blinded by a mob mentality that it will continue to attack you no matter how reasonable and rational you are.

No matter what, you should very rarely argue with an attacker. An attacker may be behaving completely unreasonably. The attacks may make you mad, and justifiably so. But starting (or continuing) an argument will make you look unreasonable to outside observers, no matter how right you may be. It is often said that the person who remains the calmest during an argument is perceived as the winner; this is just as true online as off. Further, an argument draws attention to the conflict; most online smears are not very interesting to observers, but an online argument transforms an obscure smear into a fascinating human-interest story.

Instead, simply do a better job than your attacker at creating and distributing content. If you create more positive content than he creates negative, you will have an advantage that will be multiplied when more people find your positive content than find the attacker's negative content. Your goal is to make the smear obscure; you can do it with positive content, or you can just hide it under neutral or unrelated content. One of the most effective ways to create a Google wall is to just flood the Internet with unrelated content that relates to you but doesn't obviously flatter or diminish you. In particular, see the tips in Chapter 11 regarding positive and neutral content. Create profiles on free social sites like Facebook, LinkedIn, Plaxo, and Naymz; these sites often appear very well on searches and don't repeat the smear. If you have any interests that generate passion among their adherents—such as environmentalism, fashion, car modification, sports teams, or the like—then investigate creating publicly visible blogs or profiles on sites related to your interests.

Identify Content to Try to Neutralize or Remove

In some cases, you may be able to remove some intentional false content from third-party websites such as discussion forums, business review sites, and blog hosts. Use the same careful tone described earlier in the sample letter. Some webmasters will be receptive, and others will not. For example, Google runs the blog service BlogSpot.com. Google's policy is that it will remove blogs that contain private personal information such as your home address or phone number, but it will never remove blogs simply because they contain false smears or defamation. On the other hand, some "attack sites" will never remove content because they thrive on the creation of controversy. Most sites are somewhere in the middle: You have a chance of getting content removed (or at least your side of the story appended) if you are polite, tell a compelling story, offer to help, and show empathy for the webmaster's situation (namely that the webmaster has been thrown into the position of arbitrating a dispute between strangers).

What About Wikipedia?

Wikipedia is the largest and most important reference site on the Internet. It is used by everyone from students to journalists as an authoritative reference source. But, unlike a traditional encyclopedia, Wikipedia allows anyone to create and edit articles about anything. Right now, you could go on Wikipedia and contribute your knowledge (on any topic ranging from the development of model railroading in the early 1900s, to analysis of the current political situation in Nicaragua, to news about the antics of celebrities). This "anyone goes" attitude has collected a mind-boggling amount of information in one place; allowing user contributions has created the largest encyclopedia in history.

But this model has also created huge problems for many private individuals who have been falsely attacked through Wikipedia. Anybody with a grudge can edit a Wikipedia article and insert false information or insinuations. Biographical pages about living persons are supposed to go through additional layers of review before becoming public, but it is not clear that the oversight is effective in rooting out anything beyond the most obvious attacks. False information on Wikipedia can often create a negative self-reinforcing cycle: a blogger reads false information on Wikipedia, the blogger copies the false information into her blog, and then later a Wikipedia editor uses the false information in the blog to "prove" that the false information in Wikipedia is correct. The cycle gets even worse when professional journalists rely on Wikipedia for information.

Fortunately, there is a process in place to help resolve online smears against living people (like you). However, the process is sometimes difficult to work, and you must take into account the sometimes strange culture of Wikipedia when using it; simply barging in and demanding that things be changed is a sure way to turn the community against you and make the problem worse. The same goes for simply removing the information yourself: slicing large parts out of a Wikipedia entry will likely attract the attention of an administrator, who may not understand that you are fixing a smear.

Your strategy for fixing false information on Wikipedia will depend on how the smear occurs. If somebody has created a false Wikipedia article about you, it might be possible to remove the entire article. Wikipedia is intended to contain articles only for famous people. If you are not "notable" (Wikipedia jargon for people who are sufficiently famous to warrant an entry), then the article will be deleted once an administrator notices it. If the problem is severe, take the problem directly to the group of administrators responsible for biographies. Their contact information is available at http://en.wikipedia.org/wiki/Wikipedia:Contact_us/Article_problem/Factual_error_(from_subject). The contact page describes what is expected, but it is worth repeating a few points. First, the administrators will not remove a page simply because you demand it. Instead, explain the problem in simple terms. In particular, if relevant, explain why you are not sufficiently "notable" to merit a Wikipedia article. Here's a sample:

Dear Wikipedia administrators:

I am a local businessperson with no national fame, no national news coverage, and I am generally of no interest to encyclopedia readers. It looks like an article was created about me on Wikipedia at [URL]. The article contains several false allegations that have not been sourced. I would propose the article be deleted from Wikipedia pursuant to Wikipedia's notability policy. I would be happy to provide any additional information. Thank you very much for your help.

If you are sufficiently notable to merit an article, you may not be able to get the article removed entirely. For example, if you have been involved in a high-profile news incident or have achieved some degree of national fame (or notoriety), Wikipedia editors will be unlikely to delete the entire article. But, you may still be able to remove false smears and allegations from the article. If the smear is obviously vandalism (for example, an all-caps "JOE SMITH IS A H8R" in the middle of an otherwise factual article) then you may remove it yourself. Create a Wikipedia account (be honest and use your own name), click the "Edit" button on the page you want to fix, and remove the vandalism.[3] There is a guide for new editors that walks you step by step through the editing process here: http://en.wikipedia.org/wiki/Wikipedia:How_to_edit_a_page . You may also remove false allegations about you that are not backed up by any sources: Because Wikipedia is an encyclopedia, all facts must be verified by links to outside sources. If there is a false allegation in a Wikipedia article about you, you may immediately remove it if there is no link to a reliable outside source.[4]

But, *use extreme caution* if you attempt to remove false information that has a link to an outside source, even if you know that the outside source is completely and obviously wrong. Wikipedia policies make it difficult for people to make serious edits on articles about themselves. Self-edits will draw the ire of administrators and may result in your account being locked and your changes being undone. When you make the change to the article, remove the false content and *explain why* in the "talk" page for the article; give links to verifiable and reliable sources that show why the information is false. Do not add any new positive content about yourself; it is sure to look biased. If another editor undoes your changes, *do not start an "edit war"* where two (or more) editors repeatedly undo each others' changes. Instead, you may need to seek administrative help. The fastest way to achieve resolution is to post a note on the "Biographies of Living People" noticeboard with a clear and concise explanation of why the article is wrong, along with verifiable and reliable outside sources to support your claims. Do not make allegations about other editors, do not start a personal conflict, and do not be drawn into the personal battles that are an inevitable part of collaborative editing at a site like Wikipedia. Instead, be calm and rational, and use objective facts to help fix your problem. If all else fails, you may contact the Wikipedia legal department, but this is an absolute last resort and will foreclose all other forms of resolution, many of which may be faster and easier.

There are also many other Wikipedia policies that can be used to remove false information about you, but these policies (and their enforcement) are constantly shifting. You may need to resort to expert help if you believe that your Wikipedia entry is fatally flawed but the problem is more complex than just obvious vandalism. If possible, commit to professional help *before* you try to edit yourself; once you have edited yourself, you may draw more attention to the page, and administrators may be suspicious of any future edits that attempt to fix its content.

In the end, you may not be able to completely remove all false information if there are outside sources that appear to support it (no matter how wrong those outside sources may be). In that case, your best bet may be to balance the false negative information with truthful positive information. Doing so will make the negative information less noticeable and may prevent other people from relying on the negative information.

Use these same principles to guide your efforts to resolve other issues that arise when your name appears on other pages within Wikipedia, such as in articles about news events and companies. If your name is not essential to the story, you may be able to have it removed on the basis of the "notability" criteria. If your name appears only as a result of vandalism ("Joe Smith stole my wallet" in the middle of a completely unrelated article), you may remove it yourself. Use extreme caution when editing information related to yourself that is not obvious vandalism; you may draw the ire of editors who are constantly on the watch for changes that attempt to hide true information.

You should *never* create a Wikipedia article about yourself or add substantially to one that has been posted. No matter how objective you try to be, your edits will inevitably be seen as biased by other editors. Your edits may be undone, your account may be locked, and the page that you were attempting to fix may even be tagged as "biased." Nothing good can come of such an effort. Instead, if you must, provide information on the article's "talk" page that other editors may choose to integrate into the article. You can provide positive resources (such as positive news stories) that can help other editors create a balanced profile of you.

Should I Sue My Attacker?

When faced with extreme online defamation, some people consider a lawsuit against their attackers. After all, the standards for defamation online are the same as those that apply offline: if you are a private individual and an attacker has maliciously spread a hurtful lie about you, the attacker may be liable for defamation. But, as many recent cases have shown, the legal process is slow and often does not lead to a satisfactory resolution. Online defamation is much harder to solve through legal action than is traditional libel by a newspaper or slander by a TV station.

No book can substitute for the advice of a licensed lawyer practicing in your jurisdiction, who will be aware of local laws that may impact your case. There are, however, several common themes that apply across all jurisdictions.

First, it is often difficult to find the attacker. Many online attackers hide behind a pseudonym or even create their attacks completely anonymously. In some cases, it may be possible to track down a pseudonymous or anonymous attacker through technical means, such as by using electronic "fingerprints" to try to match an IP address to an ISP subscriber. But, trying to play whodunit online can be as hard as solving real-world crimes with no eyewitnesses; sometimes electronic fingerprints lead to a suspect, but other times the trail runs cold. It may take a substantial investment in time, energy, and money to begin the process of tracking down a suspect, just to find out that the person has disappeared into the online shadows.

Second, a lawsuit may not bring resolution even if you find the person who defamed you. The person you sue may be broke ("judgment-proof," in the jargon of lawyers) and unable to pay a single dollar in damages. She also may not be able to remove or fix the smears she created; it may be too late to put the genie back in the bottle. Once a smear goes online, it often takes on a life of its own outside the control of the original attacker. Even if the original attacker wants to help fix the problem, it may be too late to take it back: the smear may have been copied-and-pasted by bloggers, linked to from Web discussion forums, or picked up by Google Cache, or it may have found a permanent home in the Internet Archive. The act of suing may even make the problem worse: The so-called Streisand Effect describes the fact that attempts to remove content from the Internet often inspire other bloggers to copy the content and make it more prominent. In these cases, there is nothing that the attacker can do to take the content back; it is out of her control. The attacker cannot force Google to remove links to the smear and often cannot force other bloggers to remove it.

Third, lawsuits often take years to finish. Justice may be blind, but it is also incredibly slow. Filing a lawsuit can create years of stress before reaching a resolution, and it may require an extensive commitment of time or money from you to support your lawyers.

On the other hand, there is a strong sense of vindication that comes from winning in court, and a victory in court can serve as proof that the smears are inaccurate. News coverage of your victory will often displace the false negative content in Google results. You will also be helping to clean up the Internet and to make it clear to online bullies and harassers that their conduct will not be tolerated. To give just one example, education counselor Sue Scheff won a multimillion-dollar lawsuit against an online harasser. She and Internet expert John Dozier wrote about the lawsuit and the additional steps she took to clear her reputation in the book *Google Bomb*.[5]

Discuss your situation with a licensed attorney with experience in Internet-based defamation. In some situations, a lawsuit may be a viable part of a larger strategy to manage online defamation—the lawsuit may lead to direct redress, and it may also send a very strong signal that you believe the attack to be entirely false and are willing to go to court to prove it. This strategy is especially powerful when you can objectively disprove the content of the attack: News reporters looking for an Internet story may be able to verify the falsity of the attack against you and help spread the word, and you can help echo their words by creating your own positive content. Ask your lawyer what the chances of success legally are, and then consider what the reputation effect might be. A lawsuit alone is rarely enough to solve an online reputation problem, but it may be a part of a successful strategy.

Why Can't I Sue Google?

Many people who have been attacked online are angry at Google for linking to an obviously false attack. But, unfortunately, there is nothing that can be done under current U.S. law. No search engine has ever been held liable in the United States for defamation because it has linked to online attacks. No Web discussion forum or blog host (such as Google's Blogspot or the independent site LiveJournal) has been held liable for attacks posted by other users on its site. This situation is a sharp contrast from that pertaining to offline law, where newspapers can be held liable for the content of false or defamatory advertisements that they run.

In the United States, the difference is largely the result of a federal law known as Section 230 of the Communications Decency Act of 1996. So far, U.S. courts have held that the law completely exempts websites from liability for the actions of their users—including defamation and other torts against private individuals. But there are some signs that this is starting to change. Several high-visibility online attacks have highlighted the strange results of Section 230, and Congress is beginning to reconsider the broad grant of immunity to websites. Other regions of the world, including Brazil and the European Union, allow lawsuits against online intermediaries; the Internet has not come crashing to a halt in those places, and Congress is taking note of their examples.

Removing Content from Archives

Information on the Internet is often automatically cached and archived in a variety of ways. The impact is that smears on one site may be stored on other sites without any human intervention. These copies of the original smear can live on long past the original.

Several archived copies of smears will expire on their own, with no need for intervention in most circumstances. For example, Google automatically stores a copy of web pages and automatically deletes the stored copy if the underlying page is deleted or altered. Normally this process occurs on its own, but it may take several weeks for Google to discover that the underlying page has been altered or removed. You may speed up the process by following this link: https://www.google.com/webmasters/tools/removals?pli=1. If the offensive page has been removed entirely, then choose the option for an "outdated or dead link" and provide the requested details. The only other way that Google will remove a page from its index is if it contains your social security number, bank account number, or credit card number. These requests can be submitted at the same URL, but choose the "remove information" link instead.

On the other hand, some copies are permanent. The "Wayback Machine" at Archive.org makes permanent copies of historic web pages. If you would like a page removed from the Wayback Machine, you will need help from the owner of the site where the page used to reside (for example, if you were smeared at [fictional] "bloghost.com/nastysite," you would need help from the owner of "bloghost.com"). Instruct the webmaster to use the guide at http://www.archive.org/about/exclude.php to retroactively remove the negative content. If you are unable to get a webmaster's help, your job is much more difficult; the Wayback Machine claims to support only automated requests. But, there is a human editor who may be amenable to requests to remove pages that display personal information, especially if that information was given in confidence. It never hurts to try to send a polite email explaining the problem and to try to work toward a resolution: info@archive.org.

Notes

1. The cartoon never specifies what the other half is. *G.I. Joe: A Real American Hero* (1980s television program). The catchphrase is still in use in current pop culture. **Go:** http://wildwest2.com/go/1007.

2. Unnamed Wikipedia contributors, "The Clinton Doctrine," *Wikipedia.* **Go:** http://wildwest2.com/go/1008.

3. As of this writing, removing vandalism was approved behavior for users themselves. See the Wikipedia policy statement here: **Go:** http://wildwest2.com/go/1009.

4. Ibid.

5. Sue Scheff, *Google Bomb: The Untold Story of the $11.3M Verdict That Changed the Way We Use the Internet* (Deerfield, Fla: Health Communications, 2009).

CHAPTER

Protect Your Small Business and Your Professional Reputation

Small businesses and professionals face unique online challenges to their reputations. In addition to facing all of the concerns shared by private individuals, most small businesses and professionals make their living on their reputation. One study found that reputation damage is a bigger risk to most companies than natural disaster or even terrorism.[1] After all, a careful backup plan can avert most harms caused by an earthquake or fire, but damage to a reputation is long-lasting and often permanent. A different survey found that corporate executives thought it would take an average of 3.5 years to fully recover from a damaged business reputation.[2]

The risk for small businesses and professionals is even more severe because their reputations are constantly being shaped by interactions with customers, the media, and others. Any customer or client may end up being dissatisfied with your product or work—whether fairly or unfairly—and take that dissatisfaction out online through an online smear campaign. In short, your reputation is your living, and every customer interaction creates a risk of ruining it.

Fortunately, there are solutions for small businesses and professionals that can minimize the risk and help them get out in front of the dangers.

Identifying Your Online Reputation Goals

The process of identifying business reputation goals echoes the process of identifying personal reputation goals. Think about all the groups that interact with your business: suppliers, employees, potential customers, the news media, community leaders, the government, and others. Which of these audiences is most important to you? A retail business will probably focus on its customers, but an industrial business may prioritize on its image in front of community leaders and government so as to reduce the risk of getting a bad reputation on environmental or labor issues.

Also consider circumstances special to your industry or business. For example, if you are an online merchant, you will likely want to present your best image of reliability and trustworthiness to Google-savvy customers who will use Google to search for reviews and information about products. One trick for improving the Google image of an online retail business is to offer coupons. A coupon—preferably in the form of an online discount code (most e-commerce applications are set up to handle them)—will trigger a cascade of links and mentions from hundreds of websites that sort and distribute coupon codes to viewers. Some of these sites show up high in Google searches and can serve as an extra way to drive traffic toward your business.

Dealing with Criticism

Businesses and professionals frequently receive reviews and ratings that would be unheard of for individuals; consumers think nothing of posting a scathing review of your professional services, even if their review also calls your personal character into doubt. These review sites can be a boon or a bust for your reputation: positive reviews will be seen as proof of the quality of your business, but negative reviews may send consumers flocking to competitors.

For example, there are at least ten popular sites dedicated to reviewing businesses and services—Yelp and Citysearch lead the pack for retail and restaurants, while Angie's List leads for professional services. It is incredibly easy for consumers to post a review on these sites, and little verification is done to make sure that the consumer's review is accurate or complete. Because of their popularity, these sites often show up at the top of Google search results. Google has even begun to integrate consumer review sites directly into the search process for retail businesses and may soon follow suit for services; if it does so, reviews will be an even more prominent part of your online résumé.

Do not panic if you receive a negative or critical review. Criticism is a normal part of being in business, and a healthy part of a competitive economy. It is inevitable that, at some point, a customer or client will be dissatisfied. It might be your fault, or your suppliers' fault, or nobody's fault at all: Many times, consumer dissatisfaction stems from some external cause over which you have no control. But, no matter the reason, in the Internet age, a dissatisfied customer is likely to turn to the Internet to vent his frustrations.

No matter what you do, you probably cannot remove all criticism of your business or profession from the Internet. Even if it were possible to remove all criticism, it might not be a good idea to do so: Criticism can help inspire you to improve your business by inspiring you to alter your policies or by changing consumer expectations surrounding your business. But, just as important to a practical business owner, it is simply impossible to remove much criticism from the Internet, and attempts to do so will often make the problem worse.

The Air Force has developed a useful flowchart that shows some important factors for businesses and professionals to consider when responding to online criticism (see Figure 13-1). The chart was designed for use by the Air Force, but it successfully identifies many factors that will be the same for businesses. In short, the chart recommends not responding if the criticism is a "troll" (seeking attention through extreme behavior) or a "rant" (motivated by anger and not logic). The chart also recommends against responding unless you can clearly show that the criticism is incorrect; otherwise, you run the risk of drawing more attention to the troublesome content without significantly advancing your cause.

If you choose to respond, you must maintain a calm tone and a helpful demeanor. Be honest about who you are and why you are writing. Always make sure that you come across as helpful and calm, and never engage in personal attacks. If the consumer directs personal attacks at you, just ignore them and move on; responding gives legitimacy to the attacks and draws more attention to them. Never attempt to blame the consumer, even in cases in which the problem really is her fault because she misused a product or had unrealistic expectations of your services. When you respond, carefully explain what steps you took to resolve the problem, such as offering to refund the customer's money or to provide a replacement. If the problem relates to the consumer's expectations (e.g., if he complains that the chainsaw he bought from you broke when he used it for demolition work), explain how the customer's expectations should have been set (e.g., that the chainsaw box clearly says that the tool is not for demolition work and that you would have advised the consumer to purchase a different tool—such as a reciprocating saw—for that job if he had asked).

In some cases, it may make business sense to make an unusually generous offer to resolve the problem, even if you would not do so for most customers. For example, if you have a strict "all sales are final"

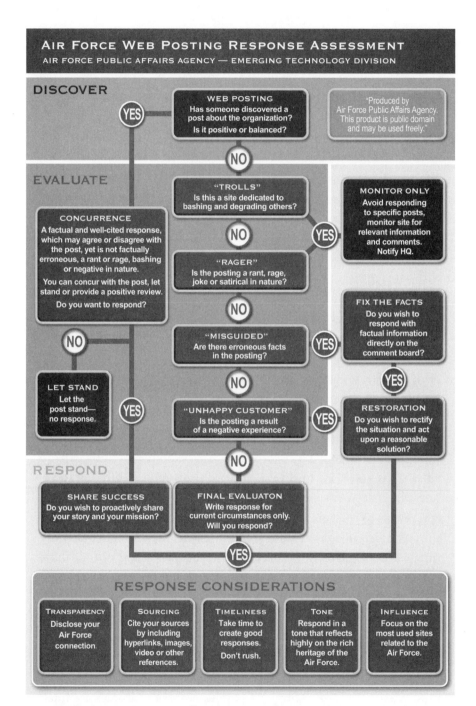

Figure 13-1. U.S. Air Force Blog Response Chart. Credit: U.S. Air Force.

policy, you might consider making an exception to it if you are faced with an angry customer who has begun to blog extensively about her complaint, especially if she has made contact with a powerful consumer-oriented blog or reviewer. If you have been contacted by a consumer blog site, especially a heavily trafficked site, it may be wise to offer a careful explanation of what steps you took to resolve the problem and then to make another generous offer to fix it; again, be sure that your tone is calm and moderate and that you do not attack the consumer. (When in doubt, you can check a site's popularity with tools like Alexa.com; if a site is among the top 10,000 global sites, it is extremely powerful; a site that is among the top 20,000 is still somewhat powerful, especially if it is focused on a region or industry.)

Online Threats Unique to Businesses and Professionals: Complaint Sites and Hoaxes

While many consumer review sites are important parts of a healthy consumer economy, not all purported consumer review sites run reputable businesses. Some businesspeople discovered that threats to a business's reputation can serve as a form of blackmail and set up sham review sites designed to bait businesses into paying effectively protection money. The idea is simple in theory: Create a sham review site, encourage users to post harsh critiques of businesses, make sure the negative reviews appear in Google, and then offer the affected business an expensive "investigative service" to remove the negative review. If the business owner doesn't pay up, the negative reviews remain prominent in Google. The pure form of this scheme is extortion and is outright illegal, but many sites tinkered with ideas around the margins of it—especially because Section 230 of the Communications Decency Act immunizes websites against liability for the content of reviews posted by users. For example, recent lawsuits have alleged that the site RipoffReport.com operates an extortionate business by encouraging negative reports and charging businesses money to rebut them; no court has yet found RipoffReport liable, but there are several cases pending, and RipoffReport is alleged to have changed some of its practices following the litigation.[3]

Businesses are particularly vulnerable to hoaxes and urban legends. Urban legends about a business can spread through e-mail, discussion sites, and even face-to-face conversations. These stories can spread especially quickly because they are often colorful tales that play on our expectations about a business or industry. As evidence of just how common these myths are, a large section of the urban-myth-debunker website Snopes.com is dedicated to myths about major corporations: For example, that there wasn't really a finger in Wendy's chili (the customer put the finger there and was sentenced to nine years in prison for attempted grand larceny),[4] that Starbucks refuses to ship coffee to Iraq (it ships coffee to every place where U.S. soldiers are stationed),[5] that Starbucks offered an online coupon for a free drink in 2004 (a hoaxster made the coupon up and spread it online without any company involvement),[6] or that the Coca-Cola Company allows people to redeem the pull tabs on its soda cans for charity dialysis treatments (the pull tab has the same scrap value as the rest of the can, and the rumor is surprisingly persistent despite the fact that Coca-Cola has no program to provide any redemption for the tabs).[7]

If you have been the victim of an online hoax or urban legend, your best bet is often to get ahead of the rumor as quickly as possible. Many major corporations have "rumor response teams" that are dedicated to extinguishing myths before they become self-sustaining; you are unlikely to have a large staff to dedicate to the project, but you can still stage an effective intervention if you are willing to put in a little elbow grease. Your first step should be to clearly debunk the rumor on your own website: Explain in a calm, rational tone why the rumor is false and try to provide verifiable facts. If you cannot yet prove that the rumor is false, find a creative way to show how confident you are that it is wrong: for example, Wendy's offered a reward of $50,000 to anybody who could identify the source of the finger in the chili, even if it came from inside Wendy's. Wendy's was vindicated when it became clear that the customer herself had added it. Make the link to this rebuttal prominent on your company's homepage: Many users will come to your company's website to verify or disprove the rumor, and you need to make the answer easy for them to find.

Next, contact any news organizations or blogs that have repeated the rumor and ask them to publish a clarification or correction. Again, use a calm and rational tone to explain why the rumor is wrong and maybe even why it is hurting your business. The goal is to set the record straight so that future reporters and readers do not incorrectly rely on early news stories; the more doubt you can inject into the earlier stories, the less trouble you will have convincing later writers to verify both sides of the story.

Next, you may want to set up a system for dealing with comments from the public. If the rumor is particularly scandalous, it is likely to trigger a fair number of complaints and comments. Use the same techniques to handle these: for e-mail or postal messages, send back a form letter that calmly explains why the rumor is false and presents as many verifiable facts as possible. For telephone complaints, you may wish to instruct employees to direct callers to the website; doing so reduces the risk of a telephone argument or a large waste of staff time. If your business is being harassed—such as by the sending of "loop faxes" or autodialer phone calls—you may wish to work with the local telephone company to identify the source of the problem.

Some hoaxes can take the form of manipulated photos or images, such as a photograph of a fast food sign edited to say something offensive or a composite of several events in one photograph. The same rules apply: Get out in front, provide a prominent rebuttal, and explain fully what really happened. The easiest way to defuse a modified image is to find the (unedited) source image that provided the base for the manipulation. If your rebuttal shows the original and modified images side-by-side, most viewers will be easily convinced. Often, digital attackers simply combine images they found through Google, which can make it easy to find the original: try searching Google

Image Search (http://images.google.com) using keywords related to what appears in the photo. If you find a close match, try Google's experimental "similar images" tool to look for other candidates (http://similar-images.googlelabs.com). You may also want to try so-called reverse image search tools like TinEye.com, which allow you to upload an image (the attack image) and search for similar-appearing images anywhere on the Internet. By analyzing the attack image, a site like TinEye may be able to find the original (unmodified) image. If you can't find the original image directly, it might be worth contacting an expert digital photographer (or even a digital forensics expert) to determine if there is any objective evidence of manipulation. Some sloppy image-editing techniques can leave obvious edges or strange blurs between parts of an image composite; if you can identify these signs, you may be able to convince others that the image is a fake.

Working Together to Fix Attacks

If other businesses have been impacted by attack similar to the one launched against your company, contact them and determine if you can work together to help overcome the problem. For example, if a new "ripoff site" begins to slander many businesses in your industry or area, it might be worth talking with the other victims to work toward a solution, perhaps even sharing the costs of litigation. Or, if other businesses have recovered from similar attacks, it may be worth contacting them to determine what tactics they used to achieve success. (Of course, if they failed to recover, it might be worth delicately inquiring to find out what tactics they used so that you can try different tactics yourself.) Our lawyers tell us that we are supposed to advise you to be careful about the antitrust implications of joining forces with competing businesses, but we think that in most cases there should be no problem with working together to overcome a persistent or nasty smear.

Special Tips for Professionals

If you are any kind of professional, your image is everything. A doctor cannot separate his personal image from his professional; a photo of a surgeon drunk when celebrating her fortieth birthday will have a negative impact on her practice, no matter how sober and careful she is almost every day of her life and always when she is at work. The same goes for false negative information about your personal life: A false smear against your personal character will inevitably affect your business.

Unfortunately, some aspects of recovery are more difficult for professionals than for private individuals. The more business-like you appear, the less sympathy you are likely to get from webmasters and others who are capable of helping to fix and remove false information. Webmasters of many sites are reasonable and want to help private individuals who have been slandered or wronged. But when it comes to professionals, their sympathy disappears, and they begin to fear that they are being played for financial gain. They may be completely wrong—a personal smear against a doctor hurts just as much as a baseless personal smear against a stay-at-home parent—but the two situations inspire completely different reactions in many website owners.

The same goes if you are a professional who has taken steps to be more visible in the public eye. If you are an actor or a model or the like, some people will say that you have decided to take the bad along with the good by putting yourself in the public eye. If you have done even some local advertising (think "The Mattress King of Weehawken" or any car dealership), some people will take it as an open invitation to attack you online—no matter how falsely or unfairly. You will get considerably less sympathy from webmasters and others who could help your cause. You can still try, but be extremely cautious and never say anything to a webmaster that you wouldn't be willing to put online: Spiteful webmasters have been known to post private e-mails in order to mock or undermine attempts to repair reputations.

Data Security for Professionals and Businesses

Reputation security begins at home . . . and work . . . and online . . . and anywhere else you store digital information.

Professionals and owners of small businesses face a double threat when it comes to data security: Often, they have digital files that contain their own personal information (such as their personal photos, their medical history, or their social security number, bank account numbers, and financial information), and they have also been entrusted with financial information that belongs to customers and clients. A failure of information can quickly lead to reputation damage for the individual, for the business, and for the business's clients. It is thus doubly important to focus on safe data-handling techniques.

The files and data that belong to many companies and individuals are not adequately protected from accidental or malicious disclosure. Some of these failures are due to user error, some are due to users taking insufficient precautions, and some are due to problems in the underlying technology. But, no matter the cause, a security breach can reveal very private or embarrassing facts, narratives, photos, and videos. Once revealed, this information can be used maliciously or just spread by users interested in saucy gossip of any kind. And, once that genie is out of the bottle, there is no way to put it back in.

Users themselves can accidentally trigger harm to their own reputation through security breaches. One of the most common mistakes made by users of file-sharing software (like Gnutella, Limewire, or Kazaa) is to make personal documents available to other users by placing them in the "shared" directory. The result is that other users of the network can view files that were never intended for public consumption. Some of these files might contain passwords or bank account information that would allow identity thieves to work. But other content might be embarrassing or incredibly private—ranging from personal diaries to intimate photos and videos. The easiest way to avoid this problem is to avoid the use of file-sharing software unless you are absolutely certain that you understand how it works and which files it will share. Be sure to double- (or even triple-) check the settings of the software to make sure that it is not sharing a directory or file that you want to keep private. And *never* place personal files in a directory that is used for filesharing.

Similarly, users can trigger reputation damage through security breaches by leaving their private files on a portable storage device ("thumb drive" or "flash drive") and then losing the portable storage device. If you walk into the nearest public library or Internet café, you will have at least a one in five chance of finding an abandoned flash drive or floppy disk near one of the computers. Some patrons are kind enough to return these abandoned drives to the "lost and found" office, but others are curious enough to start searching the contents of the drive. You can prevent this by making sure to never leave your drive in a public place. For more security, there are flash drives available that use password-based encryption to secure files against nosy strangers and even flash drives that require the owner's fingerprint to unlock the data.

When you dispose of or sell electronic devices, be sure to remove all sensitive data. Too many stories of data loss begin with a computer sold on eBay or Craigslist: Inevitably, the buyer starts poking around the hard drive and finds very personal information about the seller (or corporate records, or financial documents, or even medical histories). It is not enough to simply use the "recycle" command in Windows; it is extremely easy to recover many files that have been deleted through the recycle bin. Instead, either physically or digitally wipe the data on any hard drive you sell or trash. To physically destroy sensitive data, you can use a power drill to render any hard drive useless to all but the most determined of data thieves; the downside is that it renders the disk useless to the buyer, as well. Simply drill four holes all the way through the hard drive, being sure to puncture the round magnetized "platter" inside the drive. The holes will render the disk meaningless to all but the most sophisticated CIA-level recovery techniques. To digitally wipe data, use a "wiping" program like "BCWipe" that deletes files and then repeatedly overwrites them with random garbage. By overwriting the files with junk data, the program makes it difficult or impossible to recover files except through extremely advanced computer forensics. The advantage of digital wiping is that the drive can be used later; the disadvantage is that it is often a slow process that can take many hours.

Other security breaches occur when thieves steal passwords or access codes. One of the most common security breaches occurs when a user accidentally reveals her e-mail password by entering it in a "phishing" (fake) website designed to trick users. The scammers then have access to the victim's e-mail account (and possibly bank accounts) and can wreck financial or reputational havoc. The solution is simple: never trust a link that is sent by e-mail, especially if it appears to be from your bank or other financial institution. To help, many commercial antivirus programs now come with antiphishing "plug-ins" (helper programs) for Web browsers that alert users to potential scams; these programs are not perfect, but they can reduce the likelihood of falling for a fake e-mail.

Metadata embedded in documents have also created privacy and reputation problems. Many commercial editing systems, including the Microsoft Office™ suite, attempt to help users collaborate by automatically storing hidden information in documents. This information often includes the name of every person who edited a particular document. It also sometimes includes a revision history, including information or comments that various people removed before saving the final version of the document. This hidden information can easily be retrieved and analyzed, often revealing personal "notes to self" or embarrassing comments that should have been deleted from the file before it was made publicly available. To take a particularly colorful example, there is a website that specializes in showing cell-phone self-portraits of "hunky" men. But librarian and "Internet folk hero" Jessamyn West was among the first to make an example out of the fact that the website accidentally reveals far more information about its (purportedly) anonymous artists than intended.[8] The problem is that many of the men who submit photos use phones that automatically include the GPS coordinates of the photograph as part of the "metadata" attached to the image. Using the location information, it would be a simple matter to identify some of the models, especially for those in rural areas. For Microsoft Office documents, it is possible to avoid this problem by using Microsoft's "Remove Hidden Data" tool available at Microsoft.com: **Go:** http://wildwest2.com/go/1309. But many people are not aware of other metadata (like that in many cameraphone images), and there are not yet tools to zap all potentially embarassing metadata. Viruses, trojans, and worms can also lead to data security breaches. All three terms refer to different kinds of software infections: Viruses are malicious programs that have attached themselves to legitimate files, trojans are malicious programs that are designed to trick you into running them (like fake screensavers with ".exe" extensions that spread by e-mail), and worms are malicious programs that spread from computer to computer without user intervention (usually by taking advantage of security flaws in the Windows operating system). Some of these malicious programs simply display annoying advertisements. But others give hackers complete access to all the files on your hard drive, including any personal or confidential files. The best way to avoid falling victim to malicious software is to make sure to run an up-to-date virus scanning system, such as the free AVG system, available at http://free.avg.com, or any of the popular retail scanners from companies like Webroot or McAfee. Do not install software from unknown sources, and use extreme caution when downloading e-mail attachments; if somebody has sent you a file that ends with ".exe" that you weren't expecting, make sure that the person really meant to send it before you run it. Also, be sure to keep your operating system up to date; if you use Microsoft Windows, be sure to use the Windows Update tool to install the most recent security patches available.

Notes

1. Weber Shandwick, "Safeguarding Reputation" (Whitepaper) (2009). **Go**: http://wildwest2.com/go/1301.

2. Weber Shandwick, "Safeguarding Reputation (2)" (Whitepaper) (2009). **Go**: http://wildwest2.com/go/1302.

3. Among other sources, see Sarah Fenske, "The Real Rip-Off Report," *Phoenix New Times* January 31, 2007. **Go**: http://wildwest2.com/go/1303.

4. Snopes.com, "Finger in Wendy's Chili." **Go**: http://wildwest2.com/go/1304.

5. Snopes.com, "Starbucks Refuses Marines." **Go**: http://wildwest2.com/go/1305.

6. Snopes.com, "Starbucks Coupon." **Go**: http://wildwest2.com/go/1306.

7. Snopes.com, "Pull Tab Redemption Rumor." **Go**: http://wildwest2.com/go/1307.

8. Jessamyn West, "Social Software and Intellectual Freedom," conference talk (2009). **Go**: http://wildwest2.com/go/1308.

CHAPTER

Conclusion:
Embrace the Internet

The Internet has been one of the most powerful and disruptive technologies to emerge since the invention of the printing press. We are lucky to be able to watch its growth and development. And we all profit from the instantaneous universality of the Internet: We can research almost any topic that can be imagined, communicate with faraway friends and family, meet new people, and participate in online politics and discussion.

But this same power to instantly transmit information worldwide has also changed the rules of reputation. Thanks to the power of the Internet, everyday citizens now have more control over the reputations of their peers than at any other point in history: A single blogger working alone can make or break almost anybody's reputation. And the technology of the Internet means that people can work anonymously when shaping (or destroying) reputations.

The good news is that you can use these changes to your advantage. The Internet presents you with the opportunity to control and shape your own reputation. You can influence the information that people find about you and highlight your accomplishments and positive traits. Taking control of your reputation allows you to put your best foot forward online, whether or not you have been subject to attack. Building positive content now serves as a form of defense against negative content later—think of it as a necessary precaution, like insurance on your car or antivirus software for your computer. Building positive content also advances your image and standing in the community generally: Your online first impression is often your only first impression. If you run a small business, you can find new customers and improve the standing of your business in the community.

Anyway, the Internet cannot be ignored. It is a permanent presence in our lives, so we might as well embrace its power rather than fight against it. Get fired up, and get out there to change and improve your online image. Determine what your goals are, and then use the professional tools and techniques you learned from this book in order to proactively make your online image goals into reality. Thanks to your hard work, you are now prepared to use the Internet as an opportunity to grow and expand your personal life and your business. So get out there and put your best foot forward online!

Glossary

Amoral—Without regard for morals either way; neither immoral nor moral. The computers that run the Internet are amoral because they are not programmed to consider the impact of their actions.

Bing—A search engine run by Microsoft.

Communications Decency Act of 1996 (Section 230)—A law from 1996 that has been interpreted to immunize the owners of a website from lawsuits for attacks caused by users of the website.

Cryptoviral extortion—A specialized form of extortion that uses a computer virus to render a victim's files unusable by encrypting them. The extortionist then offers to sell the key to decrypt (unlock) the files to the victim.

E-mob—See *Electronic lynch mob.*

Electronic lynch mob—A group of Internet users who have banded together to punish some perceived wrongdoer or villain. These mobs often rush to judgment and may go overboard in their punishment.

E-lynching—The result of an *electronic lynch mob.*

Google—The largest and most important search engine and the company that runs it.

Googlebombing—A prank played through Google and other search engines. By manipulating links, pranksters make unrelated pages appear for popular search terms. The most commonly known example was that, for some time, a search for "miserable failure" returned a link to the White House.

Google of Eden—The myth that Google's search results are a pure reflection of reality. This idealized world never existed; Google's search results have always been a combination of imperfect human decisions in designing the Google algorithm and imperfect websites created by biased (or even vindictive) people.

Google Gone Wild—The self-reinforcing cycle of false negative information in Google. Many false and scandalous pages attract a large amount of attention, which confuses the Google algorithm into thinking that these pages are important, which draws more attention to them, repeating the cycle endlessly.

Google insurance—It's not "real" insurance but instead refers to the power of positive online content to prevent false negative information from ruining your reputation. If you create a positive presence today, that presence will serve as *Google insurance* against future attacks.

Googlestuffing—The act of spreading false and negative content in an attempt to fill ("stuff") the first ten links in a search engine search.

Google trail—Evidence that a person or business has been around for a while, usually in the form of a long history of results in a search engine search.

Google truth—Not the actual truth. Instead, the *Google truth* is the stylized caricature version of reality that appears in a Google search for your name or the name of your business. The *Google Truth* may appear superficially accurate, but it is often incomplete and sometimes flat wrong.

Google wall—The use of truthful positive content to make false negative content appear more obscure. Building *Google walls* by spreading truthful positive content is a popular response to online attack.

Iceberg content—False negative information about you online that is not very visible in search engines today. Much like an iceberg, it can still sink your reputation if it later rises up to the surface.

Instant universality—The power of the Internet to broadcast information to the world in tenths of a second or less.

Libel index—A way to measure the harm caused by false negative content. Roughly speaking, the harm caused by false negative content is proportional to the size of the audience that sees it, multiplied by the closeness of that audience to you.

Name collision—What happens when two people share the same name and one suffers from the other's negative online image.

Online Justice Squad—A satirical name for any group of self-proclaimed vigilantes who set out to punish apparent transgressions.

Online résumé—The first blast of content that will be seen by anybody searching for your name online. Your *online résumé* is your online first impression (and often your only first impression).

Recovery road map—Like a *reputation road map*, but targeted at recovering from an online attack.

Reputation audit—A structured investigation of how your reputation appears to a Web searcher today.

Reputation road map—A plan of action to improve your online image.

Total online profile—The sum total of all online content about you that could be found by the most dedicated Web searcher.

Wikipedia—A free community-edited encyclopedia that stores more human knowledge than any book ever written.

Wikipedia echo effect—The self-perpetuating loop that occurs when print journalists do their research on Wikipedia, which then cites the same print journalists as evidence that the article has been right all along.

Zombie site—A site that is no longer being maintained and for which no owner can be located.

Index

access codes, stolen, 246
accidental content, 218–221
accidental mistakes, intentional attacks
    vs., 214–215
accountability, 65, 75–79
active defense, 199–206
activists, 114
administrators, contacting, *see* contacting
    administrators
Adobe After Effects®, 129
advance-fee scams, 36–37
advertising, 141–142
Alexa.com, 160, 239
algorithms, 48–49, 84, 86, 208
AltaVista, 93
America Online (AOL), 39–40, 154
amorality
    of Google search results, 8–9, 48–49,
      83–87
    of Internet, 8–14
Andreessen, Marc, 33, 35
Angie's List, 236
Annan, Kofi, on impartiality vs. neutral-
    ity, 86
anonymity, 61–80
    culture of, 74–75
    as default rule, 65–69
    destruction of accountability by, 65,
      75–79
    destruction of social norms by, 63–65
    and extortion, 116
    and "Google voyeurism," 79–80
    Internet Protocol and, 69–72

and legal system, 72–74
and online vs. pre-Internet world,
    61–62
in physical world, 62–63
AOL, *see* America Online
Apple Computer, 11
Aravosis, John, 12
Archive.org, 119, 213, 232–233
archives, 51, 232–233
arguments, avoiding, 223–224
Ashley, Darlene, 131–132
Ask.com, 178
assessment of damage (to reputation),
    210–213
attachments, 247
attacks on reputation, 100–121, 123
    and bullying, 105–107
    in business context, 114–115
    content of, 124–133
    and envy, 103–104
    and extortion, 115–118
    Google and, 82–97
    historical basis of, 101–102
    and jealousy, 102–103
    legal aspects of, 73, 229–231
    measuring damage from, 150–161
    neutral content as defense against, 200
    and politics, 111–113
    recovering from, *see* restoring your
      reputation
    and revenge, 104–105
    and social gossip, 118–119
    by sociopaths, 120

attacks on reputation (*continued*)
spreading of, 133–142
and user-created content, 46–49
and vigilante justice, 107–111
audience
knowing your, 165–173
reaching, by malicious content, 156–161
audit, online reputation, *see* online reputation audit(s)
automation, of Web searches, 83–86, 88

"badger game," 117
Baumer, David, on legal measures against Internet abuses, 41
bias
and false information, 87
and Google Truth, 89
and removing Wikipedia smears, 227, 229
Bible, 101
Bing, 178, 212
blackmail, *see* extortion
BlogAds, 142
blog bonus, 87
Blogger.com, 195
blogs (bloggers)
for claiming/protecting identity, 194, 195
for creating positive/neutral content, 202
for hosting attacks, 133
identifying/neutralizing attacks from, 222, 224
measuring audience reached by, 160
and online reputation audit, 185
spreading of false content by, 87
BlogSpot.com, 224
boastfulness, 202
breach of privacy, 129–130
breaking news, 53
Buckner, Bill, 18
Bugduv, Masal, 24
bulletin boards, 46
bullying, 105–107

Bunton, Emma, on taking control, 163
Bush, George W., 137
business(es)
attacks on reputation of, 114–115
collective action to fix attacks on, 242
and complaint sites, 239–240
and criticism, 236–237, 239
data security for, 244–247
and extortion, 117
and hoaxes, 240–242
identifying online reputation goals for, 235
protecting reputation of, 234–247
value of reputation of, 17

cached copies, 55
caching, 55
Calhoun, John, 127
CAPTCHA, 96
casinos, online, 40
CDA, *see* Communications Decency Act
cell phone photos, 57, 108–109
Charles the Bald, 115
China, 139–140
Citysearch, 236
claiming your online identity, 189–196, 221
Clark, Frank A., on gossip, 118
Clinton, Bill, on fighting, 223
Coca-Cola, 240
cognitive bias, 87
collective action, 242
college admissions, 166
combat, 77–78
common names, 205
Communications Decency Act (CDA), 6
and extortion by business review sites, 239
immunity for user-created content under, 73
and libel, 74
and user-created content, 182
and website immunity, 231–232
complaint sites, 183, 239–242
conformity, 19

con men, 36–37
contacting administrators
 to correct accidental content,
  219–221
 to correct false information, 224
 to remove professional smears,
  243–244
 to remove Wikipedia smears,
  226–228
content
 of attacks on reputation, 124–133
 creating your own, 200–203
 and equality, 47–49
 identifying, 224
 reputation-enhancing vs. destroying
  power of, 21
 and simple lies, 124–126
 viral, 140–141
 in Web 2.0 world, 46–47
context, half-truths and, 126
contextual search advertising, 141–142
contributions, political, 50
control, taking, 163–165
controversy, 88, 90
"copypasta," 54
copyright violations, 6, 73–74
Coral Content Distribution Network, 55
coupons, 235
Craigslist, 40
crawler, 54
criticism, dealing with, 236–237, 239
crowd, following the, 19
cryptoviral extortion, 115–116
The Cult of the Amateur (Andrew
  Keen), 49
culture
 of anonymity, 74–75
 conflict between online/offline, 37–42
 of early Internet users, 35–37
customers, criticism from, 237, 239
customer service, 221
cyberattacks, 113
cyberbullying, 105–107
cycles, self-reinforcing, *see* self-reinforcing
  cycles

damage
 assessing, 210–213
 correcting, *see* restoring your reputation
 measuring, 150–161
Dante Alighieri, on envy, 103
data security, 244–247
debunking, 217
DEC (Digital Equipment Corporation),
  93
*Delete: The Virtue of Forgetting in the
  Digital Age* (Viktor Mayer-Schonberger), 51
Digital Equipment Corporation (DEC),
  93
digital fingerprints, 222
Digital Millennium Copyright Act
  (DMCA), 6, 73–74
digital photography, 127, *see also* manipulated photos; photographs
digital wiping, 246
directories (on the Web), 92
discount codes, 235
discussion forums, 46–47, 134, 160
Divine Comedy (Dante), 103
DMCA, *see* Digital Millennium
  Copyright Act
domain names, 195–196
DontDateHimGirl.com, 124–125, 167,
  183
doppelnamer, 161
dot.com bust, 34
Dozier, John, 230–231
Drudge, Matt, 146

election of 1860, 51
election of 2002, 146
election of 2008, 112, 141, 143, 146
electric shock experiment (Milgram),
  76–77
Electronic Frontier Foundation, 71
e-lynching, 138–140
e-mail, 36, 247
embarrassment, 153–154
e-mobbing, 138–140
emotional distance, 77–78

emotions, controlling your, 219, 224, 228
employees, anti-business smears by, 114,
    115
encryption, 72
envy, 103–104
Estonia, 113
Eternal September, 39
etiquette, 39
.exe files, 247
exploration, social, 155–156
extortion, 115–118, 239–240

Facebook
    claiming/protecting online identity on,
        192–193
    and gossip, 119
    and online image management, 166,
        167
    and online reputation audit, 184
    as paradigm for Web 2.0, 9
    and photo tags, 96–97
    and reputation road map, 170
    for spreading attacks, 134
facial recognition software, 57–58,
    96–97
"FAIL" meme, 140
fairness, profit vs., 90
faith in online content, 22
false-flag attack, 143–145
false information, 86–90
Federal Bureau of Investigation (FBI), 40
feelings, controlling, 219, 224, 228
Ferriss, Tim, on outsourcing, 186
file-sharing, 129–130, 244–245
Firefox browser, 38, 55
first impressions, 24–27
"flag this page for review" button, 218
flash drives, 245
Flickr.com, 212
Fonda, Jane, 128
Food Lion, 18
"419" fraudsters, 36–37, 40–41
Fox News Channel, 141
fraud, 40–41

frontier culture, 5–8, 35–37
The Future of Reputation (Daniel
    Solove), 45

gambling, 36, 37, 40
gay marriage controversy, 112–113
Georgia (country), 113
Gladwell, Malcolm, on Internet gold
    rush, 33
Gmail, 176
GoDaddy.com, 196
gold rush, 33
goodwill, 17
Google
    and active defense, 199–206
    amorality/neutrality of search results,
        8–9, 48–49, 83–87
    for assessing damage to reputation,
        211–213
    cached content on, 55
    and digital threats to reputation, 82–97
    and Facebook/MySpace comments,
        135
    increasing power of, 95–96
    introduction of, 93–94
    legal immunity of, 231–232
    omniscience of, 91–97
    for online reputation audit, 176–179
    and permanence of online content, 54
    and reputation road map, 170
    and self-reinforcing cycles, 86–88
    and Web 2.0, 10
    and YouTube/Viacom case, 74
Google AdWords, 142
Google Blog Search, 185
Google Bomb (Sue Scheff), 231
Googlebombing, 137–138, 215
Google Cache, 213
Google Groups, 177
Google Image Search
    for assessing damage to reputation, 212
    for defusing modified images, 241–242
    for online reputation audit, 177
"Google insurance," 189, 199–206

Google News, 12–13
"Google of Eden," 208
Google Profiles
    claiming/protecting online identity on,
        194
    for creating positive/neutral content,
        201
    and online reputation audit, 178
    for repairing online reputation, 91
Google Search Wiki, 91
"Googlestuffing," 136–137
"Google trail," 22–23
"Google Truth," 27, 88–90, 119
"Google voyeurism," 79–80
"Google wall(s)"
    and active defense, 104
    for fighting vigilantes, 110–111
    flood of content for, 224
    as part of reputation recovery plan,
        217, 221
    positive content for, 200
gossip, 101, 118–119
government data, 50–51
government interference in online
        politics, 113
Graham, Paul, on anti-spam measures, 41
greed, 114–115
Griswold, Dan, 141

Hackers and Painters (Paul Graham), 41
half-truths, 126
Hall, Joseph, on repaired reputations, 114
halo effect, 19–20
harassment, 130–132
hard drives, removing sensitive data from,
        245–246
harmful content, see attacks on reputation
header, 66, 67
heuristics, 19–20
high-speed connections, 38
hoaxes, 130–132, 240–242
Hobbes, Thomas, on nature of life, 105
hosting, of attacks on reputation,
        133–134

hosts, 69
hybrid attacks, 142–143

"iceberg content," 208
identification
    of false content, 224
    of your attacker, 221–222
impersonation
    anonymity and, 78–79
    claiming online identity as defense
        against, 190–191
    and false-flag attacks, 144–145
impressions, first, 24–27
index case, 215–216
initial public offerings (IPOs), 33, 34
instant universality, 52–53
intentional attacks, accidental mistakes
        vs., 214–215
International Red Cross, 144–145
Internet, the
    embracing, 249–250
    as new digital frontier, 1–15
    and Old Wild West, 30–35
    technology of, 65–66
Internet Archive, 54–55, 213
Internet gold rush, 33
Internet Protocol (IP), 68–72
Internet routing, 67
Internet Service Providers (ISPs), 32, 70,
        72
IP address, 67–73, 222
IPOs (initial public offerings), 33, 34
Iran, 128

James, LeBron, 132
jealousy, 102–103
Jobs, Steve, 11, 143
"joe job," 143
Johnston, Levi, 143
journals, 92–93
JuicyCampus.com, 135–136

Keen, Andrew, on Web egalitarianism, 49
Kerry, John, 128–129

Landover Baptist Church parody, 144
LANs, 70
lawsuits, 229–232
legal system (law enforcement)
    and anonymity, 72–74
    and limitations of control on Web,
      6–7, 38
    as solution to Internet abuses, 41
Lessig, Lawrence, on Internet governance,
    42
Letterman, David, 118
Leviathan (Thomas Hobbes), 105
libel, 74
Libel Index, 156–157
libraries, 71
Library of Congress, 54–55
lies, 124–126, *see also* attacks on reputa-
    tion
Lincoln, Abraham, 51, 127
LinkedIn, 9
    claiming/protecting online identity on,
      193
    and online image management, 167
    profile for Google wall, 201
    and reputation road map, 170
links, 84, 201–202, 204
Livejournal, 195
LocateCell, 181
lynch mob, online, 138

manipulated photos, 127–129, 241–242
"mark as offensive" button, 218
Mayer-Schonberger, Viktor, on deleting
    website data, 51
McAfee, 247
McCain, John, 78
McCarthy, Joseph, 128
metadata, 246–247
method, content vs., 124
microblogging, 160, 202, *see also* Twitter
Microsoft Bing, 178, 212
Microsoft Office™, 246, 247
Milgram, Stanley, 76–77
misinformation, *see* attacks on reputation
misspellings, 176–177

moral neutrality, *see* amorality
More, Thomas, on revenge, 104
Mortensen, Viggo, on unexpected events,
    120
Mosaic browser, 33, 37, 38
Motion Picture Association of America
    (MPAA), 56–57
MyEdge, 206
MySpace
    and gossip, 119
    and online image management, 166
    and online reputation audit, 183–184
    and photo tags, 96–97
    and reputation road map, 170
    for spreading attacks, 134

name collision, 214–215
NameGrab, 193
names
    common, 205
    identical, 161
NAT (Network Address Translation),
    70
negative content, *see* attacks on
    reputation
Netflix, 38
netiquette, 39
Netscape, 33, 38
Network Address Translation (NAT),
    70
neutral content, *see* positive and neutral
    content
neutrality of search results, 8–9, 48–49,
    83–87
new digital frontier, 1–15
news cycle, 52–53
New York Times, 51
911 systems, 132–133
"notice-and-takedown" system, 73–74

Obama, Barack, 141, 146
OCR (optical character recognition), 96
offline culture, online culture vs., 37–42
Oklahoma City Bombing, 131
Olympic Games (1980), 18

omniscience, of Google, 91–97
123people, 180
online anonymity, *see* anonymity
online attacks, *see* attacks on reputation
online communities, 64, 134–136
online culture, offline culture vs.,
    37–42
online identity
    claiming your, 189–196, 221
    and uncommon names, 205
online justice squad, 138
online lynch mob, 138
online profile, total, 27–28
online reputation
    attacks on, *see* attacks on reputation
    of business, 234–247
    checking up on your, 165–176, *see also*
        online reputation audit(s)
    content and, 21
    forces driving, 44–58
    and Internet as Brave New World, 45
    as means of quick decision-making,
        18–20
    proactive protection of, 188–189
    as reality, 16–28
    and real-world interactions, 16–18
    restoring your, *see* restoring your
        reputation
online reputation audit(s), 173–186
    hiring professionals for, 185–186
    personal data finders for, 180–181
    search engines for, 176–179
    of social networking sites, 183–185
    of user-created content sites, 182–185
online résumé, 25–27
optical character recognition (OCR),
    96
Othello (Shakespeare), 102
"outing," 130

packets, 66–67, 69
Palin, Sarah, 78, 143
passwords, stolen, 246
Paul the Apostle, 101
PeekYou, 179

people-specific search engines, 95,
    178–179
Pericles, 101
permanence of online information,
    53–57
personal data finders, 180–181
personal image, as part of professional
    image, 243–244
personal reputation, 151–152
phishing, 246
photographs, 57–58, 108–109,
    127–129, 241–242
Photoshop®, 127
photo tags, 57, 96–97
Picasa, 96
Pipl, 95, 179
poker, online, 36, 37
political contributions, 50, 145–146, 155
politics, 111–113, 128
popularity, search results and, 8–9,
    84–87
pornography, 130
portable storage devices, 245
positive and neutral content
    bolstering, 204–205
    claiming/protecting online identity
        with, 196–199
    creating, 200–203
    for "Google insurance," 199–206
    importance of, 198–199
    professionally-created, 205–206
    in reputation recovery plan, 217
pre-Internet era, 23, 61–62
privacy
    breach of, 129–130
    harms to, 154
    and IP addresses, 70
    through obscurity, 205
private information, online availability of,
    49–51
proactive, being, 188–189, *see also* claim-
    ing your online identity
professional directories, 203
professional reputation, protecting your,
    234–247

professionals
  data security for, 244–247
  hiring, for online content creation,
    205–206
  hiring, for online reputation audit,
    185–186
  special tips for protecting reputation
    of, 243–244
profile sites, 202
profit, fairness vs., 90
prostitution, 36, 40
protection, proactive, 188–189
proxy servers, 71–72

quiet enjoyment, 155

"rants," 237
Really Simple Syndication (RSS), 52
real-name sites, 192–193
reCAPTCHA, 96
recovery, see restoring your reputation
remailers, 71
reputation, see specific heading, e.g.: online
    reputation
ReputationDefender.com, 186, 206
reputation road map, 162–173
research, in pre-Internet age, 23
restoring your reputation, 207–233
  and assessing the damage, 210–213
  and identifying source of attacks,
    213–216
  and identifying your attacker, 221–222
  and intentional vs. accidental content,
    214–215
  and removing content from archives,
    232–233
  and responding to attacker, 221–224
résumé, online, 25–27
revenge, 104–105
"revenge porn," 129–130
RipoffReport.com, 239–240
romance, 166–167
RSS (Really Simple Syndication), 52
rumors, 6–7, 101, 126
Russia, 113, 128

sarcasm, 161
"satanic ritual abuse," 125
satiric websites, 144
scams, 36–37
Scheff, Sue, 230–231
search algorithms, 48–49, 84, 86, 208
search engines
  introduction of, 93
  for measuring audience reached by
    malicious content, 157–160
  for online reputation audit,
    176–179
  specialized, 95
  for spreading attacks, 136–138
  see also specific search engines, e.g.:
    Google
search history, 154
search results, location of attacks among,
    157–160
search terms
  importance of, 158
  and online reputation audit, 173,
    175–176
  and reputation road map, 170, 172,
    173
Section 230 (CDA), see Communications
    Decency Act
security breaches, 244–247
security patches, 247
self-reinforcing cycles, 86–88, 214–215,
    218, 225
sex, and breach of privacy, 129–130
sexual identity, 155–156
Shakespeare, William
  on jealousy, 102, 103
  on the world as a stage, 165
shortcuts in assessing reputations,
    18–20
Silicon Valley, 33
small business(es), see business(es)
smears, see attacks on reputation
Snopes.com, 240
Snow White, 103
social distance, 76, 77
social exploration, 155–156

social networking sites
  and gossip, 119
  for hosting attacks, 134
  measuring audience reached by, 160
  and online reputation audit, 183–185
  for spreading attacks, 134–136
  see also specific sites, e.g.: Facebook
social norms
  and anonymity, 63–65, 76
  in pre-Internet era, 61
  vigilante enforcement of, 107–111
"social proof" heuristic, 19, 20
social reputation, 152–153
Social Science Research Network
  (SSRN), 203
social Web, 9
sociopathy, 120
Solove, Daniel, on digital revolution, 45
South Ossetia, 113
Soviet Union, 128
spam, 36
"spider," 84, 93
Spock.com, 11–12, 179
SSRN (Social Science Research
  Network), 203
stalking, 79, 116–117
Starbucks, 240
stock prices, 11, 13
strategy, choosing, 223–224
Streisand Effect, 56, 230
students, 107
subpoenas, 73
Sullenberger, Chesley Burnett "Sully," 18
Sun Tzu, on occupying the battlefield,
  196
SWATing, 132–133

tagging (photo tags), 57, 96–97
taking control, 163–165
technology
  of Internet, 65–66
  as solution to Internet abuses, 41
Technorati.com, 185
teenagers, 106–107
Texas Hold'Em poker, 36

Thorndike, Edward, 19–20
thumb drives, 245
Tiananmen Square protests, 127
The Times (London), 23–24
TinEye.com, 242
TOR (The Onion Router), 71–72
total online profile, 27–28
trojans, 247
trolling, 145–146
"trolls," 237
trust, misplaced, 21–24
"truth," Google results as, *see* "Google
  Truth"
Twitter
  claiming/protecting online identity on,
    194
  for creating positive/neutral content,
    202
  and online reputation audit, 184–185
  and Russia, 113
Tyler, Steve, 143
typos, 175–176

uncommon names, protecting online
  identity of, 205
United Airlines, 12–13
universality, instant, 52–53
urban legends, 240
U.S. Air Force, 237, 238
U.S. Congress, 40, 232
Usenet, 32, 39, 71
user-created content
  and claiming/protecting online iden-
    tity, 192–195
  and online reputation audit, 182–183
  and potential for damage, 46–49
  see also specific headings, e.g.: blogging
user identification, 65
usernames, 192–195

vandalism, 227, 228
vectors, of Internet attacks, 124
Viacom, 74
videos, manipulated, 129
Vietnam War, 128

vigilante justice, 40–41, 107–111, 138–140

Vikings, 115

viral content, 140–141

viruses, 247

virus scanning systems, 247

vocabulary, early Internet, 35

voyeurism, Google, 79–80

war, 77–78

Watterson, Bill, on extortion, 115

Wayback Machine, 213, 232–233

Web 1.0, 9

Web 2.0, 9–11, 46–47

Web browsing, 37–38

Web design, quality of, 48

webmasters, contacting, 219–221, 224, 243–244

Webroot, 247

webservers, 69, 73

websites

for claiming/protecting online identity, 192

for hosting attacks on reputation, 133–134

for spreading attacks, 135

see also specific sites, e.g.: Archive.org

"Web spider," 93

Wendy's, 240–241

West, Jessamyn, 247

Whitepages.com, 180

Whois.net, 221

Wikipedia

claiming/protecting online identity on, 195

echo effect from, 24, 225

finding false/malicious content on, 182–183

fixing false/malicious content on, 225–229

and Google search algorithm, 84

identifying sources of smears on, 216

Windows Update, 247

Wink.com, 179

"wiping" programs, 246

wireless networks, IP addresses and, 70–71

WordPress, 195

World Wide Web, creation of, 32–33

worms, 247

Yahoo!, 93, 177, 180, 212

Yale Daily News, 51

Yelp, 236

YouTube, 74

Zeran, Ken, 131

Zillow.com, 50

Zittrain, Jonathan, on measures against Internet abuses, 41

zombie sites, 56